THE
FORGOTTEN
WAY

THE FORGOTTEN WAY

A Path to Holiness through Life's Trials

S. Marie Ristau

TATE PUBLISHING
AND ENTERPRISES, LLC

The Forgotten Way
Copyright © 2014 by S. Marie Ristau. All rights reserved.

No part of this publication may be reproduced, stored in a retrieval system or transmitted in any way by any means, electronic, mechanical, photocopy, recording or otherwise without the prior permission of the author except as provided by USA copyright law.

Scripture texts used in this work are taken from the *New American Bible with Revised New Testament and Psalms* © 1991, 1986, 1970 Confraternity of Christian Doctrine, Inc., Washington, DC All Rights Reserved. No part of this work may be reproduced or transmitted in any form or by any means, electronic or mechanical, including photocopying, recording, or by any information storage and retrieval system, without permission in writing from the copyright owner.

The poetic English translation of the *Stabat Mater* taken from the *Roman Missal* approved by the National Conference of Catholic Bishops of the United States © 1964 by the National Catholic Welfare Conference, Inc. All rights reserved.

Passages from the *Diary of St. Maria Faustina Kowalska: Divine Mercy in My Soul* © 1987 Marian Fathers of the Immaculate Conception of the B.V.M. Stockbridge, MA 01263 All Rights Reserved. Used with Permission.

Padre Pio quotes used with permission by the National Padre Pio Center, Barto, PA 19504.

Vilinius Image of The Divine Mercy © Marian Fathers of the Immaculate Conception of the B.V.M. Stockbridge, MA 01263 All Rights Reserved. Used with Permission.

Saint Faustina by Janis Balabon © Marian Fathers of the Immaculate Conception of the B.V.M. Stockbridge, MA 01263 All Rights Reserved. Used with Permission.

Images of the Sacred Heart of Jesus and Immaculate Heart of Mary; Artist, Marilyn Hamann. Used with Permission of The Apostleship of Prayer. http://www.apostleshipofprayer.org/.

Sacred Heart of Jesus (close-up image) by Leslie Langille Benson [American Painter, 1885-1972] Used with Permission of The Apostleship of Prayer. http://www.apostleshipofprayer.org/.

Scripture quotations marked (NIV) are taken from the *Holy Bible, New International Version*®, NIV®. Copyright © 1973, 1978, 1984 by Biblica, Inc.™ Used by permission of Zondervan. All rights reserved worldwide. www.zondervan.com

To protect the privacy of certain individuals, some names have been changed.

The opinions expressed by the author are not necessarily those of Tate Publishing, LLC.

This book is designed to provide accurate and authoritative information with regard to the subject matter covered. This information is given with the understanding that neither the author nor Tate Publishing, LLC is engaged in rendering legal, professional advice. Since the details of your situation are fact dependent, you should additionally seek the services of a competent professional.

Published by Tate Publishing & Enterprises, LLC
127 E. Trade Center Terrace | Mustang, Oklahoma 73064 USA
1.888.361.9473 | www.tatepublishing.com

Tate Publishing is committed to excellence in the publishing industry. The company reflects the philosophy established by the founders, based on Psalm 68:11,
"The Lord gave the word and great was the company of those who published it."

Book design copyright © 2014 by Tate Publishing, LLC. All rights reserved.
Cover design by Allen Jomoc
Interior design by Jomel Pepito

Published in the United States of America

ISBN: 978-1-63367-475-2
1. Biography & Autobiography / Religious
2. Biography & Autobiography / Medical
14.09.26

To Mary, Queen of angels and Queen of my heart
and
to my husband, with love

Acknowledgments

> Thanks be to God who gives us the victory
> through our Lord Jesus Christ.
> —1 Corinthians 15:57

I cannot even begin to thank everyone who prayed and encouraged me throughout the process of creating this book. In particular, I'd like to thank the following people for their special contributions:

Trinity Tate-Edgerton – executive director of Book Acquisitions at Tate Publishing; thank you for your readiness to invest in me and this book! Mary Cindell Pilapil – my project manager. How I relied on receiving her guidance and proficiency throughout the editing process and beyond.

Father Louis Guardiola, CPM– Fathers of Mercy. What a tremendous blessing he has been in his encouragement for me to publish this book, and for the insight he shared in confirming the subject matter of its sequel: *Love Is a Three-Letter Word—God.* A very special thank-you!

Cross & Crown Prayer Group – Thank you to Nestor Skaleski and Jerry and Dolores Schaefer for all the years of reaping their guidance and prayerful support. For the pastoral team, and all of the rest…a continuous source of blessing!

Father Kieran Hickey, OFM, Cap. – The ongoing years of his support and spiritual direction have been a remarkable source of broadening our perspective, offering us the encouragement and courage to open ourselves to God's holy

Will. In thanksgiving also for all of the wonderful priests who've blessed and encouraged us along the way!

Sisters of the Handmaids of the Divine Redeemer – Sr. Mary Assumpta Ayikue and Sr. Angela Dassinor. Iomy and Irene Engichy, Nikki Vandehey, and all of our "spiritual children;" my heart is ever so grateful for the treasure God has provided in the constancy of their loving prayers to help bring this book to completion.

Members of the Intercessors of Light prayer group – Their prayers for this book have been invaluable to me. Their ongoing commitment to pray for God's people for nearly a decade is a tremendous testament to their faith!

Debbie Wilson – What a beautiful and faithful friend God has given me in her. The epitome of what it means to live one's life for Jesus, I'm ever so thankful for being a recipient of her prayers and the constancy of her support.

Margaret Mary Ponfil, RIP – My beloved sister and the first to read this book. I'll always cherish your sweet memory, and I thank God for the honor of being able to help you store up for yourself great treasures in heaven!

Eric Ristau – My son. Thank you for your kind and generous heart and for sharing your gifts to provide me the detailed refinement necessary to finish this manuscript.

Jenelle Ristau – My daughter and best friend. Thank you for being you, and for always being there for me. God bless you for sharing your editing skills, and for your sure and steady way of reaching out to those in need of a smile.

Rob Ristau – My husband. With whom I am joined at the hip, and without whom this book would never have come to be. I love you!

Contents

The Call 20
Walk with Me...41
Ask, Seek, and Knock 54
Show Me the Righteous! 69
Come 85
Go Out 102
Behold, Your Mother 124
Intercessors of Light 144
The Apostles Blue 163
Angels Will Sing 190
Four Calling Birds 213
Hunger for Holiness 237
Celestial Choirs 255
8:2 281
Jesus, I Trust in You! 313
They Will See God 355
Notes 371

Foreword

Fr. Louis Guardiola, CPM, Fathers of Mercy

To quote a French novel, A Tale of Two Cities, "It is the best of times and the worst of times."

Our present times, so fundamentally and radically disordered in every way, are very much like the times of The French Revolution. This gives rise to much despair, confusion and a profound sense of helplessness of even many of the devout Catholic lay faithful. Yet we must recall the words of St. Paul, "Where sin abounds, grace even more abounds."

It is precisely in these fundamentally and radically disordered times, so much so that it appears we are returning to the pre-Christian pagan barbarism of the first century A D Roman empire, that great miracles and outpouring of grace occurs.

It is clearly apparent that this is the case with Susan's and Rob Ristau's witness. Theirs is truly a witness because it is a martyrdom of suffering.

Theirs is the martyrdom of worldly mortification and therefore heavenly sanctification and salvific power of suffering that is the Cross. This is the "Forgotten Way," suffering Way of the Cross. It is the Forgotten Way because it is the way so foreign to the extremely self-indulgent and therefore selfish present mentality. This is why society has lost the way, Jesus Christ, who is the Way, the Truth and the Life.

What is the essence of Jesus' suffering on the Cross that is also the essence of the Eucharist? It is self-sacrificial love. Jesus suffered His passion on The Cross because of His love for His human race, in order to expiate their sins.

Suffering is the Way of the Cross where the Love of God from all eternity comes down to meet the sinfulness of the human race in time. The Cross is where the mercy of God meets the misery of mankind.

The Cross is a plus sign, where Jesus irrevocably broke the power of Satan and issued from His pierced side the seven channels of grace to not only alleviate but to Divinely transform our human suffering into our means of salvation in union with Christ.

We all suffer. We suffer bodily, emotionally, psychologically, spiritually. We suffer persecution for our faith, rebukes, rejection from our family members as religious psychotics, and now from a majority of civil society that has become agnostic.

Susan has discovered that the power of our intercessory prayer is in direct proportion to our sacrificial suffering and emptying of our self-will.

The question is, how do we embrace our suffering? How do we embrace our cross? Do we reject it and in turn reject our faith? Or do we embrace it as a challenge to become less attached to worldly things and more attached and dependent of God and His Church?

Susan has chosen the latter way, the way forgotten to the world, and in doing so presents how a simple member of the lay faithful, a wife and mother of thirty odd years, can embrace suffering in these modern times. It is her simple, matter of fact account, entirely devoid of pride, that reveals her sincerity.

No matter how dark our times appear, God in His providence always appoints simple persons to be His light in the darkness. Jesus selects such simple persons as Susan and Rob so that the average layperson can identify with Susan and unite their sufferings to the Cross.

God has a plan for everyone, no one is created by accident. God chose Susan, appointed her, anointed her and Rob with the oils of Baptism and Confirmation to deliver His timeless message through her genetically received affliction. We see in Susan how

God chooses persons to evangelize according to their particular set of circumstances and talents. In Susan's case, it was in the midst of her family life and not in abandonment of her familial responsibilities as so many misguided women do.

Susan's message is truly of God's because in coping with her suffering she has turned to the classically Catholic sources of grace: The Holy Sacrifice of the Mass, the Holy Eucharist and Adoration, the Holy Rosary, Marian and Christological devotion such as The Sacred Heart of Jesus and the Immaculate Heart of Mary, St. Louis De Montefort's Marian Consecration, Holy Scripture, the teachings and sayings of the Saints and Doctors of the Church, and the Catechism of the Catholic Church.

Susan, in entering so deeply into the mystery of Jesus' suffering on the Cross through her own suffering, has discovered its evangelical aspect.

Yes, one may re-title Susan's work: The Forgotten Way of Evangelical Suffering.

Why is suffering evangelical? Suffering is evangelical if it is embraced as Christ did because in doing so it unleashes a huge outpouring of grace that in mortifying and washing away our selfishness, sin and self-absorption, it enables us to look beyond our own suffering and embrace and address the suffering of others.

Christ-like suffering enables us to do this because when we experience suffering, we develop sympathy, a compassion for the sufferings of others, so abundantly evident in Susan's and Rob's accounts.

Suffering is evangelical, because in our Christ-like embrace of it, we strengthen the faith of others by our own example.

We see this in Susan's husband Rob. The suffering that has broken so many marriages, strengthened the matrimonial bond between Susan and Rob Ristau. This is why I think their testimony is so edifying and needs to be broadcast to the world, because it is so extraordinary in these times. In fact, one can also entitle their work: How Suffering Strengthens and Sanctifies Marriage.

It is very edifying and indicative of the genuineness of Susan's testimony witness to witness the growth in faith and sanctity of her husband Rob, who gave her one of his kidneys. Talk about two becoming one in marriage.

Even more edifying was the fact that Susan did not force this growth upon Rob, but let the Lord, in His own time, work His miracle of conversion in Rob.

Slowly but surely, Rob became more devoted. First he returned to the practice of Confession after an absence of 20 years. This is huge in and of itself. Then Rob went to daily Mass and Eucharistic Adoration. He then started to develop his own witness by the locution, words of knowledge, etc., that the Lord gave him about Susan, the family and those around him... I found of particular interest the Lord's instruction to Rob when he attempted to block the passage way of those who were leaving the Church, that only by prayer before the Blessed Sacrament could he win souls back. I learned this lesson myself. Then, both Rob and Susan started to witness together by praying over others.

Susan not only evangelized, but taught others how to evangelize.

In both Susan and Rob, we see the miracle of unfolding grace from within and how it expands the life, prayer and practice of faith.

I have said this many times in my own Eucharistic preaching. One must first be affected interiorly in prayerful adoration by God's grace and love before one can be effectively an apostle, soldier, missionary, prophet and evangelist of the salvific love of Jesus Christ on the Cross.

It is in the forgotten and radical Way of the Cross of Good Friday that is the consummation of the Holy Sacrifice of the Mass, initiated the night before on Holy Thursday that redeemed and will continue to redeem the human race.

Redemption means "to buy back." It was our Lord's suffering on the Cross that the infinite debts of sins of the human race was paid for and purchased.

The sinfulness of today will be alleviated and the grace needed for this purchase and deliverance from evil will continue through those, who like Susan, choose to use their sufferings for this holy purchase.

In her sufferings, Susan and Rob in their solidarity in marriage, prayer, and life, have discovered that to the extent that we allow ourselves to be transformed by the Holy Eucharist, to that extent we shall transform the world.

How? Why? Eucharistic transformation is to be transformed by the self-sacrificial love of Jesus Christ on the Cross, which is the essence of the Eucharist.

When the world is full of the self-sacrificial love of Jesus Christ on the Cross, abortion will end. Euthanasia will end and all other assaults on the elderly. Selfishness will end, that is the cause of all the world's ills, and we shall share our gifts, talents and resources, not hoard them.

Susan has come to understand that when we see the Cross, we see the self-sacrificial love of Jesus Christ that motivated His suffering, and see in the Cross the Holy Eucharist that gives us power to carry our crosses.

THROUGH THE POWER OF THE HOLY EUCHARIST WE ARE GIVEN THE STRENGTH TO DO WHAT IS HUMANLY IMPOSSIBLE, BUT SUPERNATURALLY POSSIBLE.

This is what Fr. John Hardon meant when he said that God does not give us a cross we cannot bear. What we cannot bear with His grace!

Prayer before the Blessed Sacrament may not immediately take away our sufferings, but it immediately gives us the grace and therefore strength to bear it and indeed grow in faith and holiness. Like Rob and Susan, we gain a spiritual maturity and wisdom only acquired by suffering.

The Cross in this context loses its negativity. The Cross is not a sign of Divine defeat. The Cross as the supreme sign of God's self-sacrificial love becomes instead a sign of victory. Victory through suffering that defeated the power of Satan and continues to do so.

In many ways, Susan's testimony is reminiscent of John Paul II's encyclical On Human Suffering, *Salvific Doloris*. In fact, Susan gives a very astute analysis that people who try to avoid suffering by recourse to drugs, sex, pornography, alcohol and so on, in the end impose a heavier cross on themselves.

The Cross of salvific suffering, The Forgotten Way, is a countercultural sign; a sign of contradiction to a world that does not want to embrace any inconvenience such as attending Sunday Mass and Eucharistic Adoration, even if such inconvenience means their salvation.

Susan and Rob's message, namely their living experience of our Christian way of worldly contradiction, is a very timely one.

Susan's story of conversion through the fire of suffering in the holy fire of the Holy Spirit that burns away our selfishness is a desperately needed message to a world that imposes, yet rejects, suffering due to sin. Susan, in her work, poses the question: "Who and what do we suffer for? Do we suffer in union and for Christ, or do we suffer for Satan in worldly despair, anger and resentment.

I heartily and humbly endorse Susan and Rob's work and witness. It would be fitting in the end to present the summation given by Susan herself.

In speaking of her personal travel of The Forgotten Way, she says its spiritual merit will be according to our response to God's grace. "What enabled me to respond well? It was in utilizing the Sacraments and in praying Holy Scripture with an expectant faith each day that I was truly able to believe in what I could not see."

In speaking of the role of Marian intercession she said, "The Mother of God wants to be for us the guiding light to help us stay the path that will directly lead to the Heart of her Son.

In speaking of the Holy Eucharist as the Sacrament of the Divine Mercy, "Jesus is the fountain of mercy through which all mercy flows. He is the source and summit of our faith at the table of every Eucharistic banquet celebrated in all the holy Masses offered…He is the one who invites us to walk with Him in our trials and constantly reaches out to us in our pain. It is He who serves as our strength in times when we are weak and who is our healing and wholeness."

Speaking of the transformation of suffering, "Transformation takes place in the trials and sorrows of life. When God's people cry out to Him in their adversity, these are the times He uses to draw His children deeper into the Heart of Christ. Our trials are often the means most effective in catapulting us onto the path of holiness."

Susan addresses a common misperception of suffering. "God is not a sadist, nor does He take pleasure in our suffering. In some instances God allows it…for corrective purposes. When His people as a nation turn from Him and take God out of their life, disciplinary measures are sometime the only way through which His people will be saved." "For what 'son' is there whom his 'father' does not discipline?" (Heb. 12:7).

Quoting scripture again, "…but we even boast of our afflictions, knowing that affliction produces endurance, and endurance, proven character, and proven character, hope, and hope does not disappoint, because the love of God has been poured out into our hearts through the holy Spirit that has been given to us" (Romans 5:3–5).

The secret of sanctity "is in striving to surrender our will over to the Divine Will of God. It is a daily struggle, but in not striving to push forward in faith one risks the tendency to go backwards into sin."

How do we prevent backsliding? "Every opportunity for us to become like Jesus is an opportunity to become holy; to love as He loved, to serve as He served, to become holy as He is holy…but holiness doesn't just happen. It takes a long time commitment on our part to live out God's commandments in our everyday lives."

How? "With firm resolve, one must live for righteousness in full reliance of the strength and redeeming grace of God to conquer the habits that are keeping them from becoming holy."

Here is the blueprint for lifelong perseverance. "Over the course of a lifetime, the crosses will come in many shapes and sizes. In uncertain times, God will show us the way to follow and teach us to trust in ways we cannot see. We will be guided safely through the darkness of our sorrows by the steady and gentle Hand of Christ. As we walk with Jesus in a child-like faith along the Way of the Cross, we will be transformed and further changed into His likeness."

This change occurs in three ways. First, "in love of the One who first taught us how to love." Second, "in service of the One who first taught us how to serve." Third, "and in suffering with the One who first taught us how to suffer, others will follow God's people along the 'Forgotten Way' to holiness."

"Weeping as they come, to seek the Lord, their God;/ to their goal in Zion they shall ask the way./ 'Come let us join ourselves to the Lord/ with covenant everlasting, never to be forgotten'" (Jer 50:4–5).

Stations of the Cross

First Station
Jesus Is Condemned to Death

Our compassionate Lord comes lovingly to my aid when the trial is greatest, and like the loving Father He is, consoles me and encourages me to walk always more and more along the Way of the Cross.

—Padre Pio

The Call

I ran back to answer the phone as my husband Rob and I were walking out the door to go out for a nice dinner to celebrate my forty-ninth birthday. It was my doctor's office calling in regard to my annual physical. It was not good news. My heart sank as the nurse relayed the results of my lab tests, which revealed that my kidneys were functioning at only 22 percent. With a tone of urgency in her voice, she instructed me to contact one of the two major hospitals in Wisconsin that performed kidney transplants. I was numb.

At once, my mind traveled back to a vow that I had made to God nearly twenty-five years prior, promising Him that when the time came, I would humble myself and share my kidney disease openly with others. The time had come.

It was discovered that I had inherited polycystic kidney disease (PKD) soon after our second child was born when an ultrasound revealed numerous tiny cysts covering my kidneys. Although I had perfect kidney function at the time I was diagnosed, I was well aware of the dismal reality that over time, as the cysts continued to grow in size, they would eventually destroy the function of my kidneys.

Lending itself to a host of other potentially dangerous problems and side effects, PKD can also affect the liver and pancreas, as well as being systemic in its potential to be linked in causing heart defects, lung problems, and a host of other issues. A genetic disorder affecting some six hundred thousand Americans, it was beginning to show its ugly face in my generation. One by one, siblings and cousins alike were being diagnosed with the dreadful disease. The form that ran in my family typically progressed into complete kidney failure around middle age, with the grim prognosis of dialysis, kidney transplantation, or, as in the case of my dad and his siblings, early death.

Hearing for the first time what I had known for two and a half decades to be the inevitable, I was nonetheless stunned to learn that my kidneys were on a downward spiral toward complete renal failure. It all seemed surreal. In the disquiet of my soul, an unrelenting fear of the unknown threatened to consume me. I had seen my dad suffer with the symptoms of the disease growing up, and I was all too familiar with the episodes of bleeding cysts and chronic infections. His malfunctioning kidneys released poisonous toxins into his bloodstream, causing frequent bouts of nausea and vomiting from an ominous condition called uremia.

A faithful Catholic with a deep devotion to the Blessed Mother, my dad would always round up our family of ten each day to pray the rosary. "The family that prays together stays together,"[1] he'd always say.

"But, Dad," we'd sometimes protest as we were called in from outside, "we're playing with our friends."

"Bring them in," was his customary answer.

How surprised I was decades later when one of those friends from the old neighborhood called to tell me how she cherished the memory of praying the family rosary in our home.

Growing up, I had always felt such closeness to my father. I remember back to a time in my childhood when I was outside playing and upon seeing him come out of the house in dress clothes, I asked, "Where are you going, Dad?"

"To attend the Our Lady of Perpetual Help devotion at church," he replied.

"Oh. Bye."

As he turned to walk away, I instantly felt an aching within my heart to think that my dad was going alone.

"Do you want me to go with you?" I called out.

"Yes!" he said while turning back around. "Quickly, go change your clothes. And be sure to tell your mother," he added.

I recall having been taught by my father to pray my very first novena to Our Lady of Fatima at the age of nine. I had been considered to be somewhat of a tomboy as a youngster, oftentimes preferring much more to climb trees or catch tadpoles than to play with dolls. Perhaps it was because of my chosen hobbies that I picked up the virus that causes warts, as they began to appear on my hands, knees, and feet. At first they really didn't bother me much, but on one particular day I found myself examining them, counting over forty warts! It was then that I wished for them to be gone.

Walking into the kitchen, I saw that my uncle Kobe was over for a visit.

"Come here," my dad said as he motioned for me to sit on his lap.

How many times my dad had sat us kids down on his lap to tell us wonderful stories, but feeling like I was a little too old to be sitting on his lap and especially in front of my uncle, I walked over to him, saying, "Dad, I don't like having all of these warts!"

Immediately upon hearing of my concern, my uncle chimed in, "You want to get rid of your warts? Here's how to get rid of your warts: You just get a carrot from the fridge and rub it in the mud. Then, you rub the mud on your warts, bury the carrot, and your warts will go away."

What? I asked myself. With that, I went outside to play.

Later on that evening, my dad asked if I had done what my uncle had suggested in regard to my warts.

"No," I replied.

"Why not?" he asked.

"Because I thought he was just kidding around."

With a look of approval for not having taken seriously the superstitious method my uncle had proposed, my father said assuredly, "Sue, I do know of a way in which all of your warts will go away."

Trusting completely in the words he spoke, I remember wondering that if he knew how to make my warts go away, why he had not told me of it sooner!

"How?" I asked in wonderment.

"Follow me."

Pulling open the top drawer of the built in dresser in my parent's bedroom, my dad took out one of the little green vials of holy water he had ordered from Fatima.[2] On past occasions when my father brought out the Fatima water to bless the family, he articulated to us more than once of his desire to be blessed with the holy water when he died. Given that the severity of my dad's illness had been carefully concealed from the children, combined with the casual manner in which he stated his request, I simply took his aspiration at face value.

"Pray a novena to the Blessed Mother and bless yourself with this holy water for nine days," he instructed.

"What's a novena?" I asked.

"Novena means 'nine,'" he told me. "Simply pray one Our Father, one Hail Mary and one Glory Be to Our Lady of Fatima for nine days. Mary will ask Jesus to take away your warts."

Taking the bottle of holy water from his extended hand to bring upstairs, I placed it on the nightstand next to my bed in eager anticipation of praying my novena to Mary.

On the morning of the ninth day of praying my very first novena, as I was getting dressed, I noticed there was not a single wart on my entire body! Going to my father, I said, "Look, Dad, all of my warts are gone!"

Elated at the news, he wrote a letter of testimony to the *Fatima Magazine*, telling them of what the Lord had done through the faith of a child, his child. In the very next issue, the story of Our Lady's intercession for a little girl with warts was printed. From that time on, my love for Mary blossomed.

Upon finishing the eighth grade at St. John's Elementary School, my mother asked if I would be willing to spend my summer vacation at my aunt and uncle's home to help care for their young children while they built a larger home to accommodate their growing family. I had never been away from home for that long before, but the thought of getting to spend the summer with my favorite cousin enticed me into accepting my godparents' plea.

Returning back home just a week and a half before the start of my freshman year of high school, I was disheartened to find that my best friend had joined up with a few of the girls from our class whom I considered to be a little on the wild side. Also, while I was gone that summer, the other girls we chummed with had made new friendships as well. A lot had happened while I was gone, and being the "odd man out," I felt alone. Holding my eighth-grade graduation picture in my hand, I decided to turn my problem over to the Blessed Mother, asking Mary to choose for me a good friend.

On the first day of school, one of my instructors assigned an extended group project, pairing off each student with a partner to work with. Immediately, as the girl's name I was to partner with was called out, I wondered if this was going to be the means through which Our Lady would bring to me my new friend. It was this lovely girl who Mary handpicked to be my very best friend, a beautiful person both inside and out. How amazing it was to have Our Lady choose for me a precious friend, who not only possessed many of Mary's own attributes, but whose name was also Mary. Inviting me to her home that same evening to work on our project together, our friendship immediately began to flourish. To this day, we love each other as sisters.

Growing up, it was noted by my mother that I could sleep through anything. "If there's ever a fire," she'd often say, "be sure that someone gets Sue or she'll sleep right through it!"

I tell of this because of the events that took place in the early morning hours in late January that same year. As I lay in my bed sleeping, I awoke suddenly feeling thoroughly alarmed. Sitting straight up in bed, I sensed strongly within myself that something was terribly wrong. Listening intently, I heard nothing but dead silence. With great urgency, however, I threw off the covers and ran down the stairs.

Rounding the kitchen table, my eyes beheld my mother, hands shaking and paging frantically through the phone book. Looking down directly below from where she was standing, I saw my dad's body lying on the floor next to where he had been having his morning coffee. Paralyzed in fear, my mom anxiously asked, "What number do I call?"

As if enveloped in a mantle of tranquility, I remained uncharacteristically calm. Showing her the number, I then retrieved one of the small green vials of the Fatima holy water from my father's top dresser drawer. Kneeling down at his side, I honored the request he had so often made known. Making the sign of the Cross with the holy water on his forehead, I prayed from my heart, "Mary, please come and be with my dad."

Watching as the medics lifted him onto the stretcher, I stared intently in noticing his eyes open slightly in unison with seeing a tender smile form upon his face. Uplifted at what I had seen, within my heart I sensed that for me and my dad, it was our final farewell. Arranging to have the three younger children cared for, my mother prepared to follow the ambulance after instructing my older sister and myself to go to school. "Everything will be alright," she assured.

In fourth period religion class, I couldn't get the thought of my father out of my mind, nor could I concentrate whatsoever on the lesson being taught. Sitting in the very last seat of the classroom, I took out a blank sheet of paper from my folder as I began to do that which relaxed me the most. Sketching a picture for an art assignment, my mind drifted off to an art project I had done at the request of my father the year before. In recognizing my aptitude for art, my dad had asked if I would draw for him a 14" x 16" picture of Our Lady of Fatima. Handing me a small colored picture of an image of Our Lady with the three children to whom she had appeared kneeling before her—Lucinda, Francisco, and Jacinta—I couldn't help but accept his appeal to replicate it for him. Extremely pleased with the finished work, my dad meticulously hand-constructed a lovely frame for it.

Interrupted as the principal walked into the classroom, I intuitively knew that she bore news about my father. I feared the worst. Walking up to the front of the classroom to speak to the instructor, my teacher then looked up to focus on where I was sitting in the back of the room. As my eyes met with his, he spoke matter-of-factly, "Susan, please go with Sister."

Almost jumping out of my seat, I was escorted into the hallway. But before she could utter a single word I blurted out, "Is he dead?"

"No," she replied compassionately, "but your father is in grave condition. The family is being called in."

Without waiting for my older sister to be called out of class, I ran all the way home.

Arriving at the hospital with other family members, how deeply saddened we were to learn that my father had passed away just minutes before. Having suffered a massive stroke, the doctor reported to us that he had never regained consciousness. In hearing his words, I recollected the image of the sweet smile I had seen on my dad's face, pondering within myself the prospect that he had seen the face of his Heavenly Mother.

Absorbed in watching the snow swirl across the top of the road that cold January day on the drive back home from the hospital, barely a word was spoken. Walking into the house, my sister Mary Jo suggested gleefully, "Hey, why don't we all get on Mom and Dad's bed and pray a rosary together!" Not a better tribute could we have given our beloved father. As we began to pray, a peace and calmness filled the room.

A year and a half after my father's death I met the love of my life, and five years later, Rob and I married. In learning after the birth of our second child that I'd inherited the same disease that was the cause of my father's untimely death, though my initial prognosis meant only being vigilant in getting annual physicals to monitor my kidney function, my predisposed tendency was to worry. Because I didn't want to dwell negatively on what the future might hold for me, I came up with the idea to release all of my concerns back over to God. Praying directly from my heart, I asked the Lord if He would be willing to hold on to the PKD diagnosis for me so that I didn't have to fret about it. Closing my eyes, I pictured the hands of Jesus receiving my burden as I envisioned them gently closing. In return, I made a promise back to Him that when the time came, I would humble myself and share my disease openly with others. As ice on a hot summer day, my anxieties melted away, and I went on with my life.

The years raced by as our children seemingly grew straight from toddlers to teens, and it was at this time that I began to experience all kinds of adversity in my life. My stepdad had been diagnosed with terminal lung cancer and my mom with dementia and COPD, a progressive lung disease. I was acting power of attorney for both of them and would often get up in the middle of the night to work on their accounts prior to going to work. Sorting medicines, paying bills, filing for Medicare, cleaning their home, bringing meals over, and taking them to doctor's appointments were taking their toll.

Forgetting to take her nebulizer treatments to open up her lungs at the onset of dementia, my mother began also to take her medications dangerously irregularly. So many things weighed heavily on my heart, and one by one, I continued to trudge through life's problems that were coming at me from all directions. Crying out to God for His help, it was at this point in my life that I began to think about my personal relationship with Jesus. For the most part, I was merely trying to fulfill the obligatory requirements of the Church. But somewhere along the line, I had stopped going to confession. Though I don't ever remember a time in my life when I didn't pray, the real crux of the matter was that I was living out my faith only halfheartedly.

This realization came to me on my drive to work one morning as I spontaneously began praying an Act of Contrition. "O my God I am heartily sorry for having offended Thee, and I detest all my sins, because I dread the loss of heaven, and the pains of hell..."[3] Suddenly, I stopped praying in the acute awareness that I did not feel a deep sense of sorrow for my sins. In fact, I really didn't think of myself as much of a sinner at all. Exiting the highway toward work, I asked God for His forgiveness, begging for the grace to have true sorrow for my sins.

Over the years, I had come to rationalize that because I did not steal, murder, or commit adultery, I was a "good" person. "Why do you notice the splinter in your brother's eye, but do not perceive the wooden beam in your own eye?" (Matthew 7:3). Without even knowing it, I had deceived myself into thinking that I was good based solely on the standards I had set for myself, instead of those set for us by God in the Ten Commandments, and by the Church. Thus, my eyes had been blinded to the sinfulness of my own soul.

It dawned on me that it was during the years I had stopped going to confession that I had also stopped receiving the sanctifying grace necessary to keep my conscience in check. Receiving the Sacrament of Reconciliation not only gives us the grace to repent by turning from sin, but it also enables us to recognize our faults and strive to overcome them. I can clearly remember the instruction given to my elementary school class by Sister Johanna, warning us to be on guard so as not to become lukewarm in our faith. "It's a very good thing when your conscience bothers you," she said. "It's when it doesn't bother you that you have need for concern!" "So, because you are lukewarm, neither hot nor cold, I will spit you out of my mouth" (Revelation 3:16).

The voice of conscience had broken through. I heard the ever-gentle whisper of the Holy Spirit calling me onto the narrow path that leads to holiness. It's when we mistakenly think that we can stand still in our faith without perseverance that we are more inclined to go backward. I learned that the devil is more than happy to steal from us in tiny little inches, because when we're blind in recognizing his cunning tactics, those inches grow into feet and yards, until one day we find ourselves miles away from God and in danger of losing our faith. Our priorities become mixed up when He is no longer number one in our life and we fall into the allure of worldly pleasures and self-indulgence. In turn, we lose all that God intends for us. "You shall love the Lord, your God, with all your heart, with all your soul, and with all your mind. This is the greatest and the first commandment. The second is like it: You shall love your neighbor as yourself" (Matthew 22:37–39).

As my prayer life began rapidly to increase, I began also to feel a special closeness to Jesus. On my commute to work every day, I prayed for the needs of others. While on my way home, I petitioned God for my family. Seeking Mary's intercession, I prayed fervently the Memorare, another prayer taught to me by my father. I also found myself praying over and over the ejaculatory prayer; "Holy Spirit, burn in me the fire of your love." Not even knowing why I was pleading for God to set my heart on fire, it seemed more to be the Spirit praying through me in the knowledge of what I needed most.

In my night prayers, I began to feel a tug from the Holy Spirit that was calling Rob and me away from the large group of friends we'd been chumming with during the course of our entire adult lives. Finding new friendships had never been anything we'd considered, having enjoyed good times with them too numerous to count. I wondered how I'd ever be able to convey to Rob what the Lord was putting on my heart.

Returning home one evening from a night out with our friends, I was saying my night prayers after Rob was asleep. In spite of my father's constant endorsement of family prayer, the truth was that we did not pray together. I feared, in fact, that Rob's prayer life was nonexistent. As I prayed, I suddenly felt a heaviness come over me in the conviction of gossip amongst a few of our friends. I found myself feeling horrible in the interior knowledge of how greatly displeasing this was to God. Instantly, I committed myself to telling Rob.

Approaching the subject matter with him the next morning, I said gingerly, "Hon, as I was praying last night, I sensed that the Lord is leading us down another path, away from our friends."

"Oh yeah?" he responded casually. "Why's that?"

"It's because of gossip," I told him.

"What gossip?" he responded.

From that night on, my ears became increasingly sensitive in hearing little tittle-tattles of any sort, not only amongst friends but including that which went on in my workplace. On one occasion, after having gone out with our friends, I began to sob quietly on the way home. Asking me what was wrong, Rob responded to my distress by telling me once again that he had not heard any of the gossip I was telling him about. "But the things that come out of the mouth come from the heart, and they defile" (Matthew 15:18).

Failing to accomplish what the Lord was asking of me, I was torn. Every weekend, we continued to do what we had always done in hanging out with our friends. On another occasion, as I was praying upon returning home, I felt within my soul a deep sense that the Holy Spirit was calling Rob and me to a life of holiness. It had been two years since I had first heard His initial appeal for us to walk away from our friendships, and in the desperation of my heart, I answered by saying, "What more can I do, Lord? I've tried. You know I've tried." Admitting defeat, I then said, "I can't, Lord, but You can." To my amazement, it was in turning my problem back over to God in the acknowledgment that I could do nothing without Him that proved to be the breakthrough prayer!

The very next time we were out with our friends, Rob walked over and said, "We need to leave." Once outside, he explained to me that he was appalled to overhear the cruel words that were being spoken by one of the women against someone else. "I know now what you have been trying to tell me all this time," he said. "We will never come back."

I was completely shocked at the resolve of his words. "Oh, that today you would hear his voice:/ Harden not your hearts" (Hebrews 3:15). It was the Lord who opened Rob's ears in the realization of how those we spend our time with ultimately do have a huge impact on how God's plan will unfold in our lives. Not once did Rob go back on his word, and what a relief it was to have taken the first step in answering God's call.

Rob had accrued a good amount of vacation time at his job over the years, and in order for us to have the flexibility to travel together on long weekends to see our daughter play basketball at the University of Dayton, I accepted a job at a major hotel chain. My position also offered me low hotel rates for our frequent travels. A five-hundred-mile trip one way, it was typical for us to pack up and leave after work on Wednesday evenings in order to make it to the halfway point, allowing us to catch both her Thursday and Saturday night home games. It was wonderful for Rob and I to be able to spend the one-on-one time together combined with the enjoyment of watching our daughter achieve her goal of earning a scholarship to play Division I college basketball. And of no less importance was the opportunity of stirring up Rob's prayer life! Asking if he minded me praying various Scripture passages aloud as he drove, his usual nonchalant response was, "If you want to." On other occasions when I'd invite him to pray the rosary, though he declined in saying the responding half of the prayers, he'd consent for me to pray them out loud while he listened. And so I did.

The troubles of my heart were great, and I couldn't pray enough. It felt so good to confide in the Lord all my hardships, and in being able to pray with Rob for our shared concerns was even nicer. High up on my list of concerns was that our young adult son was being allured into the ways of the world. I prayed for him constantly, seeking protection from the archangel Michael. Our daughter, a gifted and talented athlete, always seemed to be plagued with sports injuries throughout her youth. Now, with the rigorous training required in playing collegiate sports, that too was also wreaking havoc on her body.

Though Jenelle suffered chronic pain in the frequency of her injuries, she'd go to the training room for continual physical therapy and, sucking up the pain, would continue to play. Having suffered from severe food allergies while still in the high chair, this was another reason for concern in the trips we had made with her to the ER when her throat began to swell shut. Having to deal with the challenges of her food allergies while flying halfway around the country with her team for away games, she'd call home frequently to talk. Advising and reassuring her, I placed my daughter into the care of her Heavenly Mother to watch over her during the times that I couldn't.

Receiving the infamous birthday call just a few years later alerting me of my imminent kidney failure, I was devastated! I was praying for less problems, not more. The shattering news opened up in me all of the worries and concerns from years past. I felt weak in the knees in dread of the cross that lay before me, a cross that I had no desire to pick up and that I only wished would go away. "Then he said to all, 'If anyone wishes to come after me, he must deny himself and take up his cross daily and follow me'" (Luke 9:23).

My spirit was broken. I'd lay awake in the terror of the night, bound in the grip of fear. My thoughts overflowed with the dread of what may or may not happen to me. Would there be a donor? Would I have to go on dialysis? I was already beyond the age in which my father lived, would I die an early death like him? I was empty and afraid.

During the time that I was overcome with fear, I quickly discovered it to be a terribly destructive vice that squeezes the life out of those who embrace it. Enveloping me in a black cloud of darkness, how soon it turned my hope into despair. Though I understood fear of the unknown to be a natural human response, I also knew that deep-seated fear was not of God. So I petitioned my family to pray for me to be set free of the foreboding gloom that held me tight within its grip. In the days following my prognosis, I remember wishing that I could retreat all by myself to the darkest, most remote corner of my house and just make the world go away. It was in this place of uncertainty that I wondered; Is God even hearing my prayers? Is He punishing me?

Trying to conceal my inner pain from Rob, as soon as the lights went out, I prayed deep from the recesses of my heart, saying, "God, it's me. I'm right here! Don't You see me, Lord? Don't You hear me calling You? I'm right here!" Feeling like nothing more than a minuscule speck in the universe, I prayed this same plea for three night's straight, begging God to hear my prayer. Unbeknown to me, it was in this heart's cry and God's impeccable timing that I was about to be set on course toward a head-on collision with His tender love and mercy. "The LORD is close to the brokenhearted,/ saves those whose spirit is crushed" (Psalm 34:19).

What threatened to interrupt the colossal pity party I had thrown for myself was the upcoming trip to Mackinac Island that I had promised to take my mother on. Since the death of my stepdad, I'd been making every effort to pick her up to spend a day at our home each week and to take her on periodic day trips and minivacations. More than willing to help out, Rob often was the first to suggest we include my mom in on various activities. What horrific timing, I thought, that the long weekend she'd been so much looking forward to all summer had been prearranged to take place just three days after receiving the news that turned my world upside down. In my unrelenting misery, it was the last thing I wanted to do.

We had planned the minivacation in mid-October in anticipation of taking in the autumn colors for the five-hour drive to Michigan's Upper Peninsula. Having to transport my mother's wheelchair and portable oxygen tanks, it was undeniably becoming more difficult for us to take her on overnight excursions. Possessing a great love for the water, my mom had voiced her excitement about this particular trip in anticipation of the boat ride over to the island. How could I cancel it now?

In hearing the weekend weather forecast for the UP was for high winds with a freezing rain/sleet mix, it occurred to me that the nasty forecast could actually work out in my favor. I'd simply tell my mom of the inclement weather prediction and let her call off the weekend herself. That way I wouldn't have to feel guilty about doing it for my own selfish purposes and could continue to drown myself in my sorrows. Calling my mom, however, I was surprised to find that her enthusiasm concerning the trip remained undaunted despite the weather forecast. Hearing the excitement in her voice, my heart melted in thinking of her being stuck in her wheelchair day after day. Feeling ashamed for even having considered denying her the chance to get out, I resolved within myself that fear was just going to have to take a back seat for a few days, and afraid or not, the trip with my mother was on. So as not to damper her spirits, I held back on telling her my bad news.

Crossing the elevated suspended bridge as we neared Mackinac City, we were thankful to view its unique structural design before hearing on the local radio station that, because of high winds, the bridge was closing. Our suite had a king-sized bed complete with fireplace and kitchenette, and off to the side was a small nook without a door, just big enough to fit a double bed with a TV mounted to the wall. Seeing my mom's eyes light up at the sight of the beautiful room, Rob and I agreed that she would have the large bed by the fireplace.

Though the sky was dark and threatening the next morning, we decided to carry on with our plans to take my mother over to the island. Having called ahead to be sure the boat was handicap accessible, we learned upon boarding that there would be no getting my mom down the set of stairs leading to the lower deck where everyone else was seated.

"Isn't the boat handicap accessible?" Rob asked. Leading us to the cargo deck, we were completely taken aback to find it was the "handicap accessible" they were referring to! It was now pouring profusely, and I quickly pulled out the blanket I had brought along to place over my mom. Alone on the cargo deck, the turbulent weather conditions and large white caps on the Great Lake made for a rough and miserable ride over to the island. Terrified as the canvas flaps whipped about violently in the repeated wind gusts that pelted us with freezing rain, I feared going overboard!

Once on the Island, the rain had finally stopped and our clothes began to dry off some. My mom was so content, and the unpleasant boat experience didn't seem to faze her in the least! Pushing her around the island to her utter delight, we stopped in shops and enjoyed the sights. Homemade saltwater taffy, my mother's favorite, had become for us a staple on all of our outings. Maneuvering her wheelchair in between the narrow aisles of the stores and restaurants, giving her meds at scheduled intervals, and searching for electrical outlets to administer her breathing treatments didn't seem to interrupt in the slightest the enjoyment of her day.

Nearing midafternoon, we decided to sport the hike up to the top of a steep walk leading up a few hundred feet to Fort Mackinac, a historical site founded during the American Revolution. Pushing on as we wheeled my mom up the hill, we stopped along the way to rest. Once at the top, we turned to take in the panoramic view of the island encircled by the waters of Lake Huron. There, I stood captivated as I watched the magnificent brilliance of the sun suddenly break through in stunning contrast to the black sky. In the luminous rays streaming out from the heavens, I was enveloped in the warmth of God's embrace.

If only for a moment, I became one with the island, surrounded not by the waters of Lake Huron, but by Jesus, the Living Water. I could neither deny the warmth of the sun on my face nor the consciousness of God's immense love shining down upon me. They were one and the same. Having carried my heavy burden up to the pinnacle of the island, it was there that I found the all-loving and never-changing God who just days before had seemed to be somewhere so very far away. As one who thirsted for God in my brokenness, the Fountain of Life extended down to me an invitation to drink generously from the inexhaustible fount of His mercy, a fount from which I would thirst no more. God had heard my call for help! "I sought the LORD who answered me,/ delivered me from all my fears" (Psalm 34:5).

Having decided to put my own problems and insecurities aside in order to keep the promise I had made to my mother, I was overcome at the way in which God had orchestrated this event in that I would be made fully aware of His presence. The stormy weather that I wanted to use as an excuse in not going was the very means through which our Lord would show to me His glory. I was enlightened to know that it is during the times when our cross is the heaviest that His light will shine through to us the brightest. Jesus, the Light of the world, had broken through the black clouds of doubt and fear to dispel the darkness that loomed in my soul!

That evening back at the hotel, I read a Scripture passage that would begin to change my perspective on suffering. "I am the true vine, and my Father is the vine grower. He takes away every branch in me that does not bear fruit, and everyone that does he prunes so that it bears more fruit. Whoever remains in me and I in him will bear much fruit, because without me you can do nothing" (John 15:1–2, 5). As I meditated on Jesus' words, my mind was opened in the blessed assurance that I was not being punished by God in my trials, but that it was through my adversity He was pruning me to bear more fruit!

The hand of God had opened back up to me the burden I had placed in it almost a quarter of a century prior. His strong but gentle hand reached out to me, offering to lighten the load of my impending kidney failure. Accepting Jesus' offer to walk with Him in the pain that accompanies adversity, I decided to hold on tightly to the one true source that would give me strength to journey into the unknown. "Take my yoke upon you and learn from me, for I am meek and humble of heart; and you will find rest for yourselves. For my yoke is easy, and my burden light" (Matthew 11:29–30).

My entire life I had viewed suffering as being more of a curse than a blessing. But God had opened my eyes to see things in a new light. I wondered if my experience on Mackinac Island served as a forerunner to the trials that lay before me. In crossing over the swaying suspended bridge in high wind velocity with my mother, would Rob and I help prepare her for a smooth passage from this life to the next? In riding the stormy waters of Lake Huron and pushing forward to the pinnacle of the island to see the sun break through the dark clouds, was God showing us that we need to persist upward in climbing the mountain of life's adversity in order for us to see the splendor of His glory upon reaching the top?

It is in the most trying of times that our faith is rebuilt and the shattered pieces of our lives put together so that we may be made whole. When the fury of life's storms blew in and threatened to sink my faith, I sought shelter in the One who calms the waves of fear and stills the winds of adversity. It was in hitting rock bottom that I looked up to God, who answered me in a way far beyond anything I had ever hoped for. "In my distress I called out: LORD!/ I cried out to my God./ From his temple he heard my voice;/ my cry to him reached his ears" (Psalm 18:7).

I was about to embark upon a five-year journey up Mount Tabor. There, I would learn of the glory that we can bring to Jesus when we allow ourselves to be further transformed into His likeness. I would discover that God had brought me up to the highest point of the island that day in order that I may one day reach the summit of eternal salvation. Through His holy plan, I was chosen to walk along the *Forgotten Way* on a path to holiness through the trials of my life. It was on this path that I would see radiant sunbeams of hope shining through along the way that would enable me to see beyond the darkness. "For God who said, 'Let light shine out of darkness,' has shone in our hearts to bring to light the knowledge of the glory of God on the face of [Jesus] Christ" (2 Corinthians 4:6).

At the cross her station keeping,
Stood the mournful Mother weeping,
Close to Jesus to the last.

—Stabat Mater

Do not be worried that the time of trial is so long. We can only reach salvation by crossing the stormy sea, which constantly threatens to overwhelm us. Calvary is the hill of saints, but from it we go on to another hill called Tabor, the Mount of Transfiguration.

—Padre Pio

Stations of the Cross

Second Station
Jesus Accepts His Cross

I have no wish whatsoever to have my cross lightened, for it is a joy for me to suffer with Jesus. When I contemplate the Cross on the shoulders of Jesus, I feel myself strengthened, and I exult with holy joy.

—Padre Pio

Walk with Me

On a day off of work, I was doing errands for my mother when I decided to listen to a Christian teaching on audio tape as I drove about. Although I had heard this particular verse many times before, it seemed this time God was speaking directly to me through His holy word: "This is the day the Lord has made;/ let us rejoice in it and be glad" (Psalm 118:24). Instantly upon hearing it, I suddenly had a deep sense that our Lord was telling me He wanted me to be happy. How often I had attributed happiness to when everything was going good in my life. I felt that God was asking me to not only trust Him in good times, but to also trust in Him amidst times of great trial, to celebrate and find joy in each new day in spite of its troubles!

To put into practice what the Lord was asking of me would require a deeper surrender of myself, to let go of my difficulties in turning them all back over to Him. Having released back the cross of my PKD after so lovingly holding on to it for me for twenty-five years, our Lord was now asking me to trust Him so fully that I should have joy.

As Rob and I traveled from our home to an all-night vigil service in Milwaukee, I picked up a brochure from a Marian Shrine we had recently visited that read; "This is the day the Lord has made, let us rejoice in it and be glad." Sitting up straight in my seat, I shared with Rob how I had felt the Lord speak those very same words to my heart the day before. During the celebration of Mass that evening, I listened in astonishment to the priest's homily centered on the very same verse. The month was November and I thought that particular psalm was one that was read exclusively during the Easter season.

In great wonderment, I decided to take a closer look at what God was trying to convey to me through the verse. Stilling my soul in front of the Blessed Sacrament following the Mass, I began to meditate on it. My thoughts brought me back to our boat ride over to the island just a few weeks prior, and of the great hope the psalm offers us during the times we find ourselves getting bounced about in the turbulent waters of life. I felt the Lord was telling me that no matter what was happening on the outside; in surrendering my troubles to Him, I'd be able to experience joy on the inside. Not when my troubles were gone, but right now—today, tomorrow, and every day! Though in my humanness my mind would sometimes wander back in focusing on all of the problems going on in my life, God was encouraging me that by focusing on the blessings that accompanied each new day, it would give me cause for rejoicing. It all made sense in my head to release my burden to God in order to have inner joy, but at the same time, it seemed to be much easier said than done! Resisting extreme tiredness as we prayed into the night, Rob and I returned home on Sunday morning feeling spiritually renewed and refreshed.

The leader of my weekly Bible group opened the study by reading "This is the day the LORD has made, let us rejoice in it and be glad!" Wow, God, now you really have my attention! That evening as I lay in bed praying, I responded to Jesus' invitation.

"Lord, there is so much pain and trial in my life right now, and I do feel inundated with sadness. But You're asking me to be joyful and trust in You in spite of my troubles. I will be obedient to Your request by making a cognitive decision to be joyful, if You will give to me the grace to achieve it."

In the distress of my situation, it was our Lord's wish to restore my inner happiness. But it first required my *yes* to follow Him along the Way of the Cross in the trials of life. He did not take my hardships away, but yet the weight of my troubles were lifted off of my shoulders by accepting to carry my cross with Jesus. He would lighten its weight. I'd been delivered from the fear of the unknown in my health status, and now I was filled with joy in spite of it! "Look to God that you may be radiant with joy/ and your faces may not blush for shame" (Psalm 34:6).

There was no other way that I could have attained the fruits of peace and joy but through prayer. Not through possessions or prestige, but only through my heart-to-heart conversation with God. It was in my brokenness that I had emptied myself out, allowing Him to fill me with His love. Jesus was my strength to persevere through life's difficulties in the assurance that He was walking right beside me. "Have no anxiety at all, but in everything, by prayer and petition, with thanksgiving, make your requests known to God. Then the peace of God that surpasses all understanding will guard your hearts and minds in Christ Jesus" (Philippians 4:6–7).

Seated in the transplant unit of the hospital's waiting room listening for our names to be called, it would prove to be a full day on top of the two-hour commute, with the scheduled lab tests, physical exam, and in meeting the surgeon and nurse coordinator assigned to my case. My physical exam revealed that, because my kidneys were enormous in size due to the numerous and large cysts that covered them, they would have to be removed. The excision of my kidneys would require them to perform a second major surgery in addition to the kidney transplant itself, which the surgeon explained would pose a much greater risk, explaining that it was not typically done unless deemed medically necessary, as in my case. It wasn't until meeting with the nurse coordinator that I began to feel an uneasiness fester within my soul. Enthused in telling her that he hoped to be my donor, she voiced to Rob rather harshly, "These husband-and-wife organ donations rarely work out." Startled when, for no apparent reason, she told him that we were not to expect any preferential treatment if he was to be a match, I lost my inner peace.

The next morning, I awakened with the disquiet of the previous day still lingering in my soul. Getting in the morning mail, a large envelope caught my eye. Inside, I found a rather large booklet containing various healing Scriptures. Not sure as to why I had received the packet, as I read the very first verse I started to laugh and cry at the same time. "Why are you downcast, my soul,/ why do you groan within me?/ Wait for God, whom I shall praise again,/ my savior and my God" (Psalm 42:12). Instantly, I knew in my heart that I would one day be praising God for the very illness that now threatened my life. I had fallen under the weight of my cross and it was through reading this soothing passage that my loving Lord had reached out His hand once again to restore my countenance.

As I continued to read the entire booklet of the wonderful promises given to us in sacred Scripture, the heaviness of my heart was lifted. Feeling as though I had stumbled onto a gold mine, I knew also that it was through God's holy providence that I received the passages. Never having requested the healing Scriptures, they arrived precisely when I needed God's peace and tranquility restored in my soul. I felt like a wounded child who was being consoled through the reassuring words of her Father. From that day on, God's word became my blueprint for living. "Heaven and earth will pass away, but my words will not pass away" (Matthew 24:35).

From the very depths of my soul, it was my desire to saturate myself in Scripture. Tears of joy would fill my eyes in the hope it offered and in the peace that was to be found. With great enthusiasm, I sat down with my Bible to highlight every verse that spoke to my heart so that I could read them every single day.

This set in motion my daily practice of reading and meditating on God's holy word.

> "My son, to my words be attentive,
> to my sayings incline your ear;
> Let them not slip out of your sight,
> keep them within your heart;
> For they are life to those who find them,
> to man's whole being they are health."
>
> (Proverbs 4:20–22)

Of the many passages I had begun to read each day, there was one that stood out to me above all the rest. "And then a leper approached, did him homage, and said, 'Lord, if you wish, you can make me clean'" (Matthew 8:2). It reminded me of the little prayer that formed in my heart in the days following my prognosis in saying to Jesus, "Lord, I know that if You're willing, You can heal me." And so amongst all of the Scriptures I read, I began reading this specific verse as my very own. Right above the word *leper* in my Bible, I penciled in "woman with PKD" in claiming it for myself. Jesus' answer to the leper who came to Him in plea to be made clean was that He would do it! But even before the leper addressed Jesus, he first paid Him homage. With that, I knew I needed to praise and thank God in advance of His response to my plea.

I was gaining understanding that the trials allowed us in turn enable us to be sympathetic to others who suffer the same. Through the comfort that God was giving me in the malady of my heart, from His consolation I would be able to comfort others in their need. "For as Christ's sufferings overflow to us, so through Christ does our encouragement also overflow" (2 Corinthians 1:5).

The year to follow was one of responding to a deeper and more courageous faith through embracing life's crosses. It was a year of spiritual surrender and of emptying myself in order to make more room for God. Jesus calls the impoverished to walk with Him because it is through our weaknesses that we are able to let go. My hardships and struggles were God's tools to help me realize my own limitations and the need for His companionship. It was in the steady flow of God's grace that I was allowed the staying power to deny myself and pick up my cross, to walk with Jesus on the path of suffering that would lead to my sanctification. This did not come easy for me by any stretch of the imagination. It required a day-to-day self-abandonment of my will in exchange to live within the Holy Will of God. Jesus, both God and man, had extended out His hand for me to walk with Him in order that my human steps could be united with His divinity. On my own, I could do nothing. But to unite my little crosses to the Cross of Christ meant power, and it meant constantly drawing from His never-ending stream of grace.

Tuning into the Eternal Word Television Network (EWTN)[1] one day, I heard for the very first time the Divine Mercy Chaplet being prayed in song. The words drew me in, and I found them echoing over and over in my mind, unaware of how it would turn out to be pivotal in my spiritual growth. Captivated by this beautiful song of God's mercy, I had to learn more.

It was back in 1931 that our Lord appeared to St. Faustina[2] in a vision in which she saw rays of mercy streaming from His Heart. In another vision, she saw an angel sent by God to punish a city. Finding her prayers to be powerless, she began pleading with God for mercy when she heard interiorly: "Eternal Father, I offer You the Body and Blood, Soul and Divinity of Your dearly beloved Son, Our Lord Jesus Christ, in atonement for our sins and those of the whole world; for the sake of His sorrowful Passion, have mercy on us and on the whole world"[3] (*Diary*, 475). As she continued saying this inspired prayer, the angel was rendered helpless, unable to carry out the deserved chastisement. Jesus told St. Faustina, "At three o'clock, implore My mercy, especially for sinners; and, if only for a brief moment, immerse yourself in My Passion, particularly in the hour of great mercy... In this hour I will refuse nothing to the soul that makes a request of Me in virtue of My Passion"[4] (*Diary*, 1320).

Deeply moved in learning of God's message of mercy to the world through St. Faustina, I began praying the Chaplet of Divine Mercy[5] (*Diary*, 754) every day at 3:00 p.m. In my meditation, I thought about Jesus' excruciatingly painful Crowning of Thorns in relation to the prideful sins of mankind. I thought of His flogging, and of the innocent blood that is shed each day around the world in the killing of unborn babies through abortion. In the nailing of Jesus' right hand, I considered aggressive sins such as sexual abuse, stealing, and murder. In meditation on His left and less dominant hand being nailed to the Cross, I thought of passive-aggressive sins, such as envy, hatred, and lust. When the feet of our Savior were nailed to the Cross, I considered the feet of so many, who turn their back on Jesus and walk the other way. Getting down on my knees before the Divine Mercy image of Jesus on the wall, I could tangibly feel my heart stir in the promise of His mercy! The simple words "Jesus, I trust in You!"[6] (*Diary*, 47) helped me to turn each day's troubles back over to Jesus in trust of His mercy. Little did I know of the significance this devotion would ultimately have in my own healing.

St. Faustina holding Divine Mercy image

Suffering is an inevitable part of life that holds the potential to sanctify our souls. Yet it is something that, without the faith of a child, can be so very difficult to embrace. Having no idea when my kidney function would fall below the 20 percent mark set by the transplant surgeon in proceeding with plans for surgery, I also didn't know whether or not my husband would be a suitable match in his desire to give me one of his kidneys. Uncertain whether I would end up on dialysis, or if I would be one of the tens of thousands of people who would be put on the national waiting list, I was content in the assurance that Jesus loved me and that He was walking with me in my trial. Whenever my humanness would take over and cause me to worry, it was in surrendering myself back into the Divine Will of God that would bring calmness back into my soul. "For we walk by faith, not by sight" (2 Corinthians 5:7).

Though I had chosen to keep private my inherited kidney disease back when I was twenty-four years old, I had every intention of keeping the promise I had made to God. I used to think that it was easier to stuff down and bury any hardship that I was experiencing under the pretext that everything was perfectly fine. But after having carried out my vow to the Lord, I better understood the value that exists in even the smallest act of humility. The outpouring of love and concern I received in sharing of my affliction far outweighed the reservation I had in doing so, and my spirit was at ease in having honored my vow to God of so many years before.

I began to live each day in the moment, trying very hard not to look back on yesterday or being overly concerned about what tomorrow might bring. God was teaching me that He uses every situation for the good, including those involving the sick and suffering. He uses adverse situations to open the hearts of those who are far away from Him. It was my sickness that brought me closer to God, and it would be through the same infirmity that others would come closer to Him through the outpouring of their love and compassion expressed toward me. "Our hope for you is firm, for we know that as you share in the sufferings, you also share in the encouragement" (2 Corinthians 1:7).

I was scheduled to go in for regular blood draws in order to monitor my kidney function. Due to my total kidney capacity functioning at only 22 percent, the minerals in my blood were definitely out of order, allowing toxic poisons to spill into my blood. Instead of filtering them from my blood and holding on to the nutrients necessary for good health, my malfunctioning kidneys were doing the opposite. Among other things, the kidneys have an effect in controlling levels of sodium, potassium, calcium, and phosphorus in the bloodstream, as well as the production of red blood cells. My lab values revealed mineral imbalances bordering on high and low-normal, requiring meticulous food monitoring. I was determined to discipline myself in maintaining a very strict diet in order to buy my kidneys more time.

In the years since first being diagnosed with PKD, I had carefully followed a low-protein diet that was thought to slow the progression of kidney failure. But since learning that my kidney function was plummeting, my diet had become much more rigorous and complicated. Coming up with meals on this harsh food regimen was extremely difficult, and to have them actually taste good with little or no sodium to control my blood pressure was an added challenge!

That's when I began praying for the Holy Spirit to inspire me in creating delicious dishes. To form a recipe, I'd first write down the limited foods I could eat, and then I'd search out ways to combine them into dishes that appealed to me. When I found a winner, I'd bring the recipe to my next appointment to share with other renal patients who were placed on similar restricted diets. I also began praying scripturally before eating, asking for God's blessing upon literally everything I put in my mouth, as well as petitioning Him to increase the numbers of our descendants.

> "The LORD, your God, you shall worship; then I will bless your food and drink, and I will remove all sickness from your midst; no woman in your land will be barren or miscarry; and I will give you a full span of life." (Exodus 23:25–26)

In resignation to God's Will, I simply offered back to Him another small sliver of the cross allowed me. Rather than feeling slighted in my eating restrictions, I felt good in the sacrifice I was able to offer back to Jesus. It was on one of my monthly visits to my nephrologist that he voiced, "Out of all my patients, you're the most disciplined."

What he didn't know was of the vast amounts of grace I was receiving in turning my problems back over to Jesus each day. My doctor would often tell me how "lucky" I was for not having the menacing symptoms of the disease.

"Yes!" I'd confirm, adding, "I am very blessed!" Reiterating his sentiments, I'd always replace his use of the word *lucky* with "blessed." In noting my joyfulness, lab technicians alike would comment on how lucky I was and say that I didn't "look sick." Smiling, I always responded, "Yes, I've been very blessed."

A strange and wonderful thing was happening inside of me. In spite of the continued decline of my kidney function, I was beginning to see the hidden graces and blessings of my illness. With an expectant faith, I continued praying the words that so resembled those of the leper in saying, "Lord, if You are willing, You can heal me." Until the time that God's Will for me would unfold, I held on to the trust in Jesus' mercy and that He would give me strength to bear my trials with Him. Striving for a childlike faith, to believe without seeing, I grasped tightly onto the hand that promised to lighten my load. Beckoning for me to walk with Him in my trials, I was better able to accept the sufferings that God was allowing me. Jesus desires to help us during times of distress. It's in these times He wishes to lovingly guide our steps along the Way of the Cross until they become one with His. In choosing to carry the cross of adversity with our Lord on this pilgrim journey we call life, one will discover the narrow path of ongoing conversion that leads to holiness. "But may I never boast except in the cross of our Lord Jesus Christ, through which the world has been crucified to me, and I to the world" (Galatians 6:14).

Through her heart, his sorrow sharing,
All his bitter anguish bearing,
  Now at length the sword had passed.

—Stabat Mater

The road is narrow. He who wishes to travel it more easily must cast off all things and use the cross as his cane. In other words, he must be truly resolved to suffer willingly for the love of God in all things.

—Saint John of the Cross[7]

Stations of the Cross

Third Station
Jesus Falls the First Time

The most certain proof of love is to suffer for the one we love, and since the Son of God suffered so much for pure love, there can no longer be any doubt that the crosses we carry for Him become lovable in proportion to our love.

—Padre Pio

Ask, Seek, and Knock

It was in realizing the ill effects of neglecting to move forward in my faith in the hustles and bustles of life that I began to prolong my daily prayer life. Praying from my heart, my alone time with Jesus was what allowed me the way out of any situation or burden that seemingly had no escape. Before putting my feet on the floor to get out of bed in the morning, I first prayed the morning offering taught to me by the Sisters of St. John's Elementary School, offering all my thoughts, all my words, and all of my actions of the new day to Jesus. By setting aside times throughout the day to forget all of my worries and concerns by resting in God, I was able to put aside my problems and know that, for right now, nothing else mattered.

At night before going to sleep, I got down on my knees to pray one of the most beautiful novena prayers I'd ever come across, *The Efficacious Novena to the Sacred Heart of Jesus*.[1] The same prayer that St. Padre Pio recited daily for those who asked for his prayers, I found it to be the ultimate way of surrendering back to Jesus all my cares and concerns. Restoring my peace at day's end, it was especially valuable in transforming everything into joy during times when the storm waters of life managed to rise up above me. Complimenting my devotion to reading my Bible each day, the three Scripture verses in the novena helped me to place the torments of my soul before the throne of God's mercy.

Sharing with Rob one night of the tremendous quietude I found in praying the novena, I asked if he'd be willing to say it with me. Reluctant at first, he ultimately got out of bed to kneel next to me in placing all the troubles of our hearts within the

Sacred Heart of Jesus. Something he had initially thought to be so awkward would become for him as routine as brushing his teeth. No longer trying to focus on the right words to say, he simply prayed out loud that which was in his heart.

"Ask and it will be given to you; seek and you will find; knock and the door will be opened to you" (Matthew 7:7). From the smallest of difficulties to the greatest of concerns, we set no boundaries on the mighty power of God. No longer concerned about asking for "too much" or for things of insignificance, we left out nothing.

"Amen, amen, I say to you, whatever you ask the Father in my name he will give you" (John 16:23). We began to realize more fully the magnitude of what Jesus has given us in the authority to use His name, as though it was Jesus Himself asking! Calling out to our Heavenly Father through the power of the holy name of His Son, the name above all names, how could He refuse us of even the smallest of things as long as they would not go against the good of our souls?

"Heaven and earth will pass away, but my words will not pass away" (Matthew 24:35). From the very depths of our heart, we thanked Jesus for our many blessings, and of our gratefulness for having been led into Scripture, believing with all our heart that God's holy word is true. More than that, we believed that God is always true to His word! Offering glory, honor, and praise to the Father for giving us His Son, the Word made flesh, we thanked Him in all of the circumstances of our day. In the knowledge that we were exactly where we needed to be, we expressed to God our trust that all things would work out for the good of those who love Him, just as Scripture promises!

Suffering for years from migraine headaches caused by hormonal fluctuations, I was unable to take aspirin products because of my kidney disease. With their potential of getting out of control, the migraines became agonizing at times, causing me to become very sick. I had been experiencing signs of premenopause for nearly ten years, when everything began to go awry. Initially, it was only in experiencing heavy and irregular periods with more cramping. An ultrasound at my gynecologist's office revealed three large fibroids on my uterus as the source of causing the excessive bleeding. I remember one night in particular when I awoke with pain in my abdomen so intense that I couldn't get back to sleep. Getting out of bed to go to work, I doubled over in pain. Unable to stand up straight, my gynecologist's office advised me to come right in for a biopsy, which, thanks be to God, was benign. Month after month as the symptoms grew worse, it escalated into a continual onslaught of one adverse symptom after another.

With the Advent season being my favorite time of the year, I awoke on Christmas morning in great anticipation of the joy it brought with it. Right away, however, I felt the menacing cramps and heavy clotting from a menstrual cycle that would not end. Just when the bleeding seemed to be stopping, it would start up all over again. I had a bad feeling inside of me and I knew this was becoming serious. I had been flowing for much too long. With the onset of heavy bleeding once again, I went over to my calendar to learn that the start of my flow had begun twenty-one days prior!

As I was preparing to celebrate Christmas Mass with my family, I decided I'd wait to tell Rob of my health concern until we returned home. During the offertory of the Mass, I felt myself begin to hemorrhage so profusely that I didn't know what to do.

In not wanting to leave Mass or to spend Christmas day in the emergency room, I prayed with all of my heart. "Baby Jesus lying in the manger, please make this hemorrhaging stop!" To my relief, no sooner did I finish my petition when the bleeding all together ceased. "Thank you, sweet Jesus!" I prayed, recollecting the Bible story of the woman who suffered with hemorrhages for twelve years. Upon touching the cloak of Jesus, her bleeding stopped. Grateful for what Jesus had done for me, I marveled at the gift I received in not having to interrupt our family Christmas celebration! I resolved to call my gynecologist the next day.

Rob received a call regarding the testing necessary to determine if he'd be a compatible candidate to donate one of his kidneys to me. Having already been established to be of the same blood type, Rob had been adamant all along in saying that *he* was going to be my donor. Suddenly, the prospect of receiving one of his kidneys stirred my emotions.

"Hon," I asked, "do you remember what you said to console me twenty-five years ago when I first found out that I had PKD?"

"Yes," he said. "I told you not to worry, because when the time came I'd give you one of mine!"

How wonderful it would be for him to be a match after vowing to be my donor all those years back! God knew the desires of my heart, and I had come to a place of surrender in knowing that He was in control. To maintain inner peace, I constantly surrendered my will in trust of His perfect plan for me. I'll never forget the joy on Rob's face when the results came in. His antigens matched mine like we were siblings! Laughing happily, he hugged me and spun me around as though we'd just won the lottery! He was then set up for a number of tests to determine the overall status of his health to further qualify him as my prospective donor.

One by one, he passed them with flying colors, with only one test remaining.

It had been determined years prior that Rob had what they referred to as an "athlete's heart." Being very athletic, his heart muscle was strong and able to pump effectively at a much lower rate. His pulse ranged in the low fifties, and we felt confident in the scheduled chemical stress test. To our dismay, however, the outcome was not as we had hoped. Noting three areas of concern, the cardiologist recommended he undergo a heart catheterization.

The long and drawn-out day at the hospital was worth its weight in gold upon hearing the news that Rob's heart was healthy. In the recovery room, he had to lie perfectly still for a length of time to allow the artery in his leg to close before going home. In not wanting to cause him further stress, I had neglected to tell him that I'd been hemorrhaging throughout the day like never before. As Rob was preparing to be released, I had a sickening feeling inside of me that I should be admitted.

Feeling exhausted, it was closing in on 7:00 p.m. when we got home. Telling Rob what was going on, he said, "Hon, I'm supposed to be on bed rest and I think you need to do the same." We'd barely eaten a thing all day, and calling Jenelle, she offered to bring us some food.

Lying perfectly still and afraid to move, when I told her of the heavy bleeding I'd been experiencing, she said, "Mom, you need to call your doctor!"

I knew that my situation had become serious, and so I promised her that if the bleeding didn't stop soon, I'd seek medical attention. Hanging up the phone, I prayed from my heart, "Dearest Jesus, just as You stopped my hemorrhaging on Christmas day, please do the same for me now." All at once, the bleeding stopped. "Cast all your worries upon him because he cares for you" (1 Peter 5:7).

Calling my gynecologist's office the next morning, his nurse instructed me to come right in. My iron tested extremely low from the loss of blood and another biopsy was done. My doctor then relayed to me that things had escalated to the point where surgery was necessary. Knowing he was correct in his assessment, I voiced my concern of going under anesthesia. It would surely deplete the small amount of kidney function I had left.

"Having a hysterectomy and renal failure would not be a good scenario for me," I said.

"Yes," he agreed. "But I cannot let you bleed to death." Standing up, he concluded, "We will see with the results of your biopsy and I want you to schedule yourself for an ultrasound in the very first opening. Then we will decide. I suspect that your fibroids have grown, and at the very least, they will have to be removed."

Stopping off at the front desk on my way out, I was so relieved to learn of the two-week wait that would allow me extra time to storm heaven! Immediately, I sought out the prayers of my family, friends, and all the prayer chains that I knew. Throughout each day, I made the sign of the Cross over my uterus, asking God to heal me.

The day had arrived and Rob insisted on coming with me to my appointment. When the nurse called out my name to take me back for the ultrasound, he whispered, "I'll be praying for you, hon."

With the ultrasound finished, I was led into an exam room to wait for my doctor. Walking into the room with my chart in his hands, he silently reviewed the results. Pausing for a moment, he turned abruptly, and without uttering a word, he walked out of the room!

My heart sank as I became exceedingly concerned that something was terribly wrong. From my heart, I began to recite my favorite prayer, the Memorare. Relying on Our Lady's intercession, I prayed the words my father had taught me. "Remember O Most Gracious Virgin Mary, that never was it known that anyone who fled for thy protection, implored thy help or sought thy intercession was left unaided..."[2] What had impressed me the most as a child was in hearing the emphasis my father had placed on the word *never*. I remember thinking; *Mary will* never *let me down!* "Holy Mother," I prayed as I awaited my doctor's return, "I do believe that you'll come to my aide by bringing my petition to Jesus!"

Minutes seemed like hours until my doctor's return. Smiling, he told me that upon reading the results of my ultrasound, he was convinced he'd been given the wrong chart. It showed not a single fibroid left to be found! Even more remarkable was from that day on, I never had another episode of excessive bleeding. Going through menopause was a breeze, a holy breeze bestowed on me through the miraculous healing of my uterus! Tears of thanksgiving formed in my eyes as I prayed, "Never was it known, Mary, that anyone who fled for your protection was left unaided." I had seen the power of God through the aide of His Mother!

In the eyes of faith, glimpses of light were poking out from the darkness. Each day, I sought to incorporate the simplistic yet powerful words that Jesus spoke to Peter and the disciples. "Have faith in God!" (Mark 11:22). Walking out on the water to meet Jesus takes faith, and like Peter, there were numerous times I'd lose sight, and in doubt, would begin to sink. For so long it had seemed that the harder I'd pray for the storms of life to let up, the harder it would rain! Getting battered and pelted from all directions, I clung on tightly to the rock of my faith. "The rain fell, the floods came, and the winds blew and buffeted the house. But it did not collapse; it had been set solidly on rock" (Matthew 7:25).

Jesus is the rock that calms the storms of life, and the rock on which I had been solidly set on through the fundamental teachings of my Catholic faith. And though the house of my faith was being pummeled and tested in the various trials I was undergoing, it did not give way because He was my sure foundation. How tempting is it for us to ask God to take our crosses away immediately upon receiving them? I was certainly no different in my desire for Him to do so. But yet I was gaining understanding that I was receiving something far greater in the fruit of long-suffering. Jesus set the example of suffering for us some two thousand years ago. How can we not expect there'll be times when we're asked to do the same?

I found myself thinking of a trip that Rob and I had made three months before I learned of my failing kidneys, and how it seemed to relate to what was going on now. After watching a segment on EWTN by Bob and Penny Lord on the St. Joseph Oratory in Montreal, Canada, I had instantly felt a strong desire to go there. Though it would be over a thousand miles for us to travel to the Shrine, I was content in knowing we wouldn't have to get on a plane to get there. Preferring to travel by car, the long hours would allow Rob and I ample time for conversation and prayer. With gentle persuasion, I asked if going to the oratory was something he'd be willing to do. To my delight, he said yes!

Not a stranger to road trips, it was over the course of four years that we had traveled cross-country to see our daughter play collegiate basketball. In hindsight, it was becoming apparent that God was using our long-distance travels as the means for us to travel closer to Him. In the way intended for us in the Sacrament of Marriage, we were becoming "one" in spiritual unity. Looking back on the words chosen for our wedding invitation twenty-eight years prior, it read, "Two minds with but a single thought, two hearts that beat as one." How splendidly wonderful it was to have God leading us mutually together on the same page of our Catholic-Christian faith! "So they are no longer two, but one flesh" (Matthew 19:6).

My hope for our trip to the St. Joseph Oratory was that it would be for Rob another opportunity to grow deeper in his prayer life. For the first time, we would travel not as tourists but as pilgrims! How exhilarating it was to be embarking upon this spiritual expedition with my husband! Navigating out a travel route to see all five Great Lakes, we included various stops of interest along the way. Pulling out my rosary an hour into our trip, I was awestruck to see beautiful prisms of multicolored light radiating throughout the car as the sun hit its crystal beads. Symbolic, perhaps, of the many rosaries we would pray together throughout the course of our pilgrimage. Praying them with Rob was, for me, the high point of the long hours spent in the car. I could feel God's presence. Being cautious not to inundate him with my constant craving for prayer, I spaced out the times I'd ask if we could pray a rosary or to read from my Bible. "For where two or three are gathered together in my name, there am I in the midst of them" (Matthew 18:20).

Stopping periodically to stretch our legs, we decided it would be nice to take a stroll in the sand on the shores of Lake Michigan. Barely saying a word, how lovely it was to walk together on the beach, hand in hand. Reminiscent of Mary's blue mantle, I became captivated in the tranquility of the gorgeous blue sky. Watching as the sea gulls flew about so freely, they seemed to be flying in sync with the driving force of the thunderous waves pounding onto the shoreline.

As we walked on the dock that extended out into the Great Lake, something awakened inside of me to see in my surroundings the magnificent handiwork of the Lord. "Praise him, sun and moon;/ give praise, all shining stars./ Praise him, highest heavens,/ you waters above the heavens./ Let them all praise the LORD's name;/ for the LORD commanded and they were created" (Psalm 148:3–5). In contemplating the vastness of God's designs, my mind began to think of the goodness and beauty of His creation that could also be seen in every continent and on countless shorelines around the entire universe! Reflecting on the magnificence of the sunrises and sunsets that take place every day globally, with all the wildlife, the majestic mountains, the trees and foliage, I was in awe of God's creation! "O Lord, our Lord,/ how awesome is your name through all the earth!" (Psalm 8:10).

Driving into Montreal, we could see from afar the spectacular site of the great basilica and its huge copper dome. Built in honor of St. Joseph, it continues to be the site where pilgrims from all over North America stream in to pray for the intercessory healing of Blessed Andre Bessette.[3] It was in visiting the sick that he quickly gained status among the people as being a miracle healer through his prayers of intercession to St. Joseph. In one year alone, there had been hundreds of cases of healings reported.

Upon arriving, I was deeply moved at the sight of pilgrims who were climbing up on their bare knees the set of steep concrete steps that led up to the St. Joseph Oratory. In spite of elevated temperatures in the 90s, I just couldn't resist doing the same. Getting on my knees, I climbed the steps to the top, all one hundred of them! On the following day, we walked along the outdoor wooded trails lined with stunning sculptures of the Passion of Christ, praying together the Stations of the Cross. Inside the oratory, there were glass cases displaying the many crutches, canes, and wheelchairs left behind by those who walked away healed after being prayed for by Brother Andre.

Touring the basilica, we first stopped in front of two sculptures that depicted Jesus in the "Carrying of the Cross" and "The Crucifixion." As I reflected on the bitter Passion of Christ, it was a pinnacle moment for me, when for the first time in my life, it became personal. I thought of the ultimate price that Jesus had paid out of love for me. I became transfixed in meditation, envisioning the horrible death He suffered. A tear rolled down my cheek as I stared at the gaping wound on His shoulder. My heart ached in thinking of all the times in my life that the weight of His Cross had intensified when I had objected to even the slightest of crosses allowed me. Staring at the sculpted image of the crucifixion, I considered how my sins had driven much deeper the nails that had been pounded into the most precious hands and feet of Jesus. Looking up at the crown of thorns, I pondered the numerous times that my own selfish thoughts and desires had been the spikes that had pierced His sweet head. I stood in the realization that, in spite of my own sinfulness, it did not diminish in the slightest the love by which my merciful Savior had died for me. All the while, I was unaware that in just three months' time, I'd be asked to pick up my cross and follow Him. "Beloved, do not be surprised that a trial by fire is occurring among you, as if something strange were happening to you. But rejoice to the extent that you share in the sufferings of Christ, so that when his glory is revealed you may also rejoice exultantly" (1 Peter 4:12-13).

During the time we spent visiting the St. Joseph Oratory, I became greatly enthused about seeking the intercession of St. Joseph for my son. How my heart ached in seeing him being pulled deeper into the ways of the world and further away from God. Turning to the one chosen by God as leader of the Holy Family, I asked that he would lead my son to a good woman to marry, and that we would be blessed with grandchildren. As an act of faith, I went into the gift shop and purchased a sculpture of a mother holding up her infant son to the Lord, on behalf of Eric's future wife and our first grandchild. Incorporating my plea to St. Joseph into our nightly novena to the Sacred Heart of Jesus, I prayed also that our son would become a righteous leader of his own holy family.

It was around this time that I came across a powerful novena prayer imploring the protection of St. Michael the Archangel. Though already seeking the assistance of St. Michael for my son, I just couldn't resist praying this powerful novena. Asking for angelic intercession brought me so much comfort that I continued praying it, not just for the nine days of the novena, but ongoing as with my prayer to St. Joseph. Knowing the logging industry to be a dangerous occupation, my prayers for protection over a son who was far off from God were well warranted. In my

Bible, I placed a childhood picture of him next to this verse from Jeremiah to claim it for him every day.

> Thus says the Lord:
> "Cease your cries of mourning,
> wipe the tears your eyes,
> The sorrow you have shown shall have its reward,
> says the Lord,
> they shall return from the enemy's land.
> There is hope for your future, says the Lord;
> your sons shall return to their own borders."
>
> (Jeremiah 31:16–17)

One night, as Rob and I were praying our novena prayer before going off to sleep, my heart was aching about a particular situation involving my son. Convinced that it would be a sleepless night for me if I failed to surrender my worries back to God, I placed all of my concerns into the Sacred Heart of Jesus. Only in letting go was I able to drift off to sleep. Early the next morning before opening up my eyes, I found myself crying out to God for my son from the very depths of my heart. "Lord Jesus! You left the ninety-nine sheep to go after the one who'd gone astray. That sheep's name is Eric. Please, Lord, rescue him!"

At Mass that same morning, I was amazed in hearing the gospel reading. "What man among you having a hundred sheep and losing one of them would not leave the ninety-nine in the desert and go after the lost one until he finds it?" (Luke 15:4–5). Feeling my peace return to me, I rested in the assurance that Jesus, the Sheep-gate, had heard my prayer.

Calling me on the phone a couple years later, Eric said, "Mom, did I ever tell you about what happened to me last summer?"

"What's that?" I asked.

He went on to tell me that he'd been working on a particular logging job, and was in the process of cutting down an enormous tree when he ran into trouble. Having been in the logging business for several years, he was adept in strategically cutting trees to fall in a specific direction. But as the mammoth tree began to go down, Eric realized in horror that it was falling directly toward him! Knowing that he could not outrun the tree threatening to crush him, he instinctively looked to the sky and cried out to the top of his lungs, "Saint Michael!" Instantaneously, he heard another loud crack, as the tree fell in the opposite direction.

"It's really strange," Eric commented. "I rarely pray to St. Michael. But that day I did, and he protected me from being crushed by that tree!"

My eyes glistened with tears. In thanksgiving to God for sparing my son's life, I continued praying every day the powerful novena prayer in seeking St. Michael's protection! "Then war broke out in heaven; Michael and his angels battled against the dragon. The dragon and its angels fought back, but they did not prevail and there was no longer any place for them in heaven" (Revelation 12:7–8).

In reaping the fruits of my sorrows, Jesus was showing me how our crosses can become valuable relics when they're united with the Cross of His redeeming grace. Our sufferings then contain Jesus because they're directly connected to Him. He is living in us and we are living in Him. "Do you not know that your body is a temple of the holy Spirit within you, whom you have from God, and that you are not your own?" (1 Corinthians 6:19–20). Our Lord longs to walk with us in every cross we carry, promising that He will never abandon us. For Rob and me, it was in responding to the sound of Jesus knocking on the door of our heart that He opened for us a spiritual door we never knew existed.

The serenity that comes from bearing our sufferings with the Cross of Christ can be compared with the analogy of living in the eye of a hurricane. The outer and vicious whirlwind of chaos and pain that can surround us in the vortex of our lives cannot succeed in destroying the inner peace and calm within our souls when we walk with Jesus in our trials. It's only when we take our eyes off of Him that we become sucked back into the worries and disquiet of the world around us.

As I appealed for His mercy, Jesus continually extended out His hand to guide me along a path so often feared. Having found Him in the midst of sorrow, my ears had been unlocked to hear His call, and my eyes opened to see the beauty of His handiwork. In the changing of seasons in nature, I was able to see how they mirrored the continual changing of our souls in the seasons of life. In traveling with Jesus on a path of transformation, He gifts to us the unearned grace to bravely endure every affliction. "Make known to me your ways, Lord;/ teach me your paths./ Guide me in your truth and teach me,/ for you are God my savior" (Psalm 25:4–5).

> Oh, how sad and sore distressed,
> Was that Mother highly blessed
>   Of her sole begotten One!
>
> —Stabat Mater

> Suffering can bring you closer to God and His creation, all you have to do is trust Him.
>
> —Saint Francis of Assisi[4]

Stations of the Cross

Fourth Station
Jesus Meets His Mother Mary

May the most holy Virgin obtain for us the love of the Cross, of suffering, and of sorrows, and may she who was the first to live the Gospel in all its perfection and in all its severity, gain for us the willingness to follow her completely.

—Padre Pio

Show Me the Righteous!

It was closing in on a year since I had learned of the decline of my kidney function. Though I had been blessed with the grace to maintain an inner peace and joy, I now sensed the Lord encouraging me not only to tolerate tribulation, but to embrace my trials with a grateful heart. Initially, I had struggled with the conflicting thought of how I could willingly accept the same infirmity for which I was praying to be healed. But it occurred to me one day in prayer that what God was really asking of me was to simply persevere in trust. Embracing my illness in resignation to His Will was not contrary to praying for His mercy, but was complimentary to increasing my faith in trusting I would receive it. "Consider it all joy, my brothers, when you encounter various trials, for you know that the testing of your faith produces perseverance" (James 1:2).

My daily devotion of reading Holy Scripture was proving to be invaluable in the hope it offered. But the one area of the Bible I purposefully steered clear from was the book of Job. Concerned that delving into the indescribable sufferings of Job would cast a negative shadow of fear and doubt over me, I felt prompted nonetheless to read it. Pushing the inspiration out of my mind for days, I finally asked the Lord straight out if this was what He was asking of me. Randomly, I opened my Bible to the prologue of the book of Job! Still resistant in my willingness to read of the overwhelming temptations that he experienced, I willfully passed it off as mere coincidence. Later on that same day, I turned on the TV at the precise moment to hear the following comment being spoken: "And who of us really wants to read the book of Job?"

It confirmed to me without a doubt what God was asking of me, deciding right then that I best be obedient. The more I read, the more I began to see how God was able to test Job's obedience and submissiveness to Him by allowing evil attacks of unspeakable sorrow to oppress his soul. The key was that in looking to God to help him in his troubles and temptations, he was more richly blessed, and his virtues and faith flourished.

Our Lord was teaching me to rely on Him in my illness and to be submissive to His holy Will. Contrary to my initial speculation that reading the story of Job would bring my spirits down, instead, it filled me with an intense feeling of hope and trust in God. Though my trials paled in comparison to those of Job, I felt that God was telling me that the problems I was encountering also had the potential to bring me into a deeper awareness of His presence and power in my life. He was encouraging me to trust that He would further bless me in every adversity that came my way. "Once more will he fill your mouth with laughter,/ and your lips with rejoicing" (Job 8:21).

One morning as I was praying the rosary on my daily walk, a specific Scripture verse popped into my mind from out of nowhere. "The fervent prayer of a righteous person is very powerful" (James 5:16). There was something especially commanding about these words that instantly caused my soul to long to be connected to God's holy ones, to those He considers as "righteous." In response to the sudden desire I felt pounding in my heart, I prayed, "Where are Your righteous ones, Lord? I don't know where to find them. Please, show me the righteous!" Spontaneously, I added to the prayer of my heart, "Lord, You already know that Rob has been going along with me to holy places and agreeing to pray more, but I feel as though I have to tug on his ear to get him on board with me. I earnestly ask You, Jesus, instill in Rob his own burning desire to grow closer to You. Let him crave more of You so that, as husband and wife, we can be of the same mind and heart in traveling on our spiritual journey together."

Receiving a call from a friend the following day, she asked if I'd be interested in coming with her to a Monday evening prayer group called Cross and Crown. They were hosting a Life in the Spirit seminar. Instantly remembering my prayer, I thought to myself, Could this be God answering me already? Learning the group had been meeting for thirty-plus years in the basement of the same church that Rob and I attended, I decided to go. Because my plea to God had been twofold in not only asking for Him to lead me to righteous people, but also for my husband's conversion, I held my breath in asking Rob if he'd come.

"You check it out," he said, "if it's any good I'll go with you next week."

I was greatly relieved that he didn't say no. Accompanying my friend to the introductory night of the seminar, I felt comfortable in the knowledge that the Charisms and Gifts of the Holy Spirit were biblically based. Nearing the end when it was announced that prayer stations were set up for anyone in want of prayer, the Scripture verse echoed in my mind once again: "The fervent prayer of a righteous person is very powerful." In fulfillment of my prayer, I humbly walked over to request the ardent prayers of God's righteous ones.

How pleased I was for Rob to honor his promise to accompany me on the following week. Greeted warmly by one of our neighbors, Rob smiled in saying, "I'll stick this out for the seven weeks of the seminar, but I'm not making any promises after that."

Turning to Carol, I said, "Unless the Holy Spirit gets a hold of him, that is!"

"What do you think about taking a weekend jaunt to Galela?" I posed to Rob that same week. We'd been talking about making the scenic drive to northwestern Illinois to visit the historical sites among the colorfully painted Victorian homes, shop the farmers' markets, and go on a Mississippi River boat tour. Having already taken my mom on our yearly drive north to Door County to purchase cherries and view the rustic autumn colors, this was an opportunity for just the two of us to see more of the same in traveling southbound. Hearing of a Christian conference that was going on in Milwaukee that same weekend, I suggested we stop off one night to attend the Thursday evening session before heading out the next morning to travel the rest of the way to Galena.

"I guess we can do that," Rob agreed.

Unaware of what God had in store for us that night at the conference, we sat thoroughly enjoying the beautiful music. Nearing the end of the evening, the host made a plea to those in attendance who had not yet fully given their lives over to Jesus, asking them to choose openly for Him by coming up to the stage area. To my astonishment, Rob got up from his seat and said, "Sue, I have to do this." Instantly becoming choked up, I nodded my head. With tears in my eyes, I watched as he made his way up to the stage. Sitting ahead of me were three women who turned around, introducing themselves to me as sisters.

"Is he your boyfriend?" they asked in regard to Rob going up to the stage.

"No," I replied, "he's my husband of twenty-nine years!"

Sharing with them of my heartfelt prayer a couple of weeks earlier in asking our Lord to instill in Rob a burning desire to serve Him, they all stood up and hugged me. Upon reaching the stage area, Rob proclaimed out loud his desire to give his life entirely to Jesus before returning to his seat with an audio tape he'd been given. Arriving back home on Sunday evening after enjoying a wonderful weekend together, how happy we were to have first taken the time to experience God in the three hours spent at the conference.

Returning home from my Bible study that week, Rob was already in bed an hour earlier than normal. Reaching for the television remote to catch the news, I asked, "Are you feeling all right?"

"Yes," he said. "But if you turn on the TV I won't be able to tell you what happened to me."

My arm froze in midair as I rescinded my finger from the Power button. Somehow, I sensed that whatever he was about to tell me was going to be something spiritual. Walking toward him, I asked, "Tell me what?"

"While you were gone," he began, "I decided to put in the tape that was given to me this past weekend in deciding to turn my life over to Jesus. As I listened to it," he went on, "I was instantly filled with the Holy Spirit beyond anything I've ever experienced. I began to speak in tongues for a half-hour straight. Afterward, I decided that I would watch TV. But you must've had it tuned into the Catholic television network, and I turned it on just as the rosary was being prayed by Mother Angelica and the Nuns of Our Lady of the Angels Monastery. Sue," he said, his voice quivering, "I sang the entire rosary in tongues!" "These signs will accompany those who believe...they will speak new languages" (Mark 16:17).

As Rob told me of the peace that permeated his heart, my heart overflowed in thanksgiving of the marvelous way in which our Lord had answered my prayer. I could hardly imagine His swift response of not only leading us to His righteous ones, but also in having instilled in Rob a deep yearning to serve Him.

The Lord had also placed on his heart that night that he was to abstain from drinking alcohol, which from that time on, he did.

Our lives were unfolding in a way we never knew existed on a "hold onto your seatbelt" kind of ride on the fast track to God! Right away, I noticed a tremendous change in Rob. It was after attending week three of the Life in the Spirit seminar that he made a comment unlike any I'd ever heard him make before: "I'm not sure exactly what it is," he told me, "but I have a deep sense that God has something very big planned for us." Not only was I stunned to hear those words come out of his mouth, but I was impressed at the conviction in which he said them!

The following Saturday after raking leaves together in our backyard, we decided to stop in at a charismatic event that was scheduled to take place that same afternoon. Taking place at a neighboring Catholic church in conjunction with the seminar we were attending, there were prayer stations set up around the room. As we were being prayed over, Rob fell backward onto the floor, "resting in the Spirit" for the very first time. This was all new to me, as I stood beside him, seemingly unmindful to his surroundings. The woman who prayed with us voiced that she sensed God was going to be using us in a very powerful way. Instantly, I remembered Rob's statement earlier in the week in saying that God had big plans for us.

Taking our seat for Mass near the front of Holy Name Church, I noticed a young man with severe autism who was sitting with his mother a few pews ahead of us. My heart ached for him in seeing his attempt to communicate with his mother in the realization that he was mute. As I prayed for them, I was unaware of the profound spiritual experience Rob was having at the same time. Afterward, he told me that during Mass he had heard very clearly the voice of God speak within his heart. In regard to the autistic youth sitting ahead of us, he heard the words, "Why don't you lay hands on him and heal the boy?" Deeply moved at the experience, Rob's joy spilled out as we spoke of the spiritual course of direction our lives had taken. Our focus had completely switched over from seeking to please ourselves to wanting for nothing more than to live our lives in a way that was pleasing to God.

The small group leader at the Life in the Spirit seminar that Monday night told us she'd do her best to be there on the following week, but because of her early Tuesday morning flight for a return pilgrimage to Medjugorje, she may not be there. Having read a book on Medjugorje, I was enthused about her trip. Though I had not known Debbie previous to the seminar, I felt comfortable with her from the start. Her leadership reflected her love and zeal for God and Our Lady. The entire week following her announcement, I longed for her to bring me back a rosary from Medjugorje! Regretting I had lacked the courage to ask her, I decided to bring money with me to the next meeting in the hope she'd be there. But my hopefulness was quickly diminished in learning that, because of her early flight, she had opted for the more sensible choice in preparation for her long journey.

It was week five of the seminar, the pivotal week in which the leaders pray with the Life in the Spirit candidates to receive the gifts of the Holy Spirit. My prayer was that Rob and I would open our hearts to receive all the Lord had for us in His designs. I asked God that our individual gifts would work together in serving the Church in a way that He found pleasing. As they began praying, Rob started speaking in tongues. Sitting right next to him, my heart felt as though it would burst from pure joy. I could feel the undeniable presence of the Holy Spirit.

Two weeks later, Rob and I arrived early for the Mass that concluded the seminar. Debbie made her way to where I was sitting and said, "Here, I thought you'd like this. It's from Medjugorje."[5] Handing me a velvet pouch, I pulled out a beautiful "Jacob's ladder" rosary. Double chained on the sides of the beads in resemblance of a ladder, its striking blue color reminded me of Mary. Completely astonished, no one other than Rob knew of my heart's desire for her to bring me back a rosary from the place where the Mother of God appears. "It's already been blessed," she said, "by a priest and the Blessed Mother." Going on to explain how all sacramentals brought to the apparition site during Our Lady's apparitions to the visionaries receive her Motherly blessing, I had received the longing of my heart. "Find your delight in the LORD,/ who will give you your heart's desire" (Psalm 37:4).

Familiar with the story of Medjugorje, I had read of the little mountain village in Bosnia-Herzegovina where a modern-day miracle was taking place every day. It all began back on the feast day of John the Baptist on June 24, 1981, when six children from the village of Medjugorje reported the Virgin Mary had appeared to them and continues to this day. Absolutely thrilled in having received a rosary from Medjugorje, I could barely contain my joy as I prayed on it. Tears streamed down my face in the closeness I felt to Mary in meditating on the life of her Son. After dinner one evening, I went for a walk to pray my rosary. Clutching onto the crucifix to keep it from swinging, the palm of my hand suddenly began to burn, feeling as though it was on fire. In not knowing the cause, I thought back on my daily heart's cry of begging the Holy Spirit to burn in me the fire of His love. I wondered, Could this be the Holy Spirit?

In the weeks following the Life in the Spirit seminar, I began praying earnestly for the Spirit to guide me as to whether or not I should quit work. The frequent doctor's appointments and medical testing was making it difficult for me to juggle my work schedule and care for my mother's needs while continuing my responsibilities at home. I enjoyed my job, and in not wanting to be hasty in my decision, I entrusted it to the Spirit's direction.

The Advent season was fast approaching and I received an e-mail telling of a St. Andrew Advent prayer.[6] I could hardly wait to begin! In my growing enlightenment that to be a friend of the world translates into being an enemy of God, all I wanted for Christmas was to receive the spiritual gifts that only God could give. Asking Rob and Jenelle if they'd like to join me in the twenty-six-day Advent prayer, I was delighted with their acceptance. And so it was with great diligence that we prayed what would traditionally become for us an annual Christmas prayer.

Asking our Lord for an abundance of spiritual gifts, I prayed also for my dear mother's failing health. In the progression of her COPD, she struggled with breathing issues and chronic bouts of bronchitis. It pained my heart to see her in such a pitiful state. Spending day and night in her recliner, she was unable to lay down flat. In purchasing a hospital bed to better enable her to sleep in an elevated position, the further decline in position decreased her oxygen flow enough to force her back into her chair. In the deterioration of her health, she was placed on oxygen around the clock.

Days before Christmas, my mom's bout of infectious bronchitis progressed into full-blown pneumonia. The news distressed my heart terribly, because I didn't think her weakened lungs were strong enough to fight off the megavirus. From the very depth of my heart, I prayed, "Jesus, You already know how difficult it would be for me to lose my mom at Christmas, but if it is Your Will to take her, please provide me the grace to help me through." As an afterthought, I made a promise to God that if my mother recovered from the pneumonia that threatened to take her life, I would read sacred Scripture to her every single day for the rest of her life on this earth.

In the ominous weeks to follow, the pneumonia reached its plateau before my mom slowly gained strength on the road to recovery. Though I never before read the Bible to her, I didn't forget the vow I made to God on her behalf. Feeling a bit awkward at first, I began with the four gospels of Matthew, Mark, Luke, and John. Stopping over to visit with her nearly every day, I'd also give her a call in the evening to check how she was doing. Just about the time I was beginning to feel at ease in reading Bible stories to my mother each day, I noticed she'd always ask if I could wait until later on to read Scripture to her. Even when I'd call her in the early evening before Rob and I headed out to a prayer meeting or such, she continued very kindly to ask if I'd do the readings later. In telling her we wouldn't be home until after 9:00 p.m., she'd respond, "That's okay, I'll be awake."

Becoming increasingly concerned as to the reason why my mom was putting off the Scripture readings, I came right out and asked her one day, "Mom, don't you like it when I read the Bible to you?"

Her answer stirred my heart. "Oh, yes!" she exclaimed. "The stories bring me so much peace that I'm no longer afraid at night when my breathing becomes labored. That's the reason I always have you call me back, so that you can read them to me right before I go to sleep!"

What a blessing it was to see the fruit of my Advent promise to God. And what a treasured gift to minister His word to my mother, becoming for her the source by which she obtained peace in her infirmity. Together with Rob and Jenelle, we affectionately cared for my mom's every need, loving her, visiting her, and bringing her out on weekly visits to our home.

Reading Scripture to her heart's content, I'd oftentimes choose stories that fit in with the current struggles of her day. Along with the biblical readings, I also read to my dear mom the inspiring stories from the trilogy book *Through the Eyes of Jesus*.[7] Having purchased it at one of Alan Ames's mission talks, it was like reading her an extension of the gospels that she had come to love. Despite her declining health, I never saw her at such peace. It wouldn't be until years later that I'd gain insight of the magnitude of God's gift to my mother that Christmas. Placed on the road to recovery, our merciful Lord then placed her on the path of holiness through her sufferings.

Though it wasn't easy for me to talk with my mom about the value and merit her suffering held in uniting them with the sufferings of Jesus, I continuously assured her that Jesus would help lift the weight of her cross. Tenderly explaining how the discomfort of her illness could serve to purify her own soul as well as to bring relief to the holy souls in purgatory, I could sense the comfort it brought her. On days when she was feeling worse than others, she'd tell me of the joy she had in the knowledge that her suffering could benefit the holy souls. "For it was fitting that he, for whom and through whom all things exist, in bringing many children to glory, should make the leader to their salvation perfect through suffering" (Hebrews 2:10).

After summoning a priest to hear my mom's confession and administer to her the Anointing of the Sick, I decided to beseech the Holy Spirit in asking Him to reveal any sins I may have suppressed that could interfere with receiving the healing grace of God. That same evening, I was awakened from sleep. With my eyes still closed, it was as though a film was being played before my mind's eye. In it, I was shown the resentment I had buried deep down in my soul, stemming back from the times in my son's youth when I felt verbally disrespected.

The love I had for my son was as great as any mother could ever have. And though I was persistently praying for him, I remained unaware that I had stuffed the hurt feelings of years past down so deep that I didn't even know they were there. Throughout the entirety of my "illumination of conscience," I could feel God's love permeating me with a deep-seated peace. While the scene was still unfolding before my eyes, I began to thank and praise

Him for the revelation shown to me. Asking forgiveness, I prayed to be released from any bitterness I had harbored subconsciously.

In the confessional, I spoke with the priest of what had transpired. He later gave me a copy of a "Forgiveness Prayer"[8] to be prayed for thirty days. Similar to what I had already done, I began praying it devoutly, asking the Holy Spirit to reveal any suppressed sins so that they may be forgiven. Going all the way back to the moment I was conceived in my mother's womb, I asked God to help me forgive all in my life who had hurt me, seeking also His forgiveness for anyone in whom I had done the same.

Because our insurance carrier switched their network of hospitals we could utilize, my follow-up kidney evaluation was scheduled at UW Madison hospital. The lab tests taken locally revealed my kidney function had dropped from 22 percent to 17 percent in one year's time. Remembering what the surgeon from the other hospital had told me in regard to the recommendation of kidney transplantation when it dropped below the 20 percent mark, I wasn't overly enthused about my upcoming appointment. Thinking the protocol of one hospital to another would be similar; I anticipated the surgeon would advise proceeding forward with the surgery.

"It doesn't matter how things appear," Rob reassured. "We're going to ask St. Joseph to intercede for God's wisdom concerning your doctors."

Taking comfort, I released my fears back into the hands of God. My heart smiled in hearing the inspiring words of counsel echoing out from Rob, the same guy that I'd been praying so desperately for his conversion only five months prior!

Arising early for the two-hour drive to Madison for a full day of testing, I was happy and content in God's plan for me. Making our way to the transplant unit, we received an itinerary of the tests and appointments that were set up for me at specific times throughout the day. With an internal map of the hospital in hand, we set out on a scavenger hunt of sorts to locate the various testing sites throughout the hospital. After meeting with a dietitian and the pretransplant coordinator, we were put in a room to meet with the head of the nephrology department. This was the pivotal moment for which we had been praying, asking that God's wisdom be imparted to this doctor.

Reviewing my case history along with the test results, he said, "It's my recommendation that we schedule surgery as soon as possible."

Accepting his advice, I commented; "It seems strange to think that I'm about to undergo major surgery when I don't feel sick or have any of the threatening symptoms that typically accompany kidney failure."

Rubbing his chin, he thought for a while before saying, "We refer to people like you as being *a-symptomatic*, meaning without symptoms."

Smiling, I replied, "I refer to it as being *a-blessing!*"

"Yes," he agreed. "With all things considered, I think that we can safely hold off on scheduling surgery if we keep a close watch on your creatinine levels."

Amazed at his sudden change of heart, it had been in surrendering myself over to God through the wisdom provided my doctor that I remained confident of walking within His holy Will. The surgeon then advised that I see my local nephrologist every month to carefully monitor my kidneys.

What a difference a year had made! It was a year that our Lord showed to me His righteous ones; devout people of good character and integrity. It was a year of continually striving to lay down my will in exchange for God's perfect plan for me. A year

He would call Rob to conversion. It was a year of hope even in the most devastating of circumstances, of learning that hope wasn't just an emotion I felt inside, but a decision to persevere through hardship in trust of God's mercy. "We know that all things work for good for those who love God, who are called according to his purpose" (Romans 8:28).

God was teaching me to see beyond the crosses of life in seeing the priceless value of picking up my cross to follow Jesus along the way to holiness. On this path of love, we're led straight to the One who willingly took up His Cross for us. In knowing I couldn't stay this path alone, I turned to Mary for help. Who else than her would be more understanding of suffering and more willing to help me in mine than the Mother of our Redeemer? Who, on the face of the earth, will ever suffer more than Jesus and the one chosen by God to be His Mother? It's in the example set for us by the Holy Family and of the saints who've gone before us that our faith will be strengthened.

We're all called to suffer during various times in our lives. It's God's desire to supply abundantly the peace that accompanies the abandonment of everyday trials to Him. Through the daily practice of "dying to self," our wounds with be filled with more of Him, serving as the ointment to soothe even the greatest of pains. Without, one may become troubled at even the smallest of trials and lose their faith entirely. In exchange for the fleeting sufferings we're called to endure in this world, our soul will gain possession of eternal glory. "The Spirit itself bears witness with our spirit that we are children of God, and if children, then heirs, heirs of God and joint heirs with Christ, if only we suffer with him so that we may also be glorified with him" (Romans 8:16–17).

Christ above in torment hangs,
She beneath beholds the pangs,
 Of her dying, glorious Son.

—Stabat Mater

The patient and humble endurance of the cross—whatever nature it may be—it is the highest work we have to do.

—Saint Katharine Drexel[9]

Stations of the Cross

Fifth Station
Simon of Cyrene Helps Jesus Carry the Cross

Jesus chooses souls for Himself and among these, in spite of my unworthiness, He has chosen me to assist Him in the great work of salvation. And the more these souls suffer without consolation, the more they lighten the sufferings of Jesus.

—Padre Pio

Come

Having entrusted the Lord to hold onto the burden of my PKD from the very onset of my diagnosis, I felt secure all these years later in releasing back to Him once again the heavy weight of my failing kidneys. "Come to me, all you who labor and are burdened, and I will give you rest" (Matthew 11:28). After Mass each day, I took Him on His word by going before Him in the stillness of the Tabernacle. There, I was able to dispose of all of my worries and anxieties and find rest in the Heart of Jesus. It was in deciding to walk with Him in the rubble of my life that I found in His Sacred Heart a refuge where I'd always be safe, and where His steady flow of grace would enable me to view life's challenges in a whole new light. I was learning that to submit all of my struggles back over to God did not mean helplessness, but power in Him. "I will rather boast most gladly of my weaknesses, in order that the power of Christ may dwell with me" (2 Corinthians 12:9). There was no escaping the cross that lay before me, yet I was beginning to discover the paradox of the cross and the love that lay behind it. In an ongoing effort to surrender my troubles back over to God's authority, I ascertained that I could give to Him all of my woes and self-doubt in exchange for His peace.

It was early February when the director of sales and catering walked into the office to announce some changes that were going to be put in effect, policies that could very well increase my hours while decreasing my flexibility. Constantly running to medical appointments, caring for my mom, and looking after my family's needs at home, I knew they were regulations that would be difficult for me to comply with. Daily, for three months,

I'd been asking the Holy Spirit to enlighten me as to when I should give my notice at work, and within my heart I felt this was the time. Considering that my kidneys were functioning at 17 percent, I figured it was only a matter of time before my doctor at UW Madison would recommend having the transplant. First discussing it with Rob, I gave my notice. Offering to work until a replacement could be trained, my last day of work turned out to be the day before Lent. Deciding to attend Mass during the forty days of Lent, that's when everything began to change.

Just a few days into Lent, I was walking and praying my rosary after Mass one morning when I heard the voice of God speak clearly within my heart saying, "You did not quit work to have surgery; you quit work to become holy." There are times in our life so profound that we remember exactly where we were and what we were doing when they happened. For me, this was one of those times.

In receiving this revelation, I speculated on the reason why the Lord told me that I did not quit work to have surgery. Mulling it over in my mind, I considered the possibility that perhaps God Himself would heal me. I didn't know. In relation to quitting work "to become holy," I thought about God's providence in not only having my job end at the start of Lent, but also of my constant prayer to the Spirit to guide me in the exact time I should quit. The message was one of calm and serenity, and it was in that same state of peacefulness that I chose to focus my thoughts. God was in charge. In the quietude of my heart, I claimed once again my personalized scripture in saying, "Lord, if you're willing, You can heal me."

Hearing the Gospel message each day at Mass, it occurred to me that transformation is truly at the heart of the Gospel! Scripture and Gospel readings suddenly came alive as the words seemed to be talking directly to me. Tears would fill my eyes as words spoken over two thousand years ago were applicable for me today. I found in them a renewed sense of hope. I began to feel within myself the true presence and power of Jesus in the Eucharist as never before, finding new meaning also in receiving the Sacraments of Confession and Holy Communion. I no longer just went to Mass, but I became a part of the Mass. Now, as I received the living body of Jesus Christ in Holy Communion, I began also to feel Jesus receiving me. "Whoever eats my flesh and drinks my blood remains in me and I in him" (John 6:56).

It had been only a few months since Rob and I had experienced a new awakening of the Holy Spirit. A life-changing event, the Life in the Spirit seminar not only deepened our awareness of the Spirit in our lives, but it also gave us a strong desire to grow together in holiness. In contrast to Rob's initial comment that he'd "stick it out" only for the duration of the seminar, we continued attending the weekly Cross and Crown prayer meetings. Not because I wanted him to, but because it was his utmost desire to live in the Spirit of God.

After the prayer meeting that Monday, an announcement was made of a Holy Spirit Conference that was coming up that same weekend. Knowing nothing about it, I instantly felt a stirring inside me that Rob and I were to attend. Telling Rob of the inspiration, though it conflicted with a floor project he had planned, he said, "It's Lent and I, too, think we should go."

Right before the lunch break that Saturday, there were designated prayer teams set up to pray for individual needs. Deciding to go up for prayer, the woman who was about to pray with me said to the catchers, "Get behind her, this one's going down." Shocked at her comment, I had no intention of falling on the floor. Though I was accepting of those who were "slain in the Spirit" and in Rob's beautiful experience a few months back, I still had my guard up. I didn't feel comfortable with it. Trying to stay focused on thinking only of Jesus as I was being prayed over, the next thing I knew, I was laying flat on the floor. Enveloped in a feeling of peace and tranquility, I didn't seem to have a care in the world. Going off site for lunch, as we were walking to the car I began to sob.

"What's wrong?" Rob asked.

Rather embarrassed, I said, "I have no idea why I'm crying, but I do know why I fell. It's because that lady pushed me. I felt her put her hands on my head and then I think she pushed me down."

Saying nothing, Rob smiled.

Returning to the conference, Rob told me of how incredibly happy he was to have postponed his project in order to attend. Even more inspiring than the remarkable witness talks spaced amongst the teachings was the main speaker's ability to invoke the presence of the Holy Spirit through his music. Before concluding on Saturday evening, the master of ceremonies announced that, due to the enthusiastic response of those in attendance, the main speaker was willing to do a one-night encore on Monday evening.

The phone was ringing as I was walking in the door after Mass on Monday morning. It was Rob. Sounding somewhat shaken, he voiced that something spiritually profound had taken place at work.

"What was it?" I questioned.

"Hon," he began, "I was sitting at my desk this morning when I heard the Holy Spirit speak within my heart. He revealed to me things involving the mission God has called us to. I was told that you will be healed of your kidney disease, and that Jenelle's eyes will be opened spiritually. The three of us will testify to the saving grace of God's healing love in our family."

I stood speechless as he went on.

"The Lord assured me that He will not send us into battle without the proper tools, revealing that I would be given the gifts of healing, prophecy, and tongues. Just like you've already been doing, I was instructed to journal these revelations down. The Holy Spirit enlightened me to get my prayer life in order. Interiorly, I was told to begin reading and studying the Bible, because with our mission there will also come persecution. He told me of the tremendous spiritual merit your nightly Scripture readings are having on your mother, instructing also that we need to bring her Holy Communion every Sunday. And one last thing," he added. "We're especially to pray for sins of the flesh and for those who rebel against God's instruction in Holy Scripture."

In the timeline given, the Lord told Rob explicitly that our mission would begin shortly after his thirtieth anniversary at his place of employment. With his anniversary date fast approaching, that meant it would be soon. Still trying to absorb what he was telling me, I suggested, "How about we go back to the encore presentation of the Holy Spirit Conference tonight to discern all of this?"

Without hesitation, he agreed.

"Do not quench the Spirit. Do not despise prophetic utterances. Test everything; retain what is good. Refrain from every kind of evil" (1 Thessalonians 5:19–22). It was an evening filled with praise and worship. At the close of the conference, we decided to go up to the altar once again for individual prayer. Standing in the line that spanned horizontally across the entire front of the altar, the main speaker was one who was praying over people. As he began to pray, I began to feel myself sway. Concentrating more on not falling than in thinking of Jesus, he then moved on to pray with Rob. Thinking of my experience on Saturday before the lunch break, I thought to myself, I knew I wouldn't fall! But before praying with Rob, the speaker then took a sideway step back to me, and he blew softly on my forehead. It felt like a 150 mph gust of wind! Lying on the floor, I was slain in the Spirit of God. "And when he had said this, he breathed on them and said to them, 'Receive the holy Spirit'" (John 20:22).

As I lay there in complete peace, the speaker who stood over me began to prophesy. "You are a woman with burning hands, hands that will burn the love of Christ in others." After three times referring to my "burning hands," he moved on to pray with Rob. Peace and happiness flooded my soul. My initial suspicion was confirmed. The burning sensation in the palm of my hands that I had first felt a couple months prior while praying on my rosary from Medjugorje was the work of the Holy Spirit! "Holy Spirit," I prayed, "burn in me the fire of Your love."

For Rob and I, there was no turning back. Accepting our summons to attend the Holy Spirit Conference, we found ourselves spiritually overflowing to the point of no return. Drawn to the encore of the conference to confirm to us our mission, we were unwavering in our resolve never to return to our old way of life. Within my heart was the acute awareness that the worst anguish anyone could ever suffer would be to become separated from God through sin.

Waking from sleep on the following morning an hour before I needed to get up for Mass, I instantly became aware of the burning within the palms of my hands. As I lay there thanking God for the gift I'd been given, I prayed for the grace to serve Him in a way that He would find pleasing. If my hands were going to "burn the love of Christ in others," I knew that would be made possible only through God's healing love flowing out through me. From that time on, I was more attentive to the times my hands would spontaneously begin to burn; sometimes in hearing the Gospel being read, and other times in the presence of individuals for whom I needed to pray. One day in bringing a meal over to a woman who was homebound, the moment I walked in, the palms of my hands began to burn. Connecting the physical burning in my hands with God's desire for me to pray for His people, I humbly asked if she was open to prayer.

Our hearts had been set ablaze with a burning desire to serve God, first in being led to attend the Life in the Spirit seminar,[1] and a few months later, in the prompting to attend the Holy Spirit Conference. In obedience to what the Lord had asked, Rob and I began right away to bring Holy Communion to my mother every Sunday. Finding it more favorable for her to receive Jesus in the evening, we also began attending a 6:00 p.m. Sunday evening Mass at St. Pius X Church located near to where she lived.

It was at one of these Sunday evening Masses we heard it announced that Eucharistic Adoration[2] was set to begin on Divine Mercy Sunday.[3] Named the Chapel of Divine Mercy, the newly built chapel housed a first-class relic of St. Faustina.[4] Because of my devotion to praying the Chaplet of Divine Mercy at 3:00 p.m. each day, my heart was stirred with excitement. Expressing to me his interest in adoration before the Blessed Sacrament as well, Rob and I mutually agreed on utilizing the chapel. But as to signing up for a specified hour every week, we decided to pray.

Following his morning meeting at work the next day, Rob called me in saying, "While I was praying this morning before getting up, the Lord put it on my heart that we are to make the weekly commitment to spend time with Him in Eucharistic adoration."

Thrilled to hear the news, I could hardly wait to call the number from the church bulletin to sign us up. "When he returned to his disciples he found them asleep. He said to Peter, 'So you could not keep watch with me for one hour? Watch and pray that you may not undergo the test'" (Matthew 26:40–41). What neither of us realized in our promise to give back to Jesus just one hour of our time each week was of the tsunami of graces that would be at our constant disposal!

It wasn't long before our weekly visits to the Chapel of Divine Mercy began greatly to increase. Having been enlightened that I quit work "to become holy," I thought of how I first became centered on Jesus' true presence in the Sacrament of the Eucharist at Mass, followed by an infilling of the Holy Spirit at the Life in the Spirit seminar, and how we now spent time with the "Eucharistic Jesus" in the Blessed Sacrament of the altar. I began to realize that the more time we spent in Eucharistic adoration, the more we became one with Jesus in Holy Sacrifice of the Mass! Nowhere else could we go to find greater peace than to come before our Lord in the Monstrance of love. It was there that He melted away the weaknesses and flaws within our souls, freeing up more room for Him.

Speaking with my friend on the phone concerning the food I prepared each week for her to pick up to bring to Father Carr's Place-2-B,[5] Debbie mentioned that she was organizing a bus of pilgrims to attend the National Medjugorje Conference[6] in Notre Dame, Indiana. The instant she told me of it, my heart began to pound as though it would explode in excitement. "It's on Pentecost Weekend," she added, "and there are seats available if you want to go."

"Pencil us in," I responded. "I'll ask Rob and let you know for sure."

Telling him of the conference the moment he got home from work, he asked, "Who's speaking?"

Realizing for the first time that I hadn't even asked any of the specifics, I answered, "All I know is that when Debbie told me about it I got the same feeling as I did when the Holy Spirit Conference was announced. I don't know anything concerning it other than it's to do with Medjugorje and that I feel we're being called to go."

"Go ahead and sign us up," he said, based solely on my enthusiasm alone. But that was about to change. Driving home from the chapel one evening, Rob told me of the divine insight he had received. "Something spiritually significant is going to happen to us at the Medjugorje Conference," he said with conviction.

As we anxiously awaited the bus trip to the National Medjugorje Conference, Rob and I were invited to a one-day workshop sponsored by the Charismatic Renewal Center.[7] Enthused about the event, while getting ready for bed on the night before it was to take place, Rob looked at me and said; "You know, I've heard a lot from God over the past several months, but as of yet, I've not heard a single word from Mary."

Chuckling at his comment, I asked, "Do you expect to hear from Mary?"

"Yes, I really do," he replied unassumingly.

Held at St. John's Church, the theme of the day-long workshop was entitled "A Call to Holiness."

Funny, I thought to myself, remembering the interior message I received upon quitting work, that even though we weren't leaders, we'd been invited to a leadership workshop that focused on holiness! Hearing of Jim Murphy's quest to crusade across America shouldering a six-foot "Cross of Christ"[8] and the incredible stories that went with it, he captivated our attention. As he told of his tangible journey along the Way of the Cross, I couldn't help but relate it to my spiritual journey of carrying my cross with Jesus.

Before heading back to our seats after the lunch break, we decided to stop off and pray before Jesus in the Tabernacle. There, alone and down on his knees in prayer was the speaker. No wonder his teachings are so inspired, I thought to myself. Throughout the day, I could feel the presence of the Holy Spirit so strong that, at one point, I found myself scanning the room to see if others were experiencing the same. My heart smiled, when in the middle of his afternoon session at exactly three o'clock, Jim Murphy stopped his teaching briefly to pay homage to Jesus' most sorrowful Passion. "Through the Chaplet you will obtain everything, if what you ask for is compatible with My will"[9] (*Diary*, 1731).

With the conclusion of the workshop, we got up from our seats to leave when the speaker approached us in conversation. Telling Jim of his conversion, Rob also told him of how we were being led to walk with Jesus in the cross of my failing kidneys.

"Really?" he questioned, sharing with us his own health issue concerning one of his kidneys. Looking at me, he asked, "Can I pray with you?"

"Yes, I'd be honored."

Joining hands in prayer, a woman walked over and asked if she could join in our prayer. Not even knowing her name, I immediately recognized her as the woman from the charismatic gathering at Holy Name Church six months prior when Rob had fallen in the Spirit for the very first time. She told us back then of her inspiration that the Holy Spirit was going to manifest Himself in our lives in a big way.

Bowing our heads, Jim began to pray. After a minute or so, he stopped unexpectedly and said, "I've just been made aware that the Blessed Mother has joined in on our prayer."

I was stunned. No one could have known what Rob had articulated to me the night before in expressing his inspired thought that he was going to be hearing from Mary! Words cannot express how I felt in knowing the *Mother of God* had made her presence known to us in our circle of prayer. Leaving the church, we went straight to the Chapel of Divine Mercy to spend time with Jesus in Eucharistic adoration. A holy day it was.

On the evening before our trip to the National Medjugorje Conference, I asked Rob if he thought we'd be able to make it to morning Mass before driving to the pickup point to board the bus.

"That would be cutting it too close," he answered apologetically. "We sure don't want to be late and have the bus leave without us!"

"All right," I said, giving in to his logic. More than anything, I wanted to be able to attend Mass. During our nightly novena, I found myself asking the Holy Spirit if He would wake me up one hour before the time we had our alarm clock set if it was in God's holy designs for me to go to Mass. Then I asked Rob, "Is that all right with you?"

"That'll be okay," he said.

Opening my eyes upon waking up, it was 6:00 a.m., exactly one hour to the minute before the alarm was set to go off. Before getting out of bed, I prayed within myself, "Thank You, Holy Spirit, for the wake-up call!" Waking up and seeing that I was already showered and dressed, Rob quickly got out of bed to get himself ready to accompany me to Mass.

With only minutes left to spare before the designated departure time, we boarded the bus. Walking all the way back to take the last seat, I was saddened to learn that Debbie would not be on the trip due to a family emergency. With the span of pickup locations for those who had signed on stretching out a hundred miles along the highway, we recognized only a few familiar faces.

It was our very first bus pilgrimage, and I was so excited to learn that we'd be praying rosaries and chaplets together along the journey. As the first rosary was being prayed, Rob whispered to me that he had sensed Our Lady walking down the aisle of the bus toward our seat in the back. "I could smell a beautiful scent of roses that grew stronger as Mary approached and now it's gradually fading off." Right after telling me of this, a few other people sitting intermittently in seats going up to the front of the bus began voicing out loud of the beautiful floral scent they smelled.

How amazing, I thought, that Rob had heard from Mary once again, this time having received the wonderful grace of smelling roses in the presence of the "Mystical Rose."[10]

Following the opening ceremonies that evening, everyone participating received a lit candle as we convoyed with hundreds of others in Eucharistic procession to the Lourdes Grotto. Reciting the holy rosary, the prayers rang out through the speaker system. Viewing the spectacular sight of the priest holding the Monstrance[11] beneath the handheld canopy with the altar boys holding up tall candles alongside brought back fond memories of the annual Corpus Christi processions of my youth. Truly, it was a night to be cherished.

Once at the grotto, benediction was said. Large numbers of people knelt down on the bare concrete while others lit special intention candles before the statue of Mary. Darkness was fast approaching and most everyone from our bus had already headed back to the dorms while Rob and I chose to linger on a little longer at the beautiful grotto, praying for Mary's intercession. It was so peaceful. It was there at the grotto that Rob and I first met Joyce Lightner. Working with Debbie in planning the bus pilgrimage to the conference, in her absence, Joyce had taken over. Having led over eighty pilgrimages to Medjugorje at that time, what a blessing it was for us to encounter this true apostle of Mary!

Recognizing us as her bus pilgrims, she quickly linked arm in arm as the three of us attempted to navigate our way back to the dorms through the maze of sidewalks. It was the darkest of nights, and it was in making a wrong turn that Joyce immediately prompted us to stop, hold hands, and pray three Hail Marys for

Our Lady's intercession. The University of Notre Dame literally means "Our Lady's University," and Mary did not let us down. Finding our way back to the dorm, Joyce's "three Hail Mary" solution had made a lasting impression. To think of the Blessed Mother bringing one Hail Mary each to God, her Father; to Jesus, her Son; and to the Holy Spirit, her spouse; in asking for our Triune God to shed light on adverse situations was powerful! Getting lost that night made me stop and think of how we are all called to be a beacon of light in our everyday lives to those who have lost their way in the darkness of sin.

Sitting in attendance of our fourth religious conference in just eight months' time, we were bowled over at the fabulous lineup of speakers who presented phenomenal testimonies. Most amazing to me was the remarkable conversion story given by Father Donald Calloway[12] involving Our Lady of Medjugorje's intervention. In addition, the conference was inclusive to the celebration of Holy Mass, Eucharistic adoration, recitation of the holy Rosary, and the Sacrament of Reconciliation.

For the first time in well over twenty years, Rob went to confession. And while it may seem out of sequence for him to have been so powerfully blessed with the gifts of the Holy Spirit seven months before receiving the Sacrament, it was nonetheless the process through which the Spirit moved. The Lord had taken us just as we were and placed us onto a path of transformation, both for the good of our souls and to be of service to Him. As if the weight of the world had been lifted from him, on our way to spend time with Jesus in the exposition of the Blessed Sacrament, he professed, "Sue, I've sinned against God and I'm forgiven." Confession roots out sin. In the knowledge that Jesus Christ had died for his sins, Rob was filled with an overwhelming sense of gratitude. "Then I declared my sin to you;/ my guilt I did not hide./ I said, 'I confess my faults to the LORD,'/ and you took away the guilt of my sin" (Psalm 32:5).

Having followed the Spirit's prompting to attend the Medjugorje Conference, I never bothered checking out the lineup of speakers. What a pleasant surprise it was to learn that Mirjana Soldo, one of the six visionaries of Medjugorje, was on the conference itinerary! Not a sound could be heard in the auditorium as she shared her personal testimony. Humbly, she gave witness of the apparitions of the Blessed Virgin in the communist-ruled village of Medjugorje that first began on June 24, 1981. Listening intently, I became convinced that everyone everywhere needed to hear the messages of Our Lady of Medjugorje! Mary's message is one of peace, conversion, prayer, and penance, not to exclude works of charity. In referencing the biblical story of David and Goliath, Mary told the visionaries in one of her appearances of the "five little stones" that we're to use as weapons in fighting against "our own Goliath of sin and temptation:"

1. Pray with the heart, rosary
2. Eucharist
3. Holy Bible
4. Fasting
5. Monthly confession

In regard to fasting, Mirjana stated that Mary asks that we fast on bread and water every Wednesday and Friday throughout the year.

Walking outside to the Notre Dame campus during the lunch break, I asked Rob, "Do you think that we'd be able to have butter on our bread when we fast?"

"Oh, I'm sure that we would," he replied.

"What about coffee?" I continued. "Do you suppose we'd still be able to have our coffee in the morning instead of water?"

"Oh yeah," he affirmed. "I think so."

Returning to the conference after lunch, Mirjana conducted a question and answer period. The very first question she read was,

"Can we still have coffee in the morning and spread butter on the bread we eat?" We burst into laughter as Mirijana smiled, saying, "This is typical American question." With exception to the sick, Mary's message is for us to fast. If not on bread and water at first, most importantly, we are to fast in some way. Once it becomes easier, it can be increased from there.

Returning back to the dorms after the Saturday evening session, it was close to 9:30 p.m. I was feeling especially tired. Being a finicky sleeper when I'm away from home, I hoped to at least catch a few hours of sleep. Surprisingly, I awoke feeling refreshed for the start of a new day. After packing up, we planned to enjoy a cup of coffee and a light breakfast before returning for the conclusion of what was proving to be a most phenomenal conference. As Rob went downstairs to load up our suitcases, I stayed back to put the last of our things in the satchel. As I was doing this, I suddenly heard spoken clearly within my soul one word, "Listen."

Hearing it, I wondered just exactly what it was that God was trying to convey. Telling Rob what had happened when he returned to the room, the thought occurred to me that it was Pentecost Sunday. Surely, if we prayed to the Holy Spirit, He would reveal to us the meaning. Joining our hands together, we prayed for God's wisdom to be revealed. In the meantime, we decided to "put our antennas up" in listening for whatever it was the Lord wanted us to hear.

Complimented by inspiring music that seemed to knit the conference together, the morning was filled with wonderful stories that offered hope in depression and brought laughter out of tears. Preceding the Mass that celebrated the birthday of the Church at Pentecost over two thousand years ago, the rosary was prayed. Watching the May Crowning of Our Lady[13] following the Mass, happy tears filled my eyes. In closing, the Blessed Sacrament was processed up and down every aisle of the auditorium. As the priest raised the Monstrance in blessing, many dropped to their knees in signing themselves in the name of the Father, and of the Son, and of the Holy Spirit. Amen. "Behold, the Lamb of God" (John 1:36).

After being led into a close and personal relationship with Jesus in the spirit of conversion, the hand of Christ was leading Rob and me along, showering upon us His great love as He beckoned, "Come." Walking with us in the hills and valleys of our lives, we would discover that it's during the darkest of times that God's light will shine through to us the brightest. It was down in the valley where we discovered the cross was within the Heart of Christ. Jesus died out of pure love. With outstretched hands, He awaits each of us in the utmost desire to help in shouldering life's crosses. "Come after me, and I will make you fishers of men" (Matthew 4:19).

Is there one who would not weep,
'Whelmed in miseries so deep,
   Christ's dear Mother to behold?

—Stabat Mater

Time is but a shadow, a dream; already God sees us in glory and takes joy in our eternal beatitude. How this thought helps my soul! I understand then why He lets us suffer.

—Saint Therese of Lisieux[14]

Stations of the Cross

Sixth Station
Veronica Wipes the Face of Jesus

If I know that someone is afflicted in body or in soul, what will I not do to see him freed from these evils? I should willingly take upon myself all his sufferings, if I could only free him from them. I should surrender in his favor the fruits of these sufferings, if the Lord were to permit it.

—Padre Pio

GO OUT

It was 3:00 p.m. as we boarded the bus in the pouring rain for the five-hour trip back home. Making our way once again to the back of the bus, I plopped down next to Rob in sheer exhaustion. Considering the spiritual high I was on, lack of sleep really didn't seem to be of much concern. I didn't want to miss out on a single thing, and it was, after all, a pilgrimage, where discomfort of some sort usually figures into the equation. As the others got themselves situated in their seats, I began praying to myself the Chaplet of Divine Mercy.

Seated at the front of the bus, Joyce got on the microphone to ask if anyone would like to give a testimony of their weekend. A middle-aged woman named Katy was the first to go up to the mic. Telling of her multiple myeloma, a life-threatening cancer affecting the plasma cells, she hoped for a cure in the bone marrow transplant she had undergone. Having already been on pilgrimage to Medjugorje, the love she possessed for Our Blessed Mother was apparent. As she told of her spiritual weekend, I glanced over at Rob to notice him overcome with emotion.

"What's wrong?" I asked.

Turning to me, he said, "God is speaking to my heart." Then, pointing toward Katy, he added, "I'll tell you about it as soon as she's finished."

But the moment Katy was through, another woman wasted no time in going up to the mic to give her witness. Janie told also of the ominous cancer that threatened her life, sharing of the renewed sense of hope she had gained in attending the Marian Conference.

As all this was going on, I began to feel an interior prompting that I was to go up to give my testimony. Plain and simple, in no way did I want to go to the front of the bus. While it felt good to honor my promise to God in sharing my diagnosis of PKD more openly once my kidneys began to fail, I certainly never considered sharing my story with a bus of complete strangers! Over the course of my entire life, I had purposefully avoided talking in front of large groups of people. Within myself, I said, "I'm not going up there." As more women went up to the front to tell of their experience at the conference, I couldn't help but notice how many of them had cancer. Looking over at Rob once again, for reasons unknown to me, he looked in great distress. A second time, the thought entered my mind to go up and give witness, but I continued more intensely to fight the prompting. Bernie, a woman who attended the Cross and Crown prayer meeting, was sitting just a few seats ahead of us on the bus. Turning around, she looked at me and said matter-of-factly, "Sue, you should go up there."

Smiling, I replied, "Yeah, I know."

But as soon as she turned back around my own will took over and I said to myself, *There's no way I'm going up there!* All at once, my heart felt heavy, feeling as though I had just disobeyed God. Feeling terrible about it, I prayed, "Lord, if You really want me to go up there, please have Bernie turn around one more time. If she does, I promise to listen."

Not but a moment later, Bernie turned around, saying, "Sue, go up there."

Wow.

Forcing myself down the aisle to the front of the bus, I had not the slightest idea as to what I was going to say. "Holy Spirit, help me!" I prayed. Sitting down next to Joyce in the front seat, I gained courage in telling of my decision to walk with Jesus in the trial of my failing kidneys. An intense heat begin to burn down my back as I explained how God asks each of us, at times, to embrace our crosses with Him for a greater good.

Wrapping her arms around me in comfort, Joyce said, "I can feel heat radiating from your back!" "But you will receive power when the holy Spirit comes upon you, and you will be my witnesses" (Acts 1:8).

In my brief message of hope, I shared with those on the bus how the Lord had enlightened me of the inner peace and joy that He longs to give us in our tribulations. Instead of complaining in times of difficulties, I told of how the Lord was guiding me to live in acceptance of His Will in full reliance of His mercy.

Breathing a sigh of relief, I was happy and relieved to be back in my comfort zone in the last seat of the bus, happy that it was over and relieved that I had finally listened to what God was asking of me! Getting back on the mic, Joyce asked if there was anyone else who wanted to come up. There was dead silence. Again, she asked, and in the quiet you could hear a pin drop. A third time, she took hold of the microphone and said, "The Holy Spirit has prompted me that there is one more person that He's called to come up here to give testimony."

It was at that moment when it finally dawned on me the meaning of the word spoken in my heart earlier that same morning, "Listen!" Leaning over toward Rob, I whispered, "If that's you who the Holy Spirit is calling up there, you'd better listen."

Shocked in seeing him bolt out of his seat, he made his way up to the front. In tears, he explained that as soon as the first woman came up to tell her story, the Holy Spirit had told him interiorly to go up and lay hands on her to pray for God's healing. "I'm so humbled to be up here," he continued. "As I was being prompted I didn't want to listen. I thought to myself, 'Who am I to go up there and pray over anyone?' Then, the next thing I knew, there was another woman up here telling of her cancer, and again, I was prompted to come up and pray over God's hurting people. But, much as I tried, I couldn't get myself to step out in faith to do it.

The more women who came up to tell of their bouts with cancer, the more I lacked the courage to listen to what the Holy Spirit was prompting me to do."

Nearly jumping out of her seat, Katy was first to come forward for prayer. Standing in the back as I watched things unfold, it wasn't my husband I saw praying with those on the bus, but in my mind's eye, it was Jesus who was ministering to His people through him. In Rob, I could see a new man, a man filled with boldness in the power and conviction of wanting only to serve God in any capacity that was asked of him. The Holy Spirit came over him as he petitioned the Lord for His healing hand to be upon Katy, asking that she receive all the healings intended for her. The second person to request prayer was the woman who was suffering from inoperable cancer. As he continued praying over various people, specific words of knowledge came into his mind in the way that he should pray for their needs. Making his way toward the back of the bus, Rob's eyes would periodically lock onto mine, signaling for me to join him. Feeling the same apprehension as I had in going up to the front of the bus to give my witness, I remained frozen in the dread of having to step outside of the boundaries of my comfort zone. Inching his way closer to me, he leaned his long body over one of the empty seats, saying persuasively, "Sue, this isn't just for me—it's for both of us. We're a team." Detecting my reluctance, he came right up to me and said, "This is the mission the Lord told me in prophesy that would unfold for us shortly after my thirtieth anniversary at work. This is it, hon. God has called us into the healing ministry."

It was Pentecost Sunday, and it was all starting to sink in. With me being the one to sense the call for us to attend the conference, it was Rob who had been enlightened that something spiritually profound was going to take place. As though a light switch had suddenly been turned on in my head, I knew this was God's Will for us. I recollected once again the word that I had heard so clearly spoken in my heart earlier that same morning,

"Listen." I realized that the Holy Spirit had put us on alert ahead of time, to take note and pay close attention to what was going to unfold by instructing us to "listen" closely to His promptings.

At once, I became compliant to pray with Rob for the needs of the people brought to us that day. The same way we'd been called onto the path that required us to take hold of Jesus' hand along the Way of the Cross, He was now asking us to pray and encourage others who found themselves traveling along the same way. As we prayed together for those who came forth, my hands began to burn. Specific Scripture verses came to my mind to share with those whose lives were being torn and shattered, offering them a renewed sense of hope.

What had transpired that Pentecost seemed surreal. Returning to our seats in the back of the bus, Katy came back to introduce the woman who she'd come to the conference with. Her friend told us that her daughter-in-law was pregnant for the third time after previously suffering two miscarriages. Asking if she could sit in proxy for her to have a full-term pregnancy, we brought her needs before God. As we were praying, Rob became emotional as he received a word of knowledge. "The baby will be born healthy," he spoke out in faith according to what the Spirit laid on his heart.

Then the young woman who was sitting with her sister in the seat ahead of us turned around. She reported that as Rob and I walked by her to take our seats in the back of the bus two days earlier, she had sensed an aura of holiness. Initially puzzled at her remark, it dawned on me that we had just received Jesus in Communion, and that it was "His presence in us" she had sensed. St. Leo the Great said, "Nothing else is aimed at in our partaking of the Body and Blood of Christ, than that we change into what we consume, and ever bear in spirit and flesh Him in whom we have died, been buried, and have risen"[1]

Rob's prophetic sense that God had something quite marvelous planned for us was fully realized on Pentecost Sunday in the amazing event that took place on the bus trip back from the Medjugorje Conference. Our healing ministry began in the timeline given him two months earlier—shortly after his thirtieth anniversary at his job. Having experienced a St. Paul "fall off of his horse" kind of conversion, God had rightfully gained the centermost place in his life. Through our personal encounter with the Holy Spirit that Pentecost Sunday, we knew in our hearts that we'd never be the same.

Less than two weeks later, Rob began receiving visions and interior locutions. Most often they would occur during the times we spent in quietude before the Blessed Sacrament and other times while we were praying the rosary or the Chaplet of Mercy together in our home. The Spirit of the Lord would come over him and reveal God's wisdom and knowledge like chapters being written in a book. In the ministry entrusted to us by the Lord, words were spoken to him interiorly for us to live by—faith, humility, trust, prepare, supernatural, and so on. It was also revealed to him that, as warriors of the faith, we needed to put on the armor of God.

> "For our struggle is not with flesh and blood but with the principalities, with the powers, with the world rulers of this present darkness, with the evil spirits in the heavens. Therefore, put on the armor of God, that you may be able to resist on the evil day and, having done everything, to hold your ground." (Ephesians 6:12–13)

From the books we were reading, we were aware that upon deciding completely for Jesus, one would meet up with opposition from the opponent of salvation. Frequenting the Chapel of Divine Mercy nearly every day, we prayed for a spiritual director who could guide and encourage us along the path chosen for us. In the burning fire of our trials and tribulations, a spark had been fueled and flamed within our hearts to grow closer to Jesus through Eucharistic adoration. Growing in trust, we surrendered our concerns back over to God. He, in turn, sent us back out to be of help to others who found themselves in precarious and despairing situations.

Seeking the advice of a local pastor who met with us on multiple occasions, he offered his support and advised that we embrace the way in which we were being led. Referring us to a retired Capuchin priest who did spiritual counseling, right from the start, Father Kieran was a perfect fit. How wonderful it was to receive the sound counsel of a priest to direct us in the powerful ways in which the Spirit of God was moving in our lives. After meeting with him for the first time, we went to the Chapel of Divine Mercy to thank God for answered prayer.

In the early morning hours of June 28 Rob sat straight up in bed. He'd been shown a vision of the face of a young woman with blond hair. Tears were running down her face. "The girl looked to be about Jenelle's age," he told me later upon calling me from work. To see such disquiet in the eyes of a girl he didn't know, we agreed to seek out God's wisdom concerning it at the Chapel of Divine Mercy. Throughout the entire hour spent in Eucharistic adoration that evening, Rob was continually prompted to pray for Katy, the first woman he prayed over on the bus trip back from the Medjugorje Conference. Returning home from the chapel, he went into the bedroom to meditate.

Coming to me later, he asked, "Does Katy have a daughter?"

"Gee, I really don't know." I responded.

"The Lord revealed to me in my prayer time that the girl with blond hair who I saw crying was Katy's daughter. Through Mary's intercession, I was told that her tears will be wiped dry. I also received the knowledge that the Lord has a special healing for Katy, and on the twenty-eighth of each month we're to pray over her and pray a rosary together."

What did it all mean? If the tears of Katy's daughter were going to be wiped dry through Mary's intercession, the obvious answer seemed to be that God would heal her of the ominous cancer that threatened her life. The one thing we knew for sure was that our focus needed to be on being obedient to what God was asking of us. Through committed prayer, we submitted Katy's needs into the Holy Will of God. "As high as the heavens are above the earth,/ so high are my ways above your ways/ and my thoughts above your thoughts" (Isaiah 55:9).

"How can we get in contact with her?" Rob asked.

Having only ever met Katy just that once, we didn't even know her last name. From the brief testimony she gave on the bus, we knew only that she lived in a small berg north of Green Bay. As Rob and I were talking, I suddenly remembered Debbie telling me a story of a woman with cancer she'd roomed with while on pilgrimage to Medjugorje, becoming close friends.

"I think her name was Katy," I told him.

"Can you call to ask her if Katy has a daughter?" he asked.

Being that I really didn't know Debbie all that well, I protested. "It's already after nine o'clock!"

Pleading, he asked again, "Please?"

In his eyes, I could see how much it meant to him. "Okay," I relented. "But I hope you pray that she's not already in bed and that she'll be open to my probing questions!"

Relieved, he promised, "I will."

First telling Debbie of what had transpired on the bus trip home from the conference, I asked, "Do you know if Katy has a daughter?"

"Yes she does," she replied.

I was astonished to learn that Katy's daughter had blond hair and that she was twenty-six years old, the same age Rob had estimated her to be. Going on to tell her of the message Rob received within his heart in that we were to pray with Katy on the twenty-eighth of each month, she said; "Katy's in Florida right now with her mom, but I know she'll be open to prayer. I'll call her when she gets back to make arrangements for us to get together."

Confirming to Rob what had been revealed to him, he felt at peace in discerning what God was asking of us.

Two weeks later, we traveled with Debbie to a restaurant about an hour north of our home. There, we met up with Katy, Joyce, and two other women who'd also been on the bus to the conference. After breakfast, we all got into one vehicle to travel to Escanaba, Michigan to see Francis, a man of humble nature who bore the stigmata wounds of Christ. On the first Tuesday of every month, he prayed over those who came in the hope of receiving healings of various sorts. Humility emanated from him. When it was our turn, Rob and I went up together. Closing his eyes in prayer, Francis stopped briefly. Smiling, he said, "Lord, You have brought me good people today." Having been summoned by God to pray with Katy, what a blessing it had been for us to receive the prayers of His righteous and unassuming servant.

On our way back home, we stopped off at a bakery where we purchased freshly baked whole wheat bread in preparation for our Wednesday and Friday fasts as advised by Our Lady of Medjugorje. Acquainting ourselves with Katy, Rob shared with her on the car ride back what the Lord had put in his heart about praying with her on the twenty-eighth of each month. Totally receptive, we exchanged phone numbers with her to make plans to meet.

Later on that day as Rob was cutting the lawn, he heard interiorly a voice asking, "Do you want to follow Jesus?" Within himself, he affirmed his desire to follow Jesus. A short time later, he was asked the same, and again he answered, "Yes. I want to follow Jesus." In his heart, he heard, "Then you must give your life up for Me." "I give my life to You, Lord," Rob promised. That night as we prayed our novena together, he heard interiorly, "Do you love Me?" "Yes, Lord. I do love You," he replied within his heart, hearing the words, "Feed My sheep."

> "When they had finished breakfast, Jesus said to Simon Peter, 'Simon, son of John, do you love me more than these?' He said to him, 'Yes, Lord, you know that I love you.' He said to him, 'Feed my lambs.' He then said to him a second time, 'Simon, son of John, do you love me?' He said to him 'Yes, Lord, you know that I love you.' He said to him, 'Tend my sheep.' He said to him the third time, 'Simon, son of John, do you love me?' Peter was distressed that he had said to him a third time, 'Do you love me?' and he said to him, 'Lord, you know everything; you know that I love you.' [Jesus] said to him, 'Feed my sheep.'" (John 21:15–19)

While kneeling in adoration before the Blessed Sacrament, Rob received an interior locution. In it, he saw a brown and tan gazebo with a single bench placed inside. Then he saw himself standing behind the bench next to me, and we were praying over a woman who was sitting on the bench. He then received a timeline that the scene shown to him would soon take place. Four days later, the prophetic vision was fulfilled.

We'd been invited by two different people to attend the upcoming Medjugorje picnic at a park in Green Bay. Hosted by Joyce, an outdoor Mass was followed by lunch and fellowship, concluding in praying a rosary and Chaplet of Divine Mercy. It did sound nice, but thinking it was reunion of sorts for all the people who'd been on one of Joyce's pilgrimages to Medjugorje, we declined both offers. It wasn't until we were invited by yet a third person that something stirred up inside of me.

"I don't know what's going on with all of the invitations to the Medjugorje picnic," I said to Rob, "but since we don't have any plans for Sunday, perhaps we should go." He agreed.

A twenty-five-minute drive from our home, we'd never been to Green Isle Park. Entering the parking lot, I immediately noticed a brown and tan gazebo positioned to the left of the pavilion. I don't know why, but I decided to wait for Rob to see the gazebo for himself. Heading over to bring our food into the kitchen, a woman exited the pavilion and walked toward us. Introducing herself, she explained that Joyce had shared with her some of the remarkable events that had taken place on the bus trip home from the Medjugorje Conference.

"Will you pray with me?" she asked.

"Sure," Rob said to her as he glanced around for a suitable place to pray. Spotting the gazebo, he looked at me in amazement. "We'll first drop off our food in the kitchen and then we'll pray with you over there in that gazebo."

Approaching the brown and tan gazebo, we were astonished to see a single park bench in the middle of it, exactly as was shown to Rob in the vision. As the woman sat on the bench, we stood behind her and prayed for God's healing. What incredible affirmation it was in knowing we were exactly where the Lord had previously shown we would be! "From now on I am telling you before it happens, so that when it happens you may believe that I AM" (John 13:19). How beautiful was the Mass and the entire atmosphere at the Medjugorje picnic that afternoon! As others asked for prayer, though it was something very new to us, it felt as though we'd been praying with God's people our entire lives.

As subsequent prophetic visions unfolded, we began referring to them as "faith boosters." Without exception, they were of holy places in which we'd never been before, and they always boosted our faith. On another occasion, as Rob and I prayed before Jesus in Eucharistic adoration, he was shown a vision of him and me talking to a small group of people under a "lollipop tree," as he referred to it.

"To the immediate right of where we were standing," he said, "was a church. There were stairs leading up around the front, and I could see wrought iron rails." In the scene shown to him, he also took note that it was a cloudless day with a full sun.

"What on earth is a lollipop tree?" I asked, laughing.

"Oh," he replied nonchalantly. "I just referred to it as that because the trunk was straight and the shape of the leaves on top was rounded. It reminded me of the shape of a lollipop, that's all."

A short time later, I called the diocesan office to inquire of where we might take my mom on a day trip.

"Have you ever taken her to the Shrine of Our Lady of Good Help?"[2] she asked.

"No. I've never heard of it," I replied.

She went on to tell me it was the site of the reported Marian apparition to a Belgian nun in the mid-1800s. She relayed that it was during the devastation of the Great Peshtigo Fire[3] twelve years later that the grounds and buildings of the site were virtually left untouched, while the surrounding land was completely scorched. Ever since the miracle, large crowds of the faithful began to gather there every year on the feast of Mary's Assumption into Heaven, celebrated with an outdoor Mass. Going to my calendar, I wrote on the date of August 15 "Mass with Mom at Our Lady of Good Help."

Two days later after attending Sunday evening Mass, we stopped off at the adoration chapel before bringing my mother Communion. Arriving at her assisted living home, Rob asked, "Would you mind if I stay in the car to read the bulletin and do some more praying? You can visit with your mom as long as you want."

"Not at all," I told him.

Returning to the car, Rob handed me the church bulletin and questioned, "Does anything on this page jump out at you?"

Being that it was already dusk, I was unable to see the small print he was holding out. "What do you want me to see?" I asked.

Pointing to one of the bulletin announcements, the subtitle read, August 15, The Feast of the Assumption. "Read this," he urged.

As I began to read of the upcoming Mass that was to be celebrated on the grounds of Our Lady of Good Help, I said, "Oh my goodness! I forgot to tell you. I've already marked this on our calendar for us to attend with my mom! I'll show it to you when we get home."

"Sue," he went on to say, "when I was reading the bulletin, this announcement stood out to me as though it was three dimensional on the page. We need to go to this!"

Inside, my heart was smiling.

With the extra hour it would take us to pick up my mom before heading to the Shrine of Our Lady of Good Help, we made certain to get an early start to attend the "Mass on the grass" in celebration of Mary's Assumption into heaven. But upon arriving, it was to our surprise to see cars already lined up along both sides of the country road, with parking attendants directing cars into the nearby fields to park. Combined with humid temperatures predicted to climb into the 90s that day, and my mom's breathing issues, we had hoped to secure a spot in the shade. But with hundreds of people already seated in their lawn chairs awaiting the Mass, it was no longer an option. Instead, we put down our lawn chairs halfway out in the field, in full sun. After getting her all situated between Rob and me, she was happy and content. Breathing in the oxygen from the tank that hung from the back of her wheelchair, she'd be the last to complain. Though Rob and I had never been there, my mother told me that she'd gone often as a child. Being that her grandmother's birthday coincided with the feast of Mary's Assumption, her parents would often take the family to the Shrine to celebrate.

Sitting back in my lawn chair, I began to look around. The very first thing that caught my eye was a tree, about fifty or sixty yards away and positioned directly in front of us.

Now that looks like a lollipop tree, I said to myself amusingly, taking note of its round top and straight trunk. Suddenly remembering the prophetic vision shown to Rob less than two weeks prior, I looked up in the sky to notice there was not a single cloud to be seen. Immediately, I turned my focus to the front of the church that was located to the right of the tree. Wanting to check if there were stairs with iron rails, the clusters of people gathered around made it difficult for me to get a clear view. Watching intently as the crowd cleared, I was amazed to see that there were indeed stairs with wrought iron rails that extended up to the front of the church!

Leaning over toward Rob, I said, "Look, hon, a lollipop-shaped tree, and there's a cloudless sky with full sun!" Pointing at the church, I added, "There are steps leading up the front with iron rails!" At the conclusion of the Mass, there was a Eucharistic rosary procession around the grounds followed with final Benediction. It was hot, and as the people filed into procession, we quickly took refuge from the blaring sun beneath the lollipop-shaped tree with my mom. Almost as soon as we got her positioned under the tree, we found ourselves surrounded in conversation by five of the people we'd recently met on the Medjugorje bus trip, including Debbie and Katy.

Introducing them to my mom, Katy knelt down on one knee to talk with her at eye level. My heart overflowed in joy of the kindness and love they showered upon my mother. After the Benediction, taking hold of my mom's wheelchair, Rob said, "Hon, the Bishop is coming out of the church and I want to see if he'll give Gloria his blessing." What a wonderfully spiritual day it had been, and how astounded we were to find ourselves exactly where the Lord had previously shown we would be, on the holy grounds of the Shrine of Our Lady of Good Help. Before leaving, we made plans with Katy to meet up with her for prayer on August 28, as the Lord had instructed us to do.

It wasn't long before we noticed a pattern begin to form as the Lord continued to show Rob prophetic visions of holy places that we would be. In every case, I'd have a spontaneous desire to go to a particular religious place or event in which the prophecies would unfold. Never did it enter our minds to figure out the possible locations of the prophetic visions, but rather it was through God's providence that they were fulfilled. Each time they came to fruition, we were surprised to find ourselves in exactly the place where God had shown we would be. It was through these divine revelations that our faith and trust in God grew in leaps and bounds!

The days had gone by quickly as we made the drive to meet Katy on August 28 at Green Isle Park. Once there, we walked over to the picnic table where she was sitting with her daughter. For Rob, it was quite remarkable to meet in person the blond-haired girl with tears coming down her cheek shown to him in the vision two months prior. Katy's face was beaming as she announced the wonderful news that her daughter was expecting her first child, and *her* first grandchild! Chatting a while before walking over to the gazebo to pray with Katy, we then prayed a rosary together with her and the daughter "whose tears would be wiped dry through the intercession of Mary."

On our way home, we decided to stop off at the Chapel of Divine Mercy to go before Jesus in thanksgiving. While in prayer, the Lord revealed to Rob specific details in regard to our ministry and the needs of the people He brought to us. We needed to listen, pray, console, comfort, and speak words of love through His promptings, quoting His word in Scripture. Our ministry was not about us. The gifts given to us were not for our credit, but for the glory and honor of God. They were to be used not for our good, but for the good of His people and for the good of the Church. Faithfully, we met up with Katy on the twenty-eighth of each month, and oftentimes in between at various religious events. With the cooler months right around the corner, we decided to change our meeting venue to the Shrine of Our Lady of Good Help.

One evening while we were in adoration before the Blessed Sacrament, Rob was shown a bright yellow star that was flashing on and off. As the star dissipated, he saw in its place a brilliant light, followed by an image of an elderly couple pictured from the shoulders up. He estimated them to be in their late seventies. Immediately sensing they were holy people, he recognized them as long standing members of the Cross and Crown prayer group. For years Jerry and Dolores had been praying for the healing of God's people on occasions too many to count. Given the knowledge they'd be instrumental in our healing ministry, we invited them along at times to pray over the people being brought into our lives for prayer. Gracious to oblige, they soon became our beloved friends and mentors.

Another time in Eucharistic adoration, Rob received a word of knowledge that we were to pray for the second woman who'd requested prayer on the return trip home from the Medjugorje Conference. Interiorly, he heard, "Because of her love for Jesus, she's been saved." Seeing us at a healing Mass for the first time since the bus trip, Janie walked over. Exchanging hugs, she told of how her tumors had shrunk in size after being prayed over on the bus three months prior.

"Would you be willing to come to Green Bay to meet my husband and pray with me again?" she asked.

Encouraged by her praise report of the healing power of God, we invited Jerry and Dolores to travel to Green Bay with us to pray with Janie.

In the months following the outpouring of the Holy Spirit on Pentecost, Rob would often be shown visions of people who God would be bringing into our lives for prayer, and other times we'd receive a phone call or be approached at church with the request to pray with someone. It was not something we set up for ourselves, but was in God's holy arrangements that we accepted His call to be vessels of prayer. Before going to pray over someone, we'd first bring them with us spiritually into Eucharistic adoration, pleading for the Blood of the Lamb to be poured out over their every need.

Rob and I were in attendance at a healing mass said by Fr. Clement J. Machado, SOLT,[4] from Italy, who was doing a parish mission at a neighboring church. A holy and devout priest possessing many gifts, his missions were always crowded. Rob took the afternoon off work so we could arrive at the church hours early to pray before the exposition of the Blessed Sacrament and go to confession. With multiple confessors present, we got into separate lines. As it turned out, I was already back in my seat while Rob was still standing in line awaiting his turn. After praying my penance, I picked up Rob's Bible and opened it randomly as I prayed, "Lord, what is it You want to say to me today?" Then, I began to read.

> "So when he had washed their feet [and] put his garments back on and reclined at table again, he said to them, 'Do you realize what I have done for you? You call me 'teacher' and 'master,' and rightly so, for indeed I am. If I, therefore, the master and teacher, have washed your feet, you ought to wash one another's feet.'" (John 13:12–14)

Returning to his seat a short time later, Rob leaned over and whispered, "While I was in the confessional line praying a rosary, the Lord showed me a vision of your feet inside a white sink. There was water trickling out from the faucet and onto your feet."

Not having yet shared with him my appeal to Jesus to speak to me through Scripture, I was utterly amazed that our Lord had shown him the visual image of the same verse He had spoken to me! Just as Jesus didn't send His disciples "out into the deep" as fishers of men without first teaching and walking with them for three years, so too, was He washing our feet before "sending us out" to pray for His hurting people.

So much had taken place since the prophetic message given to Rob of the mission we'd been called to. How true is the adage that God does not call the qualified but rather He qualifies the called. On our part, all we needed to do was to be obedient to what God was asking of us. In the spirit of service, we needed to hold on in our suffering and forget about ourselves in order to go out and be a blessing to others.

> "For 'everyone who calls on the name of the Lord will be saved.'
> But how can they call on him in whom they have not believed? And how can they believe in him of whom they have not heard? And how can they hear without someone to preach? And how can people preach unless they are sent? As it is written, 'How beautiful are the feet of those who bring [the] good news!'" (Romans 10:13–15)

It was becoming increasingly evident to me how life's tribulations can be instrumental in leading one onto the path of holiness. In uniting my trials with the Cross of Christ, I could feel within myself His constant love and consolation in every hardship. Wherever sacrifice and suffering is offered together with Jesus' sorrowful passion, great merit is attained. Our Lord had invited me to take a tiny sip of the cup from which He drank, the bitter cup of His suffering. It would be through my hardships that I'd gain the strength and understanding to offer comfort to others in theirs.

While praying our nightly novena one evening, my heart was heavy. As a wolf in sheep's clothing, the opponent of salvation desires to ensnare our youth into believing the deceptions of the culture, depicting right as wrong and wrong as right. Entrusting my children into the Sacred Heart of Jesus, I drifted off to sleep. Upon awakening the next morning, I was shown two embryos within a womb. One of them was larger and closer to the forefront of the vision, while the other embryo was much smaller and situated further behind. Opening my eyes, I heard over and over, "You'll soon be united with Jesus." Uncertain of its meaning, I prayed for God's wisdom.

As I began to pray and thank Jesus for the Blood He shed on the Cross, the Lord spoke to my heart. He revealed that the two embryos represented the two children I had borne. The message spoken within my heart was concerning them, in that they would soon be united with Jesus. The larger embryo in the forefront of the vision represented the one who would come into the knowledge of His truth ahead of the other. Immense joy flooded my heart of the saving power of the precious Blood of Christ!

A few weeks later, as we were down on our knees praying the Efficacious Novena to the Sacred Heart of Jesus, we heard the back door open. Our daughter had just returned home. Simultaneous with her arrival, Rob was shown a vision of a bottle with the cap being placed securely back onto its top. Within his heart, he heard repeatedly, "She's united with Christ." Telling me of this, I instantly recognized the familiarity of the words.

"It's the same message I received in the embryo vision!" I exclaimed. Remarkably, it was on the following morning that Jenelle told me in her usual soft-spoken manner how her heart had been opened to hearing God's truth. How good and wonderful that upon returning home physically, our Lord would reveal she had also returned home spiritually!

Praying before the Blessed Sacrament, Rob was shown a vision of our shoes being placed in the small entrance leading into the Chapel of Divine Mercy. Interiorly, he was told that we were standing on holy ground. "Remove your sandals from your feet, for the place on which you are standing is holy" (Joshua 5:15). In reoccurring visions, he was shown images of his own two feet with sandals on, with the infused knowledge that we were to go out and follow in the footsteps of Christ. Unqualified for the task, we could barely wrap our minds around what God was asking us to do, but yet we always held on to the promise that "He would equip us well."

It was in our misery that we had cried out to God. Drawing us close to Himself, He called us out of the ways of the world. Placed onto a path of transformation, we picked up our cross to follow Jesus. Now, He was sending us back out to be a witness to others, bringing them back into the fold of His love. Though God didn't expect us to minister to the four corners of the earth, He did call us to reach out in love to help those He placed in our path, to be charitable and kindhearted. "For to this you have been called, because Christ also suffered for you, leaving you an example that you should follow in his footsteps" (1 Peter 2:21).

As with His disciples, Jesus commissions His followers to walk in His shoes in the capacity in which we're called. Drawing us near, He then sends us out to wash the feet of others. In service to the One who first did it for us, Jesus did not come to be served, but to serve, and ultimately, to be a living sacrifice for the salvation of mankind.

Can the human heart refrain
From partaking in her pain,
  In that mother's pain untold?

—Stabat Mater

If we only knew the precious treasure hidden in infirmities, we would receive them with the same joy with which we receive the greatest benefits, and we would bear them without ever complaining or showing signs of weariness.

—Saint Vincent de Paul

Stations of the Cross

Seventh Station
Jesus Falls the Second Time

Yes, I love the Cross and only the Cross. I love it because I see it always on the shoulders of Jesus. Now Jesus sees clearly that all my life and all my heart are vowed to Him and to His sufferings.

—Padre Pio

Behold, Your Mother

Meeting up with Jenelle for a weekday Mass at St. Joseph's one day, she shared with me an image she saw in her heart after receiving Holy Communion. It was of a large Cross, and behind it a bright light illuminated in the form of the Star of Bethlehem, as though it was spotlighted. In front of the Cross was a Crown of Thorns.

"I think I'm supposed to design and sew a banner quilt with the image on it," she told me.

Puzzled at her comment, I responded, "But you don't sew."

"I know," she said admittedly. "But that's what I was inspired to do. I feel like it's meant to hang someplace holy, like in a church or something."

Neither possessing quilting knowledge nor sewing expertise, it was with ease that she strategically drew out on graphing paper the vision shown to her. Carefully selecting materials of various hues and cutting them into 3-inch squares, she set forth to sew her very first quilt in the image that depicted the cost of our redemption; the Star being indicative of Christ's birth, the Crown of Thorns symbolic of sin, and the Cross Jesus died on representative of the price He paid so that we might have eternal life. Coming across a life-sized Crown of Thorns, we purchased it to hang in front of the banner.

Cross banner quilt as it hangs in the Schoenstatt Wayside Shrine, Refuge of Sinners, *Quilting Cause*

Here we were, just as ordinary as people can be. Yet within the course of just a few months following Pentecost Sunday, the Lord had opened up for us the door of divine revelations. It was nothing we ever desired or asked for, but rather what God had chosen for us. "It was not you who chose me, but I who chose you and appointed you to go and bear fruit that will remain, so that whatever you ask the Father in my name he may give you" (John 15:16).

God calls each of us to become saints through living good and holy lives, and we were living proof that one does not have to be a saint to open themselves up to living within the Will of God. It is imperative to remember that gifts given so freely by the Holy Spirit are never intended for self-glory, nor are those who receive them to be held in high esteem. With humility being the foundation of all virtues and pride the source of all sin, one must embrace God's gifts as He intends, in compliance with the Magisterium of the Church.

Throughout the ages, there have been so-called "private" revelations, some of which have been recognized by the authority of the Church. They do not belong, however, to the deposit of faith. It is not their role to improve or complete Christ's definitive Revelation, but to help live more fully by it in a certain period of history. Guided by the Magisterium of the Church, the *'sensus fidelium'* knows how to discern and welcome in these revelations whatever constitutes an authentic call of Christ or His saints to the Church.[1](CCC #67)

The rosary had become for me the comfort food of my soul. In praying the family rosary as a child, my mind had often wandered off thinking about things not pertaining to prayer. On my commute to and from work each day as an adult, it remained a struggle to stay focused on the words I was saying. It wasn't until I discovered its contemplative nature that I better understood its transforming power. I was able to travel back in time two thousand years on the beads of my rosary, meditating on the lives of Jesus and Mary. I could walk with the Holy Family through their joys and sorrows in the ultimate triumph of Jesus' glorious Resurrection.

Before quieting myself in front of the Tabernacle after Mass each day, I'd first stop off to pray a rosary at the grotto of Mary. Having completed the Preparation for Total Consecration according to St. Louis de Montfort,[2] he explains that since Jesus came to us humbly through Mary, it's only logical for us to go humbly to Jesus through the same means in which He came to us, through His Mother.

Having felt such a special bond and closeness to Mary since childhood, I asked Blessed Mother to magnify my little gifts of love and present them to Jesus as something much more pleasing than what I could ever offer Him on my own. Receiving Communion each day, I'd glance up at the stained glass window of Our Lady of Sorrows behind the altar. Entreating Mary, I asked her to unite the sufferings of my heart with the swords that pierced hers, thus enhancing my gift to Jesus.

As we were leaving the Chapel of Divine Mercy one evening, Rob relayed that the Lord had shown him a vision for me. In the scene shown to him, he saw Mary. She was standing at the foot of Jesus' Cross, holding up to Him a vase. It was filled with the joys and sufferings I presented her each day to bring to Jesus. "It was a very beautiful image," he said, "to see Mary interceding in your tribulations by presenting them to Jesus at the foot of His Cross."

The following day, we drove to Green Bay to attend a special healing Mass that was taking place at Saints Peter and Paul Church. Located thirty miles from our home, it was a church we'd never been to before. Excited to see Francis again, who bore the wounds of Christ, he was going to be praying with people after Mass. As we took our seats, I looked up to see a stunning mural painted on the wall behind the altar. Taking in the beautiful image of Mary standing at the foot of the Cross looking up at Jesus, I was instantly reminded of the vision from the night before. Tears streamed down my face as I envisioned the Holy Mother of God bringing my needs directly to Jesus! This confirmed to me that the closest way to Jesus is through Mary and that everything we do in the spirit of atonement is of abundant merit. "Never be afraid of loving the Blessed Virgin too much. You can never love her more than Jesus did"[3] (Saint Maximilian Kolbe).[4]

It's in surrendering our hardships back over to Jesus through the hands of Mary that we will grow in patience and gain the endurance necessary to walk with Jesus along the path of suffering. Just as any respectful child would listen to their mother, we must listen to our Heavenly Mother in saying, "Do whatever he tells you" (John 2:5). We must strive to live out the Ten Commandments in our daily lives through loving God and in loving our neighbor. As Mary followed Jesus along the agonizing road to Calvary, she'll be there for us when the traveling gets rough. Even the worst of situations will turn into hope as we're provided the grace necessary to persevere toward our final destination. Gaining understanding along the way, in the backdrop of eternity, the trials we suffer are but a drop in the ocean of Jesus' mercy.

Image of the Immaculate Heart of Mary

Feeling miserable from a bout of bronchitis and asthma, my doctor ordered a nebulizer treatment to ease my breathing and an antibiotic to treat the infection. In bed with a fever, I tuned in to EWTN just in time to pray the rosary. Led by Mother Angelica, I closed my eyes to hear the quiet rhythm of the prayers. In meditation, I envisioned my arms wrapped around Jesus in the Garden of Gethsemane. Kissing His anguished Heart, I offered to Him my labored breathing in union with the torment of His suffering. I thought of the thorns surrounding His Sacred Heart in the pain of knowing that, in spite of His selfless gift of love on the Cross, how many would still choose hate over love? Though He paid in full the price of our redemption, how many would actually accept it?

It's in meditating on the holy rosary that our minds will be opened to comprehend the significance of the imprints that Jesus' steps left behind for us to follow. As we travel with Him through the ups and downs of life, they serve as our stepping stones to walk in His footsteps along the Forgotten Way, a path that will lead us onward in our journey toward holiness.

Finishing my rosary, I turned off the TV in hope of getting some rest. Closing my eyes, I was shown an interior locution in which I understood its sublimity. It was of a circular shape that consisted of several circles within the circle. Each of the circles were sectioned off. Contained within each section were numerous miniature shapes. Examining the circle in the very center, I recognized it as the Eucharist. Inside of the Host was a cross.

I sensed the circle in its entirety was symbolic of the human soul, and that the various circles within the circle signified the place that God is preparing for believers in His Kingdom. "In my Father's house there are many dwelling places. If there were not, would I have told you that I am going to prepare a place for you?" (John 14:2). The various shapes within the sections in each circle leading up to the Host, which is Jesus, represented the spiritual gems that are attainable for us to gain here on earth in direct relation to the level in which we'll spend all of eternity in heaven. In seeing the cross within the Host, I understood more fully the tremendous heights of holiness that can be achieved in carrying our earthly crosses with Jesus. "This is evidence of the just judgment of God, so that you may be considered worthy of the kingdom of God for which you are suffering" (2 Thessalonians 1:5).

Jesus awaits us in the sanctuary of our souls, longing to set aflame the dimly lit spark of fallen-away Christians. He's calling us to conversion before it's too late. We must strive for heaven. Hell is real and the devil works day and night to convince us otherwise! Jesus didn't come into the world to live, but to die so that we could live! Though at times we may be asked to carry a sliver of His Cross, it takes on a co-redemptive purpose, "in cooperation with our Redeemer" when united to the Passion of Christ. As in the case of Simon of Cyrene;[5] most of us don't have our hands up "to be called on" to suffer with Jesus. But when we become tired from life's struggles, it's in choosing to walk with Jesus that our burden is lifted.

Sufferings endured with acceptance are what make us worthy to share in the kingdom of God! I was praying within God's Will to heal me from my failing kidneys. "Lord, if You are *willing*, You can heal me." It didn't mean that I couldn't seek medical attention for my failing kidneys or take the medication necessary to recover from my bronchitis, but to embrace the cross allowed me by uniting it to the Cross of Christ.

Mother Mary will mentor us to walk with Jesus as she did, and nurture us to accept God's holy arrangements. The more we abandon ourselves into her care, the greater we'll discover joy amidst difficult times. In connection to Mary's "fiat," we'll draw strength from the treasury of grace to persevere in being faithful to our yes. To my blessed Mother I gave without reserve my virtues, graces, merits, and satisfactions, trusting her to dispense them in a way most pleasing to God. "Behold, I am the handmaid of the Lord. May it be it done to me according to your word" (Luke 1:38).

While in contemplative prayer before the Blessed Sacrament, Rob was shown an image of an old ship, like those from years ago. It was floating very still on a peaceful body of water.

"The message I received," he shared, "is that you're to maintain a still and peaceful spirit."

Pausing, I asked, "In regard to what?"

"I don't know." he answered.

Soon after, my yearly mammogram revealed calcifications both greater in size and in quantity than those of previous years. Called back in to undergo another round of images that would greater magnify the areas of concern, the results confirmed the need for me to undergo a biopsy. My heart sank with the news, as a number of concerns raced through my mind. How could I go through cancer at the same time my kidneys were functioning at only 15 percent? I thought back to the dear man I'd met on a PKD walk I had participated in the previous summer. He shared with me his harrowing experience of being diagnosed with cancer while awaiting a kidney transplant, having to go on dialysis during the course of his cancer treatment. When he was deemed "cancer-free," there was a three-year waiting period before he could be put back on the donor list. My heart had gone out to him, promising my prayers. Fearful I'd have to undergo the same, I lost my inner peace.

In the Chapel of Divine Mercy, we placed the cross handed me upon the altar of the Lord. In an interior locution, Rob saw a scrub pail with a mop and dirty water inside, representative of the anxiety that was causing me worry. He received the message that I was to put my trust in Jesus. After Mass the next day, we stopped off at the adoration chapel before bringing Communion to my mother. Praying for a good outcome of my biopsy, Rob was shown the open hand of God reaching out for me to place in it all of my concerns. He then saw a small wastebasket filled with Kleenex tissues. Draped atop the basket was a neon-lit rosary flashing on and off. The message was that I needed to throw away my fears and pray for Mary's intercession.

Though I was already seeking Mary's intercession every day in regard to my impending renal failure, it had been especially difficult for me to do the same in regard to my upcoming biopsy. It was as though I were perched up high on the tight rope of faith, with the balance beam of *fear* on one side and *trust* on the other, teetering back and forth between my will and God's Will for me. It seemed to me that the neon-lighted rosary was flashing to get my attention to pray, surrender, and trust! Thinking back on the serenity of the huge ship shown to Rob just days prior to having the mammogram, I realized the only way for me to stay afloat amidst times of distress was to rest in the peace of the Lord. I needed to trust that God is bigger than any hardship and that Mary would help me to rely fully on Him.

I took great comfort in the consolations given to me in my weakness. Before the Tabernacle each day after Mass, and in Eucharistic adoration on most evenings with Rob, I eagerly sought to throw away my fears. Envisioning the open hand of God, I placed in it all of my cares and concerns. Through the encouraging words of Scripture and in meditating on the mysteries of the rosary, my inner peace was restored. "Cast your care upon the LORD,/ who will give you support" (Psalms 55:23).

From the beginning, Rob insisted on rearranging his schedule at work to accompany me to my appointments. The love he showed in his constant support was beyond anything I ever hoped for. Jenelle's loving concern always shined forth in her kind and gentle ways. Praying rosary upon rosary for me, she made frequent trips to the Chapel of Divine Mercy on my behalf, though she herself suffered from chronic pain yet to be diagnosed. Assured of the prayers of my son and daughter-in-law from across the miles, how truly blessed I was to have God, family, and the prayerful encouragement of friends.

In the days preceding my biopsy, Jenelle told me she had made arrangements at work to come with me. "We can go to Mass together before your one o'clock appointment," she said.

It sounded great to me. Learning that Rob planned on being there as well, I said, "Hon, please stay at work. Jenelle will be with me." It took all I could do to convince him otherwise. He settled on taking a late lunch hour to pray for me from his desk during the time of the scheduled biopsy.

Lying face down on a hard and narrow table in preparation for the surgical procedure, I noticed right away during the prep time that it had no padding. The right side of my ribs began to hurt a lot in the uncomfortable position I was in, and I wondered how I'd possibly be able to lay perfectly still in that position for an entire hour. To alleviate the pressure from my ribs, I slid my hand beneath my right shoulder for cushioning. Noticing this, one of the nurses apologized, explaining that in most cases they're able to place a towel beneath the patient's ribcage, but with the positioning necessary for my biopsy, it was not possible.

Once the procedure began, I felt a hand sliding beneath the hand I had positioned under my shoulder. Turning my head, I saw a nurse standing at my side. The table was so close to the wall that she would've had to slide in sideways to get to me. "Thanks," I said, looking up into the most beautiful blue eyes I had ever seen. Unlike anything I'd ever experienced, her gaze permeated my soul. With a warm smile, she nodded in acknowledgement of my gratitude. Transfixed on her eyes, I couldn't help but stare. Having heard the eyes are the windows to the soul, I never expected to tangibly see the warm glow of love flowing out from the nurse's eyes and feel it infiltrate my heart. Without knowing how or why, I knew with complete certainty that the nurse standing next to me loved me. For the duration of the biopsy, I remained fixed on the beauty of her eyes.

With the procedure finished, I walked out into the waiting room where Jenelle was praying with rosary in hand. Once I exited the door, I told her of my amazing experience with the nurse who held my hand throughout the entire process.

"I know this may sound strange," I told her, "but in the radiance of the nurse's eyes, I could feel her love dispense into my heart to the point that I knew she loved me!"

Tears formed in Jenelle's eyes. "Mom," she began in her gentle tone. "The minute they called your name to take you back for your biopsy, I began praying a rosary. I begged the Blessed Mother to go along with you." Laughing and crying at the same time, she continued, "Mom, I asked Mary if she would hold on to your hand throughout the entire procedure."

Astonished at what had just transpired, we stopped briefly in the hospital hallway to embrace. Tears of joy streamed down our faces in the understanding that, in answer to her petition, I'd been holding hands and looking into the reassuring eyes of my Heavenly Mother!

Mary is the Mother who loves all of her children, and who longs to console each of us in our every need. At the foot of the Cross, Jesus entrusted His Mother to us, as our spiritual Mother. As any good mother would, Mary held on to my hand in my uneasiness, showering me with her love. "'Woman, behold, your son.' Then he said to the disciple, 'Behold, your mother'" (John 19:26–27).

It was on the Friday of Memorial Day weekend that I received the welcome news that my biopsy was benign. Getting the "okay" to carry on with our plans to do some hiking in the woods up north at our friend's cottage, I wasn't prepared for the bumpy ride in their SUV on the rough terrain of the woods. A short time later, I became aware of a trickle-like sensation internally in the area of the tissue removal of the biopsy. Suspecting it was the slow but constant drip of blood flowing from within my wound, it continued on and off throughout the weekend. On Monday morning, I was horrified to discover a huge black bruise with an enormous blood clot! Determining the internal bleeding had finally stopped, my doctor assured me there was nothing more of concern. The deep hematoma, however, was so painful that it made it difficult for me to sleep at night. Taking several weeks before it fully dissipated, I was content to offer up my discomfort in thanksgiving for what God's mercy had spared me.

Falling under the weight of my cross, the Lord was showing me that it's in those very shortcomings when we fail that we fall on our knees and cry out "Abba Father." When God's children call out to Him for help, when they acknowledge the need of his assistance, those are the times when our failures become more pleasing to Him than if we'd never fallen! It's not in the "falling" but in the "getting up" that matters. The mighty hand of Christ is always extended to help carry the burden of life's crosses on one side, with the gentle aide of Mother Mary on the other.

On the days I attended the noon mass at St. Joe's, my heart was moved at the wonderful opportunity it provided for people to be able to attend Mass during the lunch hour. Shortly after my remarkable encounter with Mary during my biopsy, I noticed total strangers began coming up to me after Mass requesting prayer or counsel. Similar to my experience of seeing love in the eyes of my nurse, I'd sometimes see in the eyes of those I encountered loneliness, inner pain, holiness, and, in one case, the darkness of evil. Specific Scripture verses would come to my mind to encourage them with God's promises.

Walking into church one day, I saw a petite elderly woman who was walking out. Wondering why she was leaving at the start of Mass, I smiled at her as I was about to pass by. Stopping, she said, "Could you please do me a favor?"

"Yes," I responded, thinking she may have become ill.

Holding out a quarter, she asked, "Would you light a candle in front of Mary for me after Mass?"

The frail-looking lady then told me that she'd left her husband home alone briefly in order to come to church and light a candle. He was suffering from Alzheimer's and she had to get right back home to attend to his needs. Unaware of the Mass, she didn't want to interrupt by walking to front of church where the Marian grotto was located.

"Yes," I said while opening my hand to receive the quarter. "I'd be happy to light a candle for you." To ease the pain I saw in her eyes, before parting ways, I said; "Jesus is hearing your prayers. He's right here with you and is aware of your pain."

Instantly, her eyes lit up, and she said, "The reason I came to light a candle was to ask Jesus to give me a sign if He was hearing my prayers. You're the angel He sent to tell me He is!" Opening up her heart, she poured out her concerns, telling me of the death of her daughter and of the great struggle her young grandson was having in dealing with it. She shared also of her granddaughter's challenges of living with juvenile diabetes, and of her own burden of her husband's failing health. Embracing the poor woman, I assured her that I'd be praying for Mary's intercession for the needs of her family.

Another occasion as I was kneeling before the Tabernacle after the Mass, I had this thought that I needed to give my bottle of St. Raphael healing oil to the tall and slender elderly man kneeling next to me. I'd been so excited to receive the blessed oil from a friend just days before, and the last thing on my heart was to give it away. More than that, it was completely out of my comfort zone to approach a complete stranger to offer him a bottle of healing oil!

The prompting in my heart continued, and so I told the Lord I'd give the oil to the man as soon as I completed my novena. But upon finishing a short time later, I looked over in dismay to discover the man had already left. My heart was heavy in the conviction of having carried on in doing what I wanted instead of obeying what God wanted of me. With all of my heart, I prayed, "Please forgive me, Lord. I promise that if the man comes back before the Tabernacle after Mass tomorrow, I'll joyfully give him the oil! Please, Lord," I begged, "bring him back."

Shortly after kneeling before the Tabernacle the following day, the tall man came up and knelt down alongside me. With all the gladness in my heart for having been given a second chance to do as God had asked of me, I felt within myself the boldness to approach him. Tapping him on the shoulder, I said, "I received this bottle of St. Raphael healing oil from a friend and I feel as though the Lord wants me to give it to you."

Appearing very pleased to receive the holy oil, he smiled before saying, "Oh, thank you! I was just reading about St. Raphael the other day." He went on to tell me that he lived in a neighboring town and attended whatever Mass he could make each day during the times that his daughter could stand by to care for his wife. "I bring her Communion every day," he told me. "She's seriously ill, but she offers her tremendous sufferings as a 'victim-soul' for Jesus." Humbled, I promised to pray for his family. Afterward, I thanked Jesus with all of my heart for the privilege of being able to give my holy oil to such a holy and devout man.

As I was praying my rosary before the Marian grotto after Mass one afternoon, a woman knelt down on the kneeler next to me and whispered, "Are you praying the rosary?"

"Yes," I responded.

"Do you want to pray it together?" she asked.

The first thing I observed about her was the twinkle of God's love in her eyes and a sense of the deep love she possessed for Our Lady. "Sure," I replied. As we began to pray, it was as though Mary and I had been introduced to each other by our Blessed Mother herself. Sitting down in the narthex afterward, we talked freely as though we'd known each other for years.

Rob and I had grown quite fond of Katy in meeting up with her for personal prayer and the rosary on the twenty-eighth of each month. We were becoming increasingly aware of the special quality she possessed in bringing those around her closer to Jesus through the courageous example she set of walking with Him in her suffering. Because she was celebrating Thanksgiving Day out of state with family members, she'd arranged to call us at a specific time on the twenty-eighth so we could pray with her over the phone. Afterward, we made plans to meet her for the Sunday Holy Hour at the Shrine of Our Lady of Good Help on December 12 to celebrate the feast of Our Lady of Guadalupe.[6]

While we were at the Shrine with Katy and some of her friends, a few began commenting on the lovely aroma of roses that filled the air. Try as I might, I simply could not detect the aroma of the heavenly scent the others were talking about. Becoming somewhat dispirited, my concern was not so much in my inability to smell the scent of roses, because I didn't feel spiritual envy for anyone. Instead, I found myself wondering if I was not virtuous enough to receive the special grace. In the disappointment and self-doubt concerning my own state of sanctity, I decided to surrender the disquiet of my soul to Our Lady in prayer.

The following day at Mass as I made my way up to receive Holy Communion, I began to pray from my heart these words:

"Dearest Lady of Guadalupe, I've loved you since I was a little child. I'm eternally grateful for your constant intercession. I do not ask you for the grace of smelling the scent of roses in your presence, if by receiving it, I'd become prideful. All I truly want is to receive sweet Jesus within your Immaculate Heart so that my heart would be opened to receive all He has for me. Help me, Mary, to receive Jesus worthily."

After Mass, I decided to use the restroom first before going to the front of church to do my prayers. Standing alone by the hand basin, I saw an elderly woman who I'd never seen before. There was something very pious about the woman standing before me that was so calming. Introducing herself as Maria, she told me she was a native of Mexico.

"I've been involved with the Society of Our Lady of Guadalupe for years," she said while reaching into her purse. Handing me a pamphlet, she then asked, "Would you like to come to a breakfast meeting we're having?" Exchanging information, she asked if I'd be willing to pray for the conversion of her son.

"I'd be happy to," I responded.

As I knelt before the statue of Mary to pray my rosary, I had a sense that the heartfelt prayer I had made to Our Lady of Guadalupe just prior to receiving Communion had resulted in my encounter with Maria. A few days later, I received from her in the mail, a beautiful print of Our Lady of Guadalupe from the basilica in Mexico. My eyes spilled over with tears. Soon after, I received the grace of smelling the scent of roses as a sign of Mary's presence.

One evening after Rob and I had spent some time before the Eucharistic Jesus in the Chapel of Divine Mercy, he said, "The Lord showed me a vision that was for you, but I'm not exactly sure of its meaning."

"What was it?" I asked inquisitively.

"I saw a peaceful looking pond that was crystal clear and as smooth and shiny as glass. Lying on top of the pristine body of water was a beautiful, long-stemmed rose. It was for you," he told me.

Knowing instantly what the vision meant, my soul was flooded with joy as tears formed in my eyes. Gaining my composure, I explained to Rob how I'd been praying an ongoing novena to St. Therese for over a year. I'd pray it for whoever the Lord would put on my heart to pray it for, oftentimes for complete strangers. In the chapel that evening, I finished praying the ninth and final day of the novena to St. Therese, "the Little Flower" for someone else, asking of her, "Please pick me a rose from the heavenly garden and send it to me with a message of love. Ask God to grant me the favor I thee implore and tell Him I will love Him each day more and more."[7] On previous occasions, there had been times when, on the ninth day of praying the novena for someone else, I'd find myself on the receiving end of the graces, even to the point of my doorbell ringing on the ninth day with an unexpected floral delivery of roses! In my heart, I knew that the rose laid out on the peaceful pond shown to Rob was another "message of love," reassuring me of Jesus' calming effect when we turn to Him in the storms of life.

It's in our faith to believe that to become Christ-like means also to share in His sufferings. Jesus became like us and took on the sufferings of mankind, and it was through His death on the Cross that we became heirs of His kingdom. When we embrace the dark times of our life in union with the Cross of Christ, we become a lighthouse to those who are lost in the blinding fog of their sins. It's the light of God's love shining through His people that serve as the gentle waves to wash up others onto the seashore of salvation. "For you were once darkness, but now you are light in the Lord. Live as children of light, for light produces every kind of goodness and righteousness and truth" (Ephesians 5:8–9).

Jesus said He wouldn't leave us as orphans, promising to send the Holy Spirit. When we receive Jesus in the Eucharist, we receive the Holy Spirit! In awareness of this, we'll begin receiving Communion more fully in awe of His true presence; inclusive to the Mass and in Eucharistic adoration. We'll gain strength and power from the Holy Spirit, not only to persevere in our sufferings, but also to ascend to greater levels of holiness on the Mount of Transfiguration! We can strive to overcome the obstacles of each new day by seeking the graces necessary to surrender our troubles back to God through His Holy Mother, the fountain through which all graces flow.[8]

The Blessed Mother always seeks to lead us closer to her Son! She promises that she will see to every soul who binds themselves and their children to her Immaculate Heart with each rosary they pray. At Fatima, Mary told the children, "My Immaculate Heart will be your refuge and the way that will lead you to God."[9] What reassurance we have in this promise, both for ourselves and for our loved ones who have fallen away from the faith. In the icon of Our Lady of Perpetual Help,[10] the fallen sandal that's hanging from Jesus' foot by only its lace is thought to be symbolic of a soul clinging to salvation by one last thread-devotion to Mary. What tremendous value it would be for us to consecrate ourselves to the Immaculate Heart of God's own Mother, who was presented to us by Jesus at the foot of the Cross. Mary will be our guide and safeguard against the snares set out against us by the adversary.

It's in our trials and sufferings that we're all called into the mystery of God's holiness so that His presence in us can be seen by others. "But set an example for those who believe, in speech, conduct, love, faith, and purity" (1 Timothy 4:12). Going to Jesus through the unblemished hands of Mother Mary serves to speed up our sanctification process. Not only will she help us to repent of our sins, but Mary will teach us the values of her virtuous life with Jesus, and the importance of uniting our free will with the Will of God. It's no wonder why so many of the saints who've gone before us who were able to achieve perfection of their souls possessed a great love for Mary! She was their true advocate and help along the way, distributing to them ample graces to fully complete the state of their sanctity. "It is difficult to become saints, difficult, but not impossible. The road to perfection is long, just as long as a lifetime. Consolation is rest along the way, but as soon as your strength is restored, you must get up diligently and continue the race" (Padre Pio).

Bruised, derided, cursed, defiled,
She beheld her tender Child,
   All with bloody scourges rent.

—Stabat Mater

If we only knew the precious treasure hidden in infirmities, we would receive them with the same joy with which we receive the greatest benefits, and we would bear them without ever complaining or showing signs of weariness.[11]

—Saint Vincent de Paul

Stations of the Cross

Eighth Station
Jesus Comforts the Women of Jerusalem

You are suffering, it is true, but fear not because God is with you. Do not offend Him, but love Him. You suffer, but believe also that Jesus Himself suffers in you and for you.

—Padre Pio

INTERCESSORS OF LIGHT

Though the days were dark and trials plenty, the light of God never failed to lift my burden. In the continual surrender of my afflictions, I was able to grow in childlike trust of His mercy. With growing awareness that the call to sanctity is not only for the religious, but for individuals and married couples alike, Rob and I understood that God was calling us to be a light by the way we lived our lives. Having received a plethora of graces and blessings that brought such hope out of misery, we asked our Lord each day to continue bringing those to us that needed Him through us. As more people asked for our prayers, we encouraged them in their suffering through the same Scriptures that we found so reassuring. "Blessed be the God and Father of our Lord Jesus Christ…who encourages us in our every affliction, so that we may be able to encourage those who are in any affliction with the encouragement with which we ourselves are encouraged by God" (2 Corinthians 1:3–4).

It was in reading the collected works of St. John of the Cross[1] and St. Teresa of Avila[2] that we first discovered the meaning of contemplative prayer. Through oral and meditative prayer, one can bring them self to God, but in contemplative prayer, they're taken deep into prayer by God Himself. In the time since our Lord first began manifesting Himself to Rob in mystical ways, it was most often before the Blessed Sacrament where he was brought supernaturally into the realm of an interior spiritual life he never knew existed.

In numerous visions, he was shown a variety of people who were in need of our prayers. Some were of the living, and other scenes were of the need to pray for the salvation of people whose lives were in imminent danger. Souls, who in the stubbornness of their hearts, had rejected the price already been paid for them on the Cross. Asking Our Lady to defend them in the hour of death, we continued praying for them for as long as the Spirit prompted—for weeks, months, sometimes for years. In the offertory of Mass each day, we pled for the Blood of the Lamb to be poured out over those brought to us for prayer, spiritually laying their souls upon the altar of salvation while enrolling them in Masses. "The Mass is the most perfect form of prayer!" (Pope Paul VI).[3]

Unaware of the reason why so many people were approaching us for prayer or why Rob was receiving vision after vision of people we needed to pray for, it was on four consecutive evenings spent in Eucharistic adoration that the answer would be revealed. On the first night as we prayed in the Chapel of Divine Mercy, Rob was told interiorly that he was to pray for the young woman kneeling two seats ahead of us, grieving her dad's impending death. Never having seen her before, he did as God had asked of him. Before leaving the chapel, he looked in the prayer request book to find that she'd requested prayer for her father, who was dying of cancer. In the car, Rob told me what had happened and together, we prayed a rosary for her on our way home.

On the following evening while in Eucharistic adoration, Rob was given the knowledge that he needed to pray a rosary for the young couple who was sitting ahead of us. They were praying for a child. Again doing as the Lord had requested, when he finished the rosary and was about to resume his private prayer, he was instructed to pray another rosary for them. Doing once again as the Lord had asked, upon leaving the chapel he saw their written request, asking for the successful adoption of a baby. Just as on the previous evening, we prayed a rosary for the couple on our way home.

On the third evening as we prayed in front of the Blessed Sacrament, Rob sensed that he was going to receive interior knowledge involving praying for the specific needs of someone who was in the chapel with us. But in thinking he already had more than enough to pray for, he decided instead to hold his hands up to his ears, figuratively speaking, so as not to hear the Lord's request. The instant we left the chapel, a great heaviness came over him as he told me of the great remorse he felt for having closed his heart to God. Visibly shaken, I offered support in telling him to simply ask God to forgive his lack of obedience. "We'll pray a rosary on the way home for the stifled message regarding the person who was in the chapel with us," I encouraged. During our night prayers, we prayed from our heart for the grace of obedience to God's Will.

The next night as we adored Jesus in the Blessed Sacrament, Rob was eager to pray for anyone the Lord would lay upon his heart. Settling into prayer, he was given an interior message to pray a rosary for a woman in the chapel who was suffering terribly from the pain of loneliness. Upon leaving the Chapel of Divine Mercy, we were filled with the exuberant joy of having been given another chance to do as God was asking of us. On the drive home, we prayed a rosary for the woman. "Holiness consists simply in doing God's will, and in being just what God wants us to be" (St. Therese).[4] In all the times we frequented the chapel, we'd never before encountered any of the four people for whom we were instructed to pray.

The pieces of the puzzle started coming together just days later when another book was randomly given to us on intercessory prayer. Reading the very first page, the Lord revealed to Rob that we were to host an intercessory prayer group. Prayer had become such an integral part of our lives that, without it, we'd never again find the peace it attained. "Our hearts are restless, O God, until they rest in You" (St. Augustine).[5] Though starting a prayer group had never crossed our mind, our deepest desire was to be obedient to what God was asking of us. Saying our night prayers that evening, we humbly accepted the Lord's summons. Inviting Mary to be the leader, we asked her to intercede in bringing us the petitions in the presence of her Son. We then asked the Holy Spirit to send out invitations by enlightening those called to be intercessors. Soon, the hearts of those chosen began to stir as we prepared ourselves to put on the armor of God. Using the sword of the Spirit, we set out to declare victory over the needs of God's people through praying His holy word. It was on February 2, 2005, on the feast of The Presentation of Our Lord, that the Intercessors of Light[6] first met in our home to present the needs of others to our Lord. Even the name had been inspired, hearing very clearly the words spoken within my heart. Fitting in perfectly with Candlemas Day in the lighting of the candles, which is also celebrated on the same day, we light blessed candles before every prayer gathering as a spark of hope and glowing ray of God's love. "I am the light of the world" (John 8:12). Petitioning Jesus to bring about holistic healings in the areas of mind, body, and spirit, we pray especially for the purification of souls in that they would inherit the kingdom.

Reciting the Chaplet of Divine Mercy, reading Scripture verses covering a variety of needs, and praying the rosary together, we not only petition for individual requests, but we fast and pray for world needs, an end to abortion, and for more priests. After making our requests known to God, we give praise and thanksgiving for answered prayer, trusting that through Mary's intercession, God is hearing our prayers. Numerous prayer requests began coming in, through e-mails, phone calls, and from people at church. Most remarkable were those received from complete strangers who approached us for prayer. Starting out small at first, the prayer ministry grew, sometimes receiving upward of three hundred prayer requests in a single week.

Following Rob's dramatic conversion, we had accepted God's call into the ministry of prayer. As prayer warriors of Christ, our goal was not only to lift up the physical and emotional needs of others, but even more importantly, to become beacons of light to the spiritual needs of those still living in the darkness of sin, who amble about in the ways of the world. How much more powerful our prayers would become through Mary's intercession and in seeking to unite them together as Intercessors of Light.

One evening, as Rob and I were exiting the Chapel of Divine Mercy, a man we'd never seen before got up and followed us outside. Starting out by making small talk, he then asked if we would pray for him. Telling us he lived about seventy miles away, he learned of the adoration chapel while in town visiting relatives. Going before the Blessed Sacrament to pray for something that troubled his heart, he relayed that as soon as we knelt down to pray, he sensed that he was to ask us for prayer.

Another such incident occurred after attending the evening Mass at Sacred Heart Church. About to drive across town to the adoration chapel, a Filipina approached and asked for prayer. A stranger to us, I found it interesting that she'd cross over to the opposite side from where she was sitting to solicit prayer.

"Did you know of our intercessory prayer group?"

"No," she replied.

Affirmed in the belief that nothing happens by coincidence, I was in awe of God's mighty providence. My heart filled with wonderment in the day-to-day witness of the magnificent ways in which He was bringing to us the needs of His people. "Whereas we shall devote ourselves to prayer and to the ministry of the word" (Acts 6:4).

Requests for prayer were coming in from distraught parents whose children had fallen away from the faith. Though for any parent to experience the unimaginable pain of the death of a child would be unbearable, how much worse to be separated from a child eternally through their spiritual demise? For this reason it's vitally important for our children to be "prayed" back into the fold. "Believe in the Lord Jesus and you and your household will be saved" (Acts 16:31).

More and more I was seeing how trials of any kind are so often the means that cause people to search inwardly, serving to bring them straight into the Heart of Christ. There within Jesus' merciful Heart they discover the safe haven to help them persevere through life's struggles. One weekend, three separate women called our home for prayer. All three of them, it turned out, were awaiting upcoming surgery, and all of them were experiencing fear and anxiety concerning it. What I found most interesting was that after being reminded of the opportunity they had to unite their suffering with those of Jesus' and of the meritorious value it would bring, their frame of mind changed and their inner peace was restored.

I received a call after returning home from Mass one afternoon. On the other end of the line was a God-fearing man who Rob and I had met through a mutual friend several months prior. Having suffered for many years from a physical ailment, Don asked if we'd be willing to pray over him. Prior to meeting up with him in an adjoining town from where we both lived, we first stopped off to pray before Jesus in the Chapel of Divine Mercy. Interiorly, Rob received a message that the Lord was well pleased with this man who'd borne his suffering with Him for so long. After praying with Don, he asked, "Would it be okay if I came to your intercessory prayer meeting next week?"

"Sure," we responded. "If you feel it in your heart to come then that's the Spirit's invitation for you to come!"

Living a distance away, it had been several months since we'd last heard from him. Calling our home, he relayed to me that he had gone to Eucharistic adoration before work that same morning. "The Lord put it on my heart to call you and Rob for prayer," he said. A soft-spoken man, as he continued to talk, I had a sense that he was despairing over his situation more than he was letting on. Blessing myself with holy water, I petitioned the Holy Spirit to guide my words.

After reassuring Don that he'd receive the grace to persevere in hope, I gently reminded him that those who suffer willingly in imitation to the sufferings of Christ venerate His Heart the most. Remembering the words spoken to Rob in the chapel, I said, "God is very pleased with you. Your faithfulness to Him in spite of your long suffering is gaining you treasures in heaven, as well as effectively doing greater things than we can possibly imagine." Confessing to me that he was at the point of wishing sometimes that he'd go to bed and never wake up, I said, "Don, Jesus loves you so much! He's walking right alongside you in your suffering and will never fail to help you carry the burden of your cross."

On the other end of the phone, there was a moment of silence. Breathing out a sigh of relief, he said, "I am so glad you told me that." After another brief pause, he added, "This morning, when I was praying before the Blessed Sacrament, I told Jesus that I felt…" He stopped again. "I felt that perhaps He didn't love me anymore."

Arranging for Rob and me to meet up with him for prayer, he then shared a vision shown to him the night he attended Intercessors of Light. He saw what looked to be the throne of God with ladders extending down on four sides, with angels traveling up and down, bringing the prayers to heaven. Meeting up with him after Mass a few days later, we prayed for Don to receive God's healing, petitioning also for the grace necessary for him to surrender his suffering in conformity to God's Will. "As a result, those who suffer in accord with God's will hand their souls over to a faithful creator as they do good" (1 Peter 4:19).

We had come to love Katy as a cherished friend. Her passion and zeal for God was contagious, as the fruit of her suffering spilled off to those around her. One morning, Debbie and I met Joyce up at the hospital to visit and pray with Katy during one of her platelet transfusions. As we were talking, a certain Scripture verse kept coming to my mind. Learning that, along with Katy's blood cancer she'd also been seriously injured in a water sport accident, I finally listened to the prompting as I opened my Bible and read. "There was a woman afflicted with hemorrhages for twelve years. She had suffered greatly at the hands of many doctors and had spent all that she had. Yet she was not helped but only grew worse" (Mark 5:25–28).

"What verse is that?" she asked inquisitively. "I can't believe how it fits in perfectly with what's been going on with me!" Noting the passage, it soon became one of her favorites.

Though we'd been fasting on bread and water since the Medjugorje Conference on Wednesdays and Fridays, Rob sensed in his prayer time that the Lord was calling him to a much stricter fast. Added to his two-day fast, he ate only one full meal a day on Mondays, Tuesdays and Thursdays. I, on the other hand, needed to change the way in which I fasted. With the multiple cysts on my kidneys growing larger, they crowded my stomach to the point where I was only able to eat small amounts of food at a time. Our Lady said everyone except the sick must fast, and I knew that accepting I could not fast in the way I desired was a fast of sorts in itself. How soon I discovered creative ways in which even the sick can do various forms of self-mortification while still maintaining healthy food intake.

After Saturday morning Mass at St. John's, we went up to kneel before Jesus in the Tabernacle. While steeped in prayer,

Rob received a revelation that he was to add Saturdays onto the days he restricted himself to one meal. He was then given the knowledge that he was to offer this extra day of fasting for Katy, hearing within his soul; "She is dying." Ever since Rob's initial vision of Katy's daughter with a tear running down her cheek and hearing interiorly, "Her tears will be wiped dry through the intercession of Mary," we prayed with an expectant faith in believing that Katy would be healed. With the news she was dying, tears flowed down from my face as I committed to doing my usual weekday mortifications for our dear friend on Saturdays as well.

In Eucharistic adoration at the Chapel of Divine Mercy that same evening, Rob received a vision that had to do with Katy. In the scene shown to him, he saw a creek with water flowing through it, but lying across the stream was a fallen tree that was preventing the water from flowing through as freely as it should. He received the infused knowledge that the water represented "Jesus" and the fallen tree, "unforgiveness." "But whoever drinks the water I shall give will never thirst; the water I shall give will become in him a spring of water welling up to eternal life" (John 4:14).

Telling me of this, my mind traveled back a time we met up with Katy at Our Lady of Good Help. Handing me a print of Jesus suspended above a large waterfall with His arms open wide, she exclaimed, "Isn't this beautiful!"

"Yes," I agreed.

Handing it to me, she said, "It's for you!" Feeling unworthy to receive it, she insisted, saying, "Please, I want you to have it."

Most often, the wisdom Rob received involving the people we prayed for was to aid in praying specifically for individual needs. But in voicing to me the vision pertaining to Katy was meant to be shared, my heart sank. "Holy Spirit, guide my words," I prayed from my heart. Sharing with her on the phone of the time when I asked the Spirit to reveal any sins I may have suppressed,

I told her of the illumination of conscience I had involving a past hurt that I unknowingly had not forgiven. Telling her of the immense love I'd felt that caused me to praise God while it was still being shown, she interjected, "That's amazing!" Taking the opportunity to gently share with her the image shown to Rob, she paused briefly before saying; "I think I know what it is. I'll go to confession in Green Bay tomorrow." Before hanging up, she said, "I love you guys."

In the time we'd known Katy, she went to confession every time she had the chance. The next night, she called to tell us of the relief she had in talking at great length to a priest concerning something buried in her subconscious. Elated, she said, "This has helped me so much! I can't thank you enough! Please tell Rob how grateful I am for his willingness to be God's vessel." Receiving the purification of her Baptismal waters through the Sacrament of Reconciliation, how greatly it benefited her to have the Living Water of Christ flowing freely within her soul.

Returning home from Eucharistic adoration one evening, Katy called, asking that we pray for a man in his forties who, after suffering from alcoholism for a number of years, was dying from advanced throat cancer. While we were praying for James in front of the Blessed Sacrament the following evening, Rob received an interior message, requesting that we go and pray for him. Given the knowledge that he was to concede that Jesus died for his sins, we immediately made arrangements to travel the thirty miles from our home to do as the Lord instructed.

From that time on, Katy was devoted to praying with James. Sitting at his bedside after receiving her own cancer treatment, she would pray out loud the Divine Mercy Chaplet. In spite of the comatose state he soon fell into, she'd read to him God's promise… "For, if you confess with your mouth that Jesus is Lord and believe in your heart that God raised him from the dead, you will be saved" (Romans 10:9). A short time later, James passed away. How humbling it was for us to have had the privilege of praying for this beloved soul who Jesus gathered back into His flock before calling him home.

It was February 28, and right after Mass we planned to meet Katy at the Shrine for prayer. Before leaving, however, we learned that she was back in the hospital with ominously low platelet levels. With each blood transfusion she received to replenish them, it became less effective in increasing the platelets and the duration of time it would last was decreasing as well. With this unexpected turn of events, our prayer venue quickly changed as we headed up to the hospital to meet Debbie and Joyce. On the drive there, I thought of what the Lord had recently shown to Rob in contemplative prayer. He saw a vision of her platelets, as though he was looking at them through a microscope. "Her platelets were so few that I could literally count them," he had told me. From that day on, Katy's deteriorating health status was on a downhill, slippery slope. After praying with her and saying a rosary together with those in the room, we made plans to visit Francis again. It was Lent, and it had been back on Good Friday in 1993 that he first received the stigmatic wounds of Christ.[7]

Dismayed in learning Katy had been admitted back into the hospital the day before our visit with Francis, Debbie came up with an alternative plan. We'd go to early Mass and stop at the hospital to visit with Katy before traveling to Escanaba.

"I'll sit in proxy for her when we're prayed with individually," she added.

Feeling melancholy as we entered Katy's room, I stood back as the others greeted and hugged her.

Patting her hand on the bed, Katy said, "Sue, come and sit next to me. I have to tell you something!" Doing as she asked, she then said, "This morning, as I was meditating on the Scripture you shared with me about the woman with the blood issues, my pastor called and read me the same passage on speaker phone! And as he was reading it, I could feel Jesus' love flowing out from the words!" Wrapping her arm around my shoulders to draw me close, she whispered, "I had a talk with Jesus this morning and told Him that if one of us were to be called home, it should be me, so that you and Rob can continue in your healing ministry."

Massaging my enlarged kidneys in my lower back and asking Jesus to heal them, I remained silent.

Breaking the silence, Katy asked. "Can you do me a favor?"

"Sure," I replied.

"When you see Francis today, will you kiss the wound on his hand for me?"

Realizing I'd agreed too soon, it was definitely something not in my character to do. On previous visits, I'd noticed the wounds on the top of his hands were bandaged. Seeing the bandage on top of Katy's hand, I said, "For you I will do it."

Joyce was motioning that we were next in line to receive prayer from Francis. When it was my turn, I got down on my knees as I had seen Katy do. Telling him what she had asked, he simply said, "Yes. I'm sorry to hear she's in the hospital." Simultaneously, as I lowered my head to kiss the bandage on his hand, Francis turned it palmside up, exposing the uncovered wound of Christ. In proxy for my dear friend, I was honored to kiss the stigmata on the holy hand of Jesus' suffering servant.

Returning home just minutes before Rob came in from work, I could barely get out the words Katy whispered to me at her bedside. "My heart feels compelled to go back up to see her again tonight with you," I told him. In agreement, what neither of us knew was that the visit with her would be our last.

Friends and relatives who came to see Katy were witness to see *her* reaching out in holy joy to those around her. "Sue and Rob," she said jubilantly, "I want to show you a little chapel where we can pray." Congregating to pray a rosary in the tiny chapel with a few close relatives, Katy was truly in her element. Walking back to her room, I told her that I'd kissed the burgundy-colored stigmata on the palm of Francis's hand on her behalf. Thrilled, she said, "Thank you! How awesome for you to kiss the wound of Christ for me!"

Taking hold of my arm, Katy led Rob and me over to a young woman with an infant in her arms. "Do you remember praying over my friend on the Medjugorje bus trip last May? She sat in for her daughter-in-law who was pregnant after having two previous miscarriages?"

"Yes," we both nodded. "The word of knowledge was that her grandchild would be born healthy," I added.

Beaming from ear to ear, she announced, "Meet Baby Connor!"

Tears filled my eyes as I held the precious little gift of God's creation, and how His holy arrangements unfolded for us to see the fruition of His spoken word back on Pentecost Sunday. "So shall my word be/ that goes forth from my mouth;/ It shall not return to me void,/ but shall do my will,/ achieving the end for which I sent it" (Isaiah 55:11).

Radiating out from Katy was an ecstasy of sort, which can only be explained in having completely abandoned her will over to the Will of God. In her complete surrender, she'd already begun to live Heaven while she was still yet here on this earth. The bittersweet side of Katy's last hospital stay was that at the very same time her life was coming to an end, her daughter was giving birth to her first grandchild in the same hospital. What allowed us to have a better understanding of the irony of the situation was in learning of her daughter's deep desire to conceive and give birth to a child before her mother's passing. A precious baby girl named after her grandmother, the first interior locution ever shown to Rob was coming to fulfillment. Through Mary's intercession, her daughter's tears would be wiped dry in the birth of Katy's first grandchild. "For the Lamb who is in the center of the throne will shepherd them/ and lead them to springs of life-giving water,/ and God will wipe away every tear from their eyes" (Revelation 7:17).

Holding a deep and binding love for the Blessed Mother, Katy had gone on pilgrimage to Medjugorje after being diagnosed with multiple myeloma. She understood that in turning her joys and her sorrows over to Mary, she'd bear fruit in her suffering. It was Mary who had planted in Katy's soul the desire to live within the Will of God above her own wants. Expressing her desire to carry the cross of her suffering with Jesus during Holy Week, never did I witness such complete abandonment of self as in Katy that night.

Tiptoeing quietly into our bedroom, Jenelle whispered, "Mom, are you awake?"

Turning over, I asked, "What is it?"

Telling me of what had transpired in her prayer time, she voiced that she had a sense we were to pray for Katy in the Chapel of Divine Mercy.

"Right now?" I questioned.

"Yes, I think so."

One thing I knew for sure was that Jenelle would not awaken us if she didn't feel it imperative to do so. Getting out of bed, we arrived at the chapel just before midnight. Kneeling before Jesus, to my left was the first class relic of St. Faustina. For Katy, I prayed the Chaplet of Divine Mercy.

Brought into contemplative prayer, Rob was shown a vision of a woman up on a balcony, shaking her rugs out over the rail. The interior locution was followed by a scene of a holy place where we would be. Seeing the inside, he sensed it was a church. There were high white walls and a large arched window on top. Through the window, he saw the image of a woman wearing a white, translucent gown, standing suspended in the air.

The next morning, I received a call from Debbie. A prayer marathon was being organized to cover Katy in continuous prayer until she could receive another platelet transfusion. Around the clock, a rosary would be prayed for her from 3:00 p.m. on Friday until 3:00 p.m. on the Monday of Holy Week.

It just so happened that the weekend of the rosary marathon was on the same weekend as our son's wedding, on the feast of St. Joseph. Unaware that I'd been praying fervently for the saint's intercession to aide Eric in finding a good wife ever since our trip to the St. Joseph Oratory, I was pleased when he met Kelly, later choosing March 19, the feast of St. Joseph, as the day they would come before God in the Sacrament of Marriage. It was upon learning this that I first shared with my son of my ongoing prayer to St. Joseph for him.

Katy was brought in our life for prayer. In spite of the doings surrounding the wedding celebration involving the same three days as the rosary marathon, the three of us pledged to pray a rosary for her during 2:00 a.m. to 4:00 a.m. on all three nights. But by the time Sunday evening rolled around, I found myself in a state of complete exhaustion. With the rollercoaster of emotional highs in the festivities of the wedding and the lows of praying for our friend who lay dying, in combination with my iron-poor blood, I questioned if I had the stamina to get up at 3:00 a.m. for my committed hour of prayer. Purposefully choosing the 3:00 a.m. hour to precede my rosary by first praying a Chaplet of Divine Mercy, I petitioned in our night prayers for God's strength to get me through. Getting back into bed, I was asleep before my head hit the pillow. Awaking to the 3:00 a.m. alarm, I slid out from under the warm covers to get down on my knees. Feeling somewhat refreshed, hearing me stir, Rob got out of bed to kneel beside me to pray for Katy. It was on the following morning that we received the news of her passing, and how happy we were to have taken part in her beautiful send-off!

Locating the church to attend the funeral Mass, we were overcome with emotion upon entering it for the first time. There were the vivid white walls with a large window off to the right of the altar, shaped precisely as shown to Rob in the prophetic vision of days prior. In connection to the lady seen shaking out her rugs over the balcony, it was in her suffering with Jesus that Katy was provided the opportunity to be washed pure and clean. How beautiful it was to envision her in the flowing gown, spiritually present with family and friends in the celebration of the Mass and of her birth into eternal life.

It had been less than two weeks since Katy's passing, and within my soul I felt an unrelenting sorrow. Hearing the heartrending news that Pope John Paul II was teetering on the brink of life and death, I immediately began praying a novena to St. Therese for him. A true shepherd who set for his flock an exemplary example of what it means to be a suffering servant for Jesus; the nations bore witness to the commendable way he carried his cross. Born to eternal life on the eve of Divine Mercy Sunday,[8] I couldn't help but think of how he had articulated publicly the launch of Divine Mercy Sunday to be the happiest day of his long reigning pontificate.

> No soul will be justified until it turns with confidence to My mercy, and this is why the first Sunday after Easter is to be the Feast of Mercy."
>
> —*Diary*, 570[9]
>
> On that day the very depths of My tender mercy are open. I pour out a whole ocean of graces upon those souls who approach the Fount of My mercy. The soul that will go to Confession and receive the Holy Communion shall obtain complete forgiveness of sins and punishment."
>
> —*Diary*, 699[10]

In spite of our beloved pope's passing, I continued praying the novena for him. On the ninth day, I knelt down before the crucifix in our bedroom upon waking to pray the final prayers, when spontaneously, I prayed, "St. Therese, if John Paul II is already in heaven, please send his 'message of love' to whoever needs it the most."

After the 6:30 p.m. Mass at Sacred Heart Church that same evening, Rob and I headed across town to spend time in Eucharistic adoration. Later on at home, after praying our nightly novena to the Sacred Heart of Jesus, Rob told me he received a word of knowledge for me.

"Really?" I questioned. "What was it?"

"You're going to be getting a message from St. Therese," he stated matter-of-factly.

"When?" I asked.

"That I don't know," he replied.

During the night I was awakened. Interiorly, I was shown a vision of the Sacred Heart. Appearing as a human heart, it grew larger as it came closer, as though I was viewing it from a zoom lens. Then, I saw a separate image of a full-bodied statue of the Sacred Heart of Jesus with His arms extended outward toward me, feeling His love permeate my heart.

Still basking in the love that lingered within my soul, I was reminded of the word of knowledge Rob had received during our night prayers. Wondering, at first, how what was shown to me was connected to St. Therese, I suddenly remembered the spontaneous request I had made of her while praying my novena prayer for John Paul II, asking her to send the consolation intended for him to whoever needed it the most—if he was already in heaven. How blessed I was to have her choose me as the beneficiary of the late pope's "message of love." Seeing the Heart of Christ pounding with love and His loving arms reaching out to me, it was God Himself who gave me comfort in Katy's passing. "I, it is I who comfort you" (Isaiah 51:12).

O sweet Mother! Font of love,
Touch my spirit from above,
   Make my heart with yours accord.

                                     —Stabat Mater

When it is all over you will not regret having suffered; rather you will regret having suffered so little, and suffered that little so badly.

                                —Saint Sebastian Valfre[11]

Stations of the Cross

Ninth Station
Jesus Falls the Third Time

At times our Lord makes you feel the burden of the Cross. This burden seems intolerable to you. But as for you, carry it because the Lord extends His hand and gives you strength.

—Padre Pio

The Apostles Blue

Enjoying our morning coffee together one Sunday, our son phoned to ask Rob if he'd like to ride along to look at a woods he was going to log. Asking me what I thought, I encouraged him that it sounded like a nice father-son outing. A three-hour round trip, he quickly decided to attend the early morning Mass before heading out, while I'd still go to the 6:00 p.m. Mass to bring Communion to my mother. Kissing me good-bye, he said, "We should be getting home right around the same time, and then we'll have a late dinner together."

Visiting with my mom for a while after Mass, I suddenly felt drawn to return to the Chapel of Divine Mercy. But it was already getting late, and having prepared one of Rob's favorite dinners as a little surprise, I was anxious to get home at the time of his estimated return. In spite of that, the sudden pull I felt to visit Jesus in the Blessed Sacrament won out.

What a gorgeous evening it was as I drove from the chapel toward home on a street lined with trees. With the rays of sun poking out through the leaves, I was steeped in God's beauty revealed through nature. Within my soul, I received the infused knowledge that my devotion to Mary would grow even deeper, and within my heart, I heard, "Medjugorje." My mind took me back to the special closeness I felt to Our Lady of Fatima since childhood, thinking of the answer I received to my very first novena. I considered the rosary from Medjugorje given to me through God's holy designs, and of the burning within my hands when I first prayed on it. I pondered the Medjugorje Conference at Notre Dame in fulfillment of the prophecy given to Rob on

Pentecost Sunday. I thought of my love for Mary, of the times I called out for the help of my Heavenly Mother, and of how she never failed to come to my aid.

Returning home within minutes of each other, I was surprised to find that Rob had also been detained in getting back home.

"Hi, hon," he said as he walked across the driveway to embrace in a hug. "Were you praying for me?"

"Well, yes," I said, telling him of my sudden inspiration to stop off at the adoration chapel when I had every intention of going straight home. "Why do you ask?"

"Because," he said, "as I was praying the rosary on my way home, I could sense that someone was praying for me, and I figured it was you. But what happened next is hard to put into words."

"What?" I asked.

"I felt as though I had an open line of communication with God. Interiorly, He was talking to me and I was talking to Him. I was told that you and I are going to be going on a trip."

"Really?" I asked curiously. "Where are we going?"

"I didn't know right away," he answered. "But as the conversation went on, I gained the courage to come right out and ask what kind of a trip we were going on."

"Did He tell you?"

"Yes," he replied. "Mary has called us to come to Medjugorje."

I could hardly believe my ears! Telling him of my own spiritual experience of hearing the word "Medjugorje" spoken within my heart on the way home from Eucharistic adoration, I exclaimed, "I didn't realize we'd actually be going on pilgrimage to Medjugorje! When will we go?"

"This fall," he answered without hesitation. That's when it hit me. Miles apart from each other, we had both received Mary's invitation to come to Medjugorje at the same time!

Stopping by to pick up the food I had prepared for Farther Carr's Place-2-B a few days later, Debbie said; "Sue, I brought along this case of VHS tapes on Medjugorje that you and Rob might be interested in watching."

"Oh my goodness!" I said, telling her of our planned pilgrimage there. "We'd love to watch them!"

How incredible, I thought, that within days after being called to Medjugorje, we'd have in our possession an entire case of videos to learn more of the spiritual happenings there! Viewing over forty videos on Medjugorje, how greatly it increased our desire to travel to the little village where Mary was still appearing!

More than thirty million people have visited Medjugorje. The visionary Mirjana Dragicevic-Soldo had daily apparitions from June 24, 1981, to December 25, 1982. During the last daily apparition, Our Lady gave her the tenth secret, telling her that she would appear to her once a year, on March 18 with a message for the world. It's been this way through the years.[1] Since the Vatican's formal investigation of the reported apparitions of the Blessed Virgin Mary in Medjugorje, it's hoped to receive the Church's stamp of approval. Encouraging many bishops to visit there, Pope John Paul II said to Bishop Paolo Hnilica, "Medjugorje is the fulfillment and continuation of Fatima."[2] In a private conversation with the visionary Mirjana Soldo, the pope said, "If I were not Pope I would already be in Medjugorje confessing."[3]

Shortly after receiving our summons to Medjugorje, Rob and I were invited to attend the ordination of Joyce's son into the priesthood. What a powerful witness he has given in testimony of his amazing call to the priesthood after submitting to his mother's request to accompany her on one of the pilgrimages she led to Medjugorje. Having grown close to Joyce since the Medjugorje Conference and in our mutual connection to Katy, we could hardly wait to tell her of our plans to sign on for her fall pilgrimage, which included a side trip to Rome.

With my kidney function hovering right around the 12 percent mark, it occurred to me that my nephrologist may not be all too keen about me making the physically demanding journey to Medjugorje. And so before my monthly appointment, we decided to lay my concern before Jesus in the Blessed Sacrament. Submitting myself into the Will of God, I was confident that if it was His Will for us to go on pilgrimage there, then the path would be cleared for it to happen. While in prayer, Rob received a word of knowledge to pray for the intercession of St. Joseph in asking God to impart His divine wisdom to my doctor. From that day on, we implored always the aid of the foster-father of Jesus to impart divine guidance involving our health care professionals.

Telling my doctor of my aspiration to go to Medjugorje in late October, which was still several months off, how pleasantly surprised I was with his immediate approval for me to go! "Looking at you," he said quite frankly, "and looking at your chart, I'd almost have to say the chart is lying!"

Stopping back at the adoration chapel to give thanksgiving, on the walls on either side of the Monstrance is an illuminated stained glass of Mary and St. Joseph. Within my soul, I could feel the presence of the Holy Family.

Inspired to make another banner quilt in honor of her favorite saint, St. Therese of Lisieux, Jenelle selected striking colors to sew together the numerous squares that formed the diagonal cross within the quilt's center, depicting the crucifix portrayed in the arms of the "Little Flower" in a popular image of her. Within the center of the cross, she applied hand-made flowers as shown in the picture of St. Therese. The same as with the "Cross Quilt," she felt interiorly that this, too, was intended to hang "someplace holy." This later came to pass when she was moved to donate them to hang in the Schoenstatt Wayside Shrine, Refuge of Sinners,[4] where the Holy Sacrifice of the Mass is celebrated on Monday mornings and on the first Saturday of every month.

St. Therese the "Little Flower" banner quilt, *Quilting Cause*

St. Therese of Lisieux banner quilt, *Quilting Cause*

    In shared enthusiasm for our upcoming pilgrimage to Europe, Jenelle picked up her quilting tablet to design two banner quilts to send along. The first was for the visionary, Mirjana, for putting up our group in her home. Made in coordinating patterns in hues of cream and plum, she sewed onto the finished banner a handmade appliqué of St. James Church in Medjugorje. Creating the appliqué of Our Lady with her arms extended outward calling her children to conversion, she meticulously completed the banner by hand, sewing it between the two towers of the church in the small village that was bringing the world to their knees. The second quilt was intended for us to bring to the Vatican in honor of the late Pope John Paul II's proclamation of the "Year of the Eucharist"[5] that was concluding that same October. Sewn in elegant custom material remnants provided her "quilting cause" by an interior designer, the hand-sewn appliqués she made of the papal mitre,[6] the golden chalice with the Eucharist positioned directly above, and of the papal cross were exquisitely stunning.

I came to discover that the muscle spasms resulting from end-stage renal failure were cramps like none other. There was no "walking them out," as I rarely made it past the side of the bed before becoming completely incapacitated in the agonizing pain of multiple cramps ravaging my feet and legs all at once. In the days following these horrendous bouts of cramps, my muscles would be so weak that I could barely pick up my feet to walk. Lasting on an average of six to seven excruciating minutes, they were brought on from exercise exertion. But now the dreadful cramps had escalated to the point that I was unable to walk even a half a block without waking up at night with contorted muscles wreaking havoc on my legs.

After overdoing it on my legs one day, I awoke in the middle of the night with brutal leg cramps. With seven spasms simultaneously forming from my feet to my thighs, it felt as though as many king cobras were biting down on my muscles with enormous ferocity. Right away, I asked Mary to bring my suffering to Jesus, because as the pain intensified, it was with a beggar's heart that I pleaded for them to stop.

Though he never let on, I knew it was a great sacrifice for Rob to assist me sometimes two and three times a night to hold ice on my legs. Quickly retrieving several ice packs from the freezer, he alternated them on the various areas of cramping. Beside myself and reeling from pain, I felt I could lose my composure at any moment. Breaking out into a cold sweat and unaware that my nightgown was soaked, I began to shiver unstoppably. Weak from exhaustion, as the spasms subsided new ones took their place.

I smile when I think back on one night in particular, when for the third time I'd awakened with horrendous leg cramps. Not wanting Rob to wake up, I tried to get to the kitchen for ice before they worsened. Stopping well short of my destination, my feet contorted into balls of unrelenting spasms. Unable to go on, I called out to Rob, who came quickly to my aid. Kneeling down at a chair on the hard ceramic tile with ice packs in each hand, he was still six feet away. Not knowing how I'd be able to maneuver myself to where he was, I noticed he was sound asleep. My heart overflowed in love of his constant self-giving. With every ounce of strength I could muster up, I put mind over matter to unite step by agonizing step with those of Jesus'. Making my way to the chair, I kissed the top of his sweet head as he awakened.

The spiraling effect of needing to back off of physical activity in order to prevent cramping was that the less I did physically, the smaller the amount of exertion it would take to bring on the horrible cramps. My heart felt heavy, wondering how my legs would possibly endure the physically challenging trip to Medjugorje. Reading a book on the memoirs of St. John Bosco,[7] I began to pray to Mary under the title he had constantly invoked her intercession, "Mary, Help of Christians." Soon after my plea for Our Lady's help, Jenelle, who held a degree in health science, came up with a plan that would help strengthen my legs for the upcoming trip. Starting me out with a mere five minutes a day, it wasn't long before I was able to increase my exercise endurance level. But neglecting to do the stretching exercises, or if I did too much, always spelled out trouble for the following night. Along with experiencing the leg cramps associated with end-stage renal failure, the level of iron in my blood was also becoming depleted. This caused me to feel very cold, and more easily fatigued.

To replenish my iron, my nephrologist arranged for me to receive iron intravenously at the local hospital once a week for a regimen of six weeks. With each four-hour IV session, Rob planned to use a half day of vacation to go along.

"That's not necessary!" I assured him. "I'll use the time to pray and read."

Driving home from my first treatment, my extremities started to feel strange, and my hands and feet began swelling up like a balloon. Seeing me drive in, Rob and Jenelle came to greet me. The soles of my feet were so swollen that they became rounded, making my trek from the car to the house extremely painful. Already unable to remove my rings, we were instructed to go back to the hospital for evaluation. Though it was the first and the last IV treatment for me, it was not the last of the little crosses I was allowed to suffer, crosses that I could offer back to Jesus.

Frequenting the Chapel of Divine Mercy, Rob began receiving numerous visions for me. "The Lord showed me a beautiful pink chrysanthemum for you," he said upon leaving the chapel one evening.

"Really?" I asked eagerly. "Were there missing petals or any that were torn or wilted?"

"No, why do you ask?"

"Well, it's strange that you'd be shown a flower for me." Getting choked up, I paused. "Just this afternoon I was reading *The Life of the Blessed Virgin Mary*,[8] and it compared the degree of holiness to the petals of a flower. As soon as I read it, I longed to be a beautiful flower for Jesus." Humbled at the vision shown him, I thought of how, just as a flower opens each day to soak in the dew and morning sun, for me to be a beautiful flower for Jesus, the "Sun of righteousness," meant fully opening my heart to soak up the droplets of grace necessary to walk with Him along the path to holiness.

Another evening after spending a holy hour with Jesus, Rob told me that he'd been shown a very special vision of me. "What was it?" I asked.

"I saw you as a child of seven, and you were being fitted in a shimmering gold dress. It was lovely, coming just below your knees. The finishing touches were being made on it, as the hem was being pinned up to be hand sewn and completed."

"What does it mean?" I asked.

"I don't know exactly, but interiorly, I knew that it was something especially good."

"Do you think it means I'm going to die soon?"

"No, why would you ask that?"

"Well, keep in mind that my kidneys are failing, and what other reason would I be fitted for a gold dress other than for heaven? Wouldn't the 'final alterations' signify it will be soon?" I asked.

"Hon," Rob said softly, "I know that's not the case. Besides, you know that we can never figure these things out on our own without first seeking God's wisdom. We'll pray for discernment on what it means."

A week and a half later while we were having our Sunday morning coffee, I said to Rob, "I've been praying persistently in regard to the meaning behind the 'the gold dress vision' and I really want to know what God is trying to convey to me."

"Keep asking," he responded. "You'll find out sooner or later."

Saying our morning rosary, it was with all of my heart that I prayed for the answer.

Planning to attend the night Mass at St. Pius X, I was looking forward to spending some time reading *Her Name Means Rose*,[9] which I could hardly put down. A suffering soul for Jesus, the

Rhoda Wise story told also of the healing Mother Angelica received through Rhoda's intercessory prayers, marking her lifelong commitment to God. Foundress of EWTN, the story of her miraculous healing from a painful stomach condition is also recounted in *Mother Angelica* by Raymond Arroyo.[10]

Picking up my book, the words that Jesus spoke to Rhoda Wise penetrated my heart as though He was speaking them directly to me, disclosing to me the meaning behind the vision of me as a young child in the glistening gold dress.

> So many ask you why you are chosen. You are chosen because you had the faith of a little child and believed everything that was told to you. Some think they believe, some want to believe, you <u>did</u> believe and for your faith, suffering, patience, and courage to carry on when all were against you, I have chosen you for a great work.[11]

The Lord was calling me to a childlike faith! He was showing me the progress I was making in striving to surrender myself fully into the care of my Heavenly Father! "Let the children come to me; do not prevent them, for the kingdom of God belongs to such as these" (Mark 10:14).

Before the start of the Mass that evening, Rob received the interior knowledge that the Lord wished to convey a message to him through the Gospel reading. Standing to hear the word of God read, Jesus' words to His Father in speaking of those with a child-like faith penetrated his heart the same as they had pierced mine earlier that afternoon.

> "At that time Jesus said in reply, 'I give praise to you, Father, Lord of heaven and earth, for although you have hidden these things from the wise and learned you have revealed them to the childlike. Yes, Father, such has been your gracious will. All things have been handed over to me by my Father. No one knows the Son except the Father,

and no one knows the Father except the Son and anyone to whom the Son wishes to reveal him.'"
—Matthew 11:25–27

After Mass, we went into the Chapel of Divine Mercy. While in contemplative prayer, Rob was shown an old-time building with sentries patrolling the area. He saw saints of long ago past, who were being brought out to be martyred. Amongst them, he saw himself. Interiorly, he heard a voice ask him if he would say yes to whatever Jesus asked of him.

"Yes, Lord," he responded within himself. "I will say yes to whatever You ask of me, even if it means dying for the faith. But what about Sue, Lord? Where will she be in all of this?"

Interiorly, he heard, "She will be your Peter, your rock."

Ten days before our trip to Medjugorje, Rob was shown a vision of me lying prostrate before the Blessed Sacrament. Seeing my arms and my legs stretched out, he received the interior knowledge that I was to begin doing more full-bodied stretching in preparation for our upcoming pilgrimage. Along with doing leg stretches each day before my walk, I got down on the floor to stretch my body muscles as the Lord instructed. He was also told that God was going to reveal something of great importance which he needed to write down.

Praying our Novena to the Sacred Heart that same evening, Rob was shown a vision of Mary holding the baby Jesus in her arms. He received the knowledge that the message would be given to him over in Europe, and that it would be on a Sunday. Shown also the priest who would advise us, it was concerning the mission we were called to, receiving the words, "Mission Sunday." In looking at the itinerary for our trip, we took note that we'd be in Medjugorje on one Sunday, and in Rome on the other. What puzzled us was in noticing that the Church's celebration of "World Mission Sunday"[12] was going to take place prior to our trip. We wondered, did "Mission Sunday" have to do with World Mission Sunday?

Leaving the house at 6:00 a.m. en route to the airport for the short flight from Appleton to Chicago O'Hare, I beckoned St. Raphael the Archangel to accompany us for safe travel. Meeting up with Joyce and rest of the pilgrims totaling thirty-three in number, we enjoyed the "meet and greet" during our layover before boarding the aircraft to our next destination, Washington, DC. Once there, we spent a three-hour layover in the Dulles Airport awaiting our connecting flight to Vienna. It was already late afternoon, and walking through the terminals was proving to be strenuous on my legs. Though I was stretching them periodically, I was beginning to feel the muscles tightening up. Already pushing myself beyond my limit, I was aware that the most physically demanding part of our travel had yet to come.

"Let's check if our seats can be moved to an area that isn't so confined," Rob suggested. How grateful I was to learn that, because the 290-seat aircraft was not entirely full, they relocated us to a more open area. Boarding the plane, the stewardess brought over a fold-out bench to elevate my legs!

"Thank you, Jesus," I prayed.

Well into our long flight, it was growing quiet as people settled down to rest. Suddenly, I felt the dreadful cramps begin seizing up in my legs. There was no stopping them, as one was followed by another. Motioning for the flight attendant, Rob asked if we could get some ice, but he never returned. Trying with all my might to bear the pain, I couldn't refrain myself from whimpering.

Going to search out some ice, he returned in learning that, for safety reasons, they couldn't allow ice. With no relief in sight, Rob began massaging my legs.

"Mary, please bring my suffering to Jesus," I prayed.

Nearly beside myself in pain, I started twisting and turning, standing, then sitting in attempt to alleviate the pain. Somehow noticing my distress from the opposite side of the jumbo jet, two women we met on our layover in DC stood before me with a bottle of St. Raphael healing oil. Kneeling down, Ginny and Dawn blessed my legs and prayed. Soon after, the muscle spasms stopped. Weak from exhaustion, I forced myself to follow my doctor's recommendation in getting up to stretch my legs every hour. "Dear children! Today I wish to tell you that God wants to send you trials which you can overcome by prayer. God is testing you through daily chores. Thus, now pray to peacefully withstand every trial. From everything through which God tests you come out more open to God and approach Him with love" (Our Lady of Medjugorje).[13]

Later on, Ginny came by to check on how I was doing. She began to tell us of the immense sufferings of a close friend. Assuring her that we'd pray for her dear friend, she asked if we'd be able to come to Green Bay to pray with her sometime. Writing down Kristin's name to pray for while on pilgrimage; we promised also to bring it in prayer before the Blessed Sacrament once we returned home. I couldn't help but relate the anguish of her friend's affliction to the immense sufferings of Rhoda Wise.[14]

Arriving in Vienna, we had a four-hour layover before boarding our flight to Sarajevo. How wonderful it was to have a local priest on pilgrimage with us, celebrating Mass in a small room located in the lower level of the airport. Receiving Holy Communion meant receiving the staying power of Jesus to help me persevere in the long journey, both in what I was enduring physically and in the spiritual journey of life.

Once in Sarajevo, it was exuberating to know that we had all four of our flights under our belt and were very close in reaching our final destination. But my relief was short-lived when we learned we still had a 3-1/2-hour bus excursion through mountainous terrain before reaching the little village of Medjugorje. Not having slept since leaving home the morning before and feeling the ill effects of the cramps from the previous night, I wondered how my feeble legs could possibly tolerate the cramped bus ride. More surrender and trust that God would provide for my needs. Lifting my legs up on his lap, Rob said, "You need to get your legs up." What love he showed me at the cost of his own discomfort, not begrudgingly, but with joy.

Arriving at the home of the visionary Mirjana after traveling some thirty-odd hours, we were greeted with a warm welcome and a hot dinner. After receiving the general itinerary for the next day, Joyce took care of the room assignments. Settling down in our dorm-sized room, I was exhausted! Because the heat registers in the rooms had not yet been turned on, with my low iron, I began shivering uncontrollably. Shoving the two single beds together, we spread both sets of blankets on top, snuggling up close in an attempt to warm up. After finishing up our night prayers, Rob drifted fast to sleep while I laid there shivering like never before. Forcing myself out of bed hours later, I put on a sweatshirt and jogging pants with my robe over that! Still too cold to sleep, I checked Rob's watch and found it was 3:00 a.m. Praying the Chaplet of Divine Mercy, I fell asleep.

Waking up at 6:00 a.m. to get ready to go down for breakfast, I felt a migraine headache coming on from the lack of sleep and the extreme conditions of our journey. Feeling groggy and slightly queasy, Rob forewarned me that the hot water ran out halfway through his shower. Forcing myself into the cold shower, I took consolation in the warm air of my hair dryer. But in attempting to connect the European electrical adaptor to the blow dryer, a ball of fire shot out from the outlet, blowing out

Rob's watch and depositing black soot on his arm. I was thankful he wasn't electrocuted. Without a watch to go by, we now faced the challenge of following the daily itineraries involving specific times. Unable to dry my wet, frizzy hair, I surrendered to the fact that I was in Medjugorje. Nothing else mattered.

What struck me about the visionary Mirjana was her humility. Joining the small staff to serve breakfast to our group, her unpretentious words were "seasoned with salt" and laced with a delightful sense of humor. An inner zeal welled up inside of me, ready to embark upon our first day in Medjugorje. Hearing Marian songs played and rosaries prayed from inside the homes and shops as we walked through the grape fields to attend Mass, it truly felt like the closest place to paradise this side of heaven. Droves of people from numerous countries packed into St. James Church for Mass, with seating and sound systems accommodating those outdoors. Counting seventeen priests celebrating Mass, with multiple confessionals available in various languages from morning to night, Eucharistic adoration, veneration of the Cross, Apparition Hill, Cross Mountain, and so much more, all on the holy ground where the Queen of Peace was still appearing!

Hearing Rob's confession, the priest said, "I knew exactly the penance I was going to give you, but it's been completely erased from my mind. I feel like I'm supposed to tell you to live in the present. Don't worry about time, things from the past, or concerning the future. Does that make sense to you?" he asked. Thinking of his watch, Rob yielded to God's holy providence.

Telling the priest hearing my confession of the challenges I'd encountered in getting there and of the difficulty in retraining my mind to view my struggles as sources of potential blessings, his words touched my heart. "Try to remember St. Therese and her little ways of offering up even the smallest of suffering," he advised. How I loved the "Little Flower!"[15] Just days before leaving for Medjugorje, I'd begun reading her autobiography, *Story of a Soul*.

"Jesus does not ask great deeds, but only for gratitude and self-surrender"[16] (St. Therese, the Little Flower of Jesus).

That's when it dawned on me that in spite of the strenuous travel and tremendous sleep deprivation, my headache was gone. Instead of feeling the fatigue of low iron, I felt energized and refreshed! Nor did I have any of the usual aftereffects of the severe leg cramps that typically made it difficult for me even to pick up my feet and walk. Walking with flashlights in hand through the grape fields to return shortly after 11:00 p.m., I'd walked the distance from Mirjana's home to St. James Church and back again three times without any indication whatsoever of the ominous leg cramps. How enjoyable it was to meet up at day's end in Christian fellowship with the other pilgrims following the evening Mass. How I longed to capture and bottle the peace found in the tiny little village where the Queen of Peace was appearing, a peace that's meant for us to bring home and retain in our daily living.

> "Dear children, today I invite you to peace. As the Queen of Peace I have come to deepen within you my motherly peace. Dear children, I love you and I wish that all of you experience God's peace which enriches every heart. I invite you to become carriers and witnesses of my peace to this unpeaceful world. Let peace rule over all the earth, which is devoid of peace and yet longs for it. I bless you with a mother's blessing."[17]
>
> —Our Lady of Medjugorje

Quilting Cause Banner of St. James Church in Medjugorje with Our Lady's open arms, calling her children to conversion.

On our third morning in Medjugorje as we neared St. James Church on our walk to Mass, I suddenly became aware of a commotion going on behind us. Turning around, I saw several people looking up and gazing at the sun.

"What's going on?"

"It's the miracle of the sun,"[18] Sister Patricia answered.

"Look at it, Sue!" Mary exclaimed.

Going against all previous instruction never to look directly into the sun, I looked up to witness the spectacular event of the spinning sun! Seeing it appear as a radiant white Host, a wide red ray extended downward from its center, seemingly within reach. Around the luminous Host, I saw three-dimensional prisms of light in the colors of the rainbow, spinning about magnificently, as though they were dancing! Instantly, I was taken back to Mackinaw Island, where I'd felt the embrace of the divine Sun.

Heading back through the grape fields after Mass to Mirjana's for lunch, Rob suggested we take a stroll to check out Apparition Hill prior to going up the mountain with the group the following morning. Uncertain if my legs would endure the hike, all I knew was that I didn't come all the way to Medjugorje without at least trying! Meeting up with an older couple from our group at the base of the hill, the next thing I knew, we were doing a trial-walk with them up Apparition Hill! Collecting stones along the way from the holy ground on which Mary had first appeared, I stopped periodically to stretch out my legs. Exhilarated, we stood silently in prayer before the statue of Mary on reaching the top.

Over the course of three days, I'd already walked more than when the cramping from end-stage renal disease first began. Since first stepping foot in Medjugorje, I didn't experience a single leg spasm. Having pushed myself to the limit by going up Apparition Hill in addition to walking to and from St. James Church three times, my legs began feeling sore and achy. During our night prayers that evening, I petitioned Mary for the grace to be able to make it up Apparition Hill a second time. Feeling the discomfort of my legs, I prayed, "I'll do my best to climb the mountain again, but if my legs won't take me all the way up, I promise to humble myself and turn back." "Ah, Jesus does not ask for great things. What pleases Him the very most are our abandonment and gratitude. With that, we can reach the summit of the mountain of love"[19] (St. Therese).

Arriving for our early morning trek up Apparition Hill on yet another beautiful and sunny day in Medjugorje, I noticed the frost still on the ground. Miki, our tour guide, cautioned the pilgrims of the potentially slippery climb up the rocks. Standing at the base of the hill, a sweet aroma of roses filled the air. Beginning our ascent uphill, my heart was overjoyed in walking hand in hand with Rob as Miki led us in the rosary. Stopping at the spot that marked the first mystery, as the reflection was voiced, the same lovely fragrance of roses filled the air. Having asked Mary for the grace to get me up the mountain, at every stop thereafter, as the mystery reflection was spoken, I smelled a perfumed bouquet of roses. Neither Rob nor those around us could smell the beautiful scent of Mary's presence.

With crowds of people on Apparition Hill that day, droves of people were gathered around the statue where Mary first appeared when we reached the top. Getting our footing on the rocks some six feet back, we prayed before the statue as we'd done the day before. Instinctively cupping my hands on my forehead so as to create a makeshift visor to block the sun from my eyes, I saw a radiantly bright light completely outline the statue of Mary! Her veil was washed in a deep blue hue, appearing as though it was swiftly being painted in, first on one side and then the other. All at once, her gown went from being stone white to slightly off-white in color, looking as though it were real.

Astounded at what my eyes beheld, I began praying spontaneously within myself; "Mary, if you're real, please move." A second time I prayed the same, followed with a third request for Mary to validate what I was seeing. With my eyes locked onto hers, the lifelike statue of Mary smiled a very broad and jubilant smile at me. Removing my hands from my forehead, I turned to Rob and asked; "Did you see that?"

"See what?" he replied.

Sitting down the rocky ground, joyful tears streamed down my face. "If you knew how much I love you you'd cry for joy"[20] (Our Lady of Medjugorje).

Within minutes, Ginny approached from out of nowhere affirming, "Sue, you experienced something spiritual, didn't you?" Looking up at her, I could only shake my head yes as I tried to take in what had happened. Staying with us up on Mount Podbrdo after the others had gone back down, Ginny showed us a shortcut down before going on ahead. As fast as my legs could take me, we reached the bottom in time to catch a cab to St. James for Sunday Mass.

In his homily, the priest spoke on the tender subject of the intrinsic dangers of cultures that embrace "sins of the flesh." Quoting various Scripture verses, his message was void of any hatred, reflecting only love. Our Lady at Fatima voiced that more people would suffer eternal hellfire from sins of the flesh than through any other sin.[21] Right after Mass, Rob whispered, "Remember the locution I received two weeks ago involving 'Mission Sunday' and that I'd be receiving an important message on one of our Sundays in Europe?"

"Yes," I replied.

"Well, today is the Sunday that God's message was revealed through the priest's sermon."

"What's the message?" I asked.

"Our mission is to be one of truth, according to God's word, and with the same charity as the priest displayed in his homily. Today is our 'Mission Sunday' in confirmation to the mission God has called us to!" Nodding towards the main celebrant, he added, "That's the priest I saw in the vision who's going to help us."

"That's incredible!" I said while leaving the church.

"Yes," Rob agreed. "Our healing ministry needs to be one of love, not judgment. It has to be set firmly on the truth of the Gospel message and not according to the views of the culture. As ministers of God's truth and Intercessors of Light, we ourselves have to reflect His love. We must stand firmly on His word in Scripture and pick up the 'sword of the Spirit,' for battle in the fight for souls. We need to heed to Our Lady of Medjugorje's request to 'Pray! Pray! Pray!'"[22]

Just as we'd both received Mary's call to come to Medjugorje individually, but on the same day, once there, we'd also learned separately of the reason she called us, also on the very same day! For me, it was in my climb of faith up Apparition Hill. Determined to reach the top, I was graced in seeing the smiling face of my Heavenly Mother. In persevering up the hill of transformation in the struggles of life, one will achieve holiness in striving to reach the summit of salvation. Rob, on the other hand, received the "message for our mission" while taking part in the most powerful prayer of the Mass at St. James Church. As we were being transformed in holiness, so, too, was Mary calling us to pray for others to do the same. "I am your Mother and so I wish to lead all of you to complete holiness. I want you to be happy on earth and then to join me in heaven. This is, dear children, my purpose in coming here, and my desire" (Our Lady of Medjugorje).[23]

Deciding to skip lunch at Mirjana's in favor of talking with the priest, Rob shared with him the interior locution shown him prior to coming to Medjugorje, and how it had been fulfilled through the words of his homily. Relieved at the genuine warmth of his demeanor, he asked, "Can you come back at 1:00 p.m. tomorrow?" Conflicting with our bus trip to see Father Yozo,[24] a Franciscan priest associated with the first apparitions, we arranged to meet with him the day after. With the extra time on our hands in not having trekked back for lunch, we thought it a good time to patron the shops around the church to purchase religious articles to bring to Mirjana's November 2 apparition.

Returning back to our room before dinner and returning for the evening Mass, we passed by the open door of Joyce's room. Cheerfully, she called out, "Hello, Rob and Sue!" With her legs propped up on pillows, she asked, "Do you two have time to pray over my feet?" What an honor it was for us to pray over this God-fearing woman who'd brought so many of God's people closer to Him through her pilgrimages. Telling Joyce of the profound experience I had on Apparition Hill that same morning, I asked if she ever heard of anyone who'd witnessed the same. Telling us stories of miraculous signs and wonders that have been occurring there throughout the years—in the sky, on the mountain, at the church, and so on she said, "Aside from the miracle of the sun, most of them are as individual and unique as yours." She added, "I once saw the eyes of the statue of Mary at the Shrine of Our Lady of Good Help appear to look real."

Noticing her hair was almost finished air drying from her shower, I offered to curl and style them as Rob brought the souvenirs up to our room. Though our electrical adaptor had blown out, I had a curling iron with me purchased in Europe that my sister-in-law insisted I bring along. How glad I was that she did! Fixing Joyce's hair, I shared with her of the love of Mary that I could feel emanating from her motherly hugs.

I'd been cutting and styling my own mother's hair for years, as I had also done for my grandmother. As I was doing my mom's hair one day years prior, my great-aunt stopped by for a visit. Though Aunt Jo lived only fifteen minutes away, my mom often invited her to spend weekends at her home to ease her loneliness. As she sat at the kitchen table watching me wash, cut, and style my mother's hair, I sensed somehow that she longed to have her hair fixed as well. Though I really wanted to get back home to get dinner started before picking the kids up from school, I asked, "Aunt Jo, would you like me to wash and style your hair when I'm finished doing Mom's?"

"Ooooh!" she responded in a high-pitched tone. "But I don't have anywhere to go."

"That's okay," I said. "I'll fix them *just because*."

"Would you really?" she said gleefully.

"Yes, I sure will." What I didn't know then was that my dear aunt Jo really did have somewhere to go that day, someplace very special. It was later on that same evening that Our Lord would call her home. How I'll always treasure in my heart the privilege of being able to fix her hair for the occasion!

One can hear the lovely sound of church bells tolling at 6:00 a.m., 12:00 noon, and 6:00 p.m. every day in the little village of Medjugorje. Wherever the natives are and no matter what they're doing, they stop to pray the Angelus. It etched in my mind a beautiful memory of how the world should be—prayerful and peaceful. At exactly twelve noon on our bus ride to see Father

Jozo, Miki got on the microphone to lead our group in saying the Angelus,[25] a prayer commemorating Mary's Fiat to God. What a special grace the Lord was allowing the world through Our Lady's messages at Medjugorje in her call to conversion. Striving daily to give Jesus our yes, He'll be born again and again in our hearts.

It was in 1992 that the Holy Father, Pope John Paul II, told Father Jozo, "I am with you, protect Medjugorje! Protect Our Lady's messages!"[26] In Meeting Father Jozo, I sensed a great ambiance of holiness in his presence. I thought of the woman in Mark's Gospel who came up from behind Jesus in the crowd thinking that if she could only touch Jesus' cloak she'd be healed. Emanating out from the holy priesthood of Father Jozo, the magnitude of God's love settled over me so strongly to the point of wanting for nothing more than to cast myself at his feet and touch the hem of his garment!

It was All Saints Day, and after my experience with Mary on Apparition Hill, I held no trepidation in attempting to take on the steeper and more difficult climb up Cross Mountain. With so many on the mountain that day, Miki instructed us to pray silently to ourselves instead of as we'd done on Apparition Hill. Hand in hand with Rob, how exhilarating it was to trudge upward in praying the Stations of the Cross and individual prayers for our loved ones back home. Just being in Medjugorje in the frail condition of my health was beyond belief. When the boulders became too steep for me to climb, I found myself looking up in apprehension of how on earth I was going to get from point A to point B. Deciding that instead of looking up and viewing the mountain as an enormous hurdle, I'd simply concentrate on taking one step at a time. Before I knew it, we were on the summit of Mount Krizevac![27]

With most all pilgrims already off the mountain, we stayed on longer to pray, take pictures, and stretch my legs in preparation for the climb back down. Surprised to find the descent to be even more difficult, coming upon some slippery rocks, I was horrified to see a woman who had slipped off the side of the mountain. With only the tips of her tennis shoes gripping down tightly onto the top of the trail, I pointed to her as I called out for Rob to help her. Afraid to move, she lay perfectly still as he found a sure footing down the side of the mountain to lift her back up to safety.

Continuing downward, we prayed a rosary together in thanksgiving for the wonderful things the Lord had done, and for our niece, whose birthday it was. Taking much longer than we'd anticipated, we opted to take a cab parked on the dirt road at the mountain's base so as not to be late for Mass. As previously arranged, we met up with Father John in his office after Mass, fulfilling the prophetic vision shown to Rob. Offering us encouragement and support in our healing ministry, he recommended two books for us to read.

It was day five in Medjugorje, and though I physically exerted myself to a greater degree each day, I still had not experienced a single cramp! Walking back to St. James well in advance of the evening Mass, we strolled the grounds on the tree-lined path behind the church to see the sculpted figure of the Risen Christ[28] with outstretched arms. Drawing closer to the monument, we saw pilgrims swabbing up the unexplained substance dripping out from the "weeping knee of Jesus."[29]

Seeing the droves of people congregated outside of the church on our walk back over, I spontaneously commented to Rob, "Wouldn't it be wonderful if we were to see Sister Emmanuel?" Viewing her on the many VHS tapes we watched, as well as listening to her audio teachings, her personal testimony involving the circumstances leading up to her vocation was incredible. No sooner had I verbalized the sudden desire within my heart when I exclaimed, "Isn't that her over there?" It was a chilly evening, and with her hood up, I couldn't be sure. Making our way through the crowd, I walked up and asked, "Are you Sister Emmanuel?"

Indeed it was, and once again, the Lord had given to me the desires of my heart.

It was November 2. Getting up early to walk with Joyce and our group to the site where Mirjana's monthly apparition was to take place, we arrived in plenty of time to get a seat up front. With Rob seated on my left, to the right of me was sitting a beautiful young girl of about seventeen years old. Upon saying hello to her and talking briefly, I noticed that she spoke English to me and Croatian to her friend on the other side. I was wearing a bracelet made up of small crosses encircling my wrist, given to me by a friend back home. I found it reminiscent of the little crosses I sought to carry with Jesus, and I was excited to receive Our Lady's Motherly blessing on it. Interiorly, I sensed I was to give my cross bracelet to the girl sitting next to me. First rationalizing every reason not to give her my bracelet, as the promptings continued, I turned to her saying, "I've purchased religious articles from your country and I'd like you to have this cross bracelet as a souvenir of mine."

Reaching out reluctantly, she said, "Are you sure?"

"Yes, please take it. Mary wants you to have it."

With tears in her eyes, the young woman named ZeZe shared with me that she'd traveled to the apparition site to pray for her terminally ill aunt. But after using her spending money to buy a gift to bring for Our Lady's Motherly Blessing, she somehow lost it. Nearly crying, she said, "It's been very upsetting for me and I asked Mary for her help. Now, I'm so very happy to have this beautiful cross bracelet to bring back for my aunt!"

Leaning over to embrace her, I knew I'd gained much more than I was asked to give. During Mirjana's apparition, raindrops fell from the sky as tears rolled down her face.

It was All Soul's Day, and visiting the cemetery to pray for the holy souls in purgatory, what a blessing it was to kneel at the gravesite of Father Slavko to pray for his intercession. As pastor of St. James, he climbed to the heights of Cross Mountain daily, and it was up on the same holy mountain where he died. On the day after his death in November 2000, Our Lady of Medjugorje gave this message: "Dear children…I rejoice with you, and wish to tell you that your brother Slavko has been born again in heaven, and intercedes for you."[30]

My most prized possession from Medjugorje were the stones I collected from Apparition Hill in commemoration of Mary's message concerning the five stones of conversion. It was up on the mountain's top where our Lady appeared to the visionaries that I understood that those who go to Medjugorje are not there by chance. They've been hand selected by Mary as her "Apostles Blue" called to be true disciples of Jesus in becoming part of her "Blue Army" as a continuation of what she established in Fatima. Through transformation and living out her messages in love and truth, others will want the same. "I have given you my love, so that you may give it to others" (Our Lady of Medjugorje 1985).[31]

Holy Mother, pierce me through,
In my heart each wound renew
    Of my Savior crucified.
                                —Stabat Mater

In suffering, love, and in loving, suffer!
                —Blessed Maria Lopez of Jesus[32]

Stations of the Cross

Tenth Station
Jesus Is Stripped of His Garments

Keep your eyes fixed on Jesus who is your guide to the Heavenly country, where He is leading you. Why worry whether it is desert or meadow through which you pass, so long as God is always with you, and you arrive at the possession of a Blessed Eternity.

—Padre Pio

Angels Will Sing

How charming was the convent that Joyce had arranged for us to stay during our time in Italy. Located in the flurry of activity within the city, once inside its doors the pious atmosphere was a breath of fresh air. Arising that first morning, we spent time in Eucharistic adoration in the beautiful little chapel before the celebration of Mass. At breakfast, being waited on by the Selesian Sisters reminded me that to serve others is to serve God.

Excited to receive the blessing of the Vicar of Christ on earth, I was greatly looking forward to being in the papal audience. I planned to purchase scapulars ahead of time to have blessed by the Holy Father to give out back home as the Spirit prompted. Concerning the pope, Our Lady of Medjugorje once said to the seers, "Have him consider himself the father of all mankind and not only of Christians. Have him spread untiringly and with courage the message of peace and love among all mankind."[1]

"Year of the Eucharist" memory quilt in honor of Pope John Paul II, *Quilting Cause*

Rich in history and a gold mine of spiritual endeavors, touring the four major basilicas, I was awestruck in visiting one of Rome's most inspiring churches. St. John Lateran is where popes are consecrated and the Bishop of Rome presides. Lying beneath the altar is what remains of a small wooden table on which it's said that St. Peter celebrated Mass. What an amazing opportunity presented itself in being able to kneel before the casket of Pope John Paul II.

Our spirit-filled pilgrimage over in Italy brought along with it a few incidents that brought us ever so abruptly back into the real world. Chaotic and worldly, our travel through the busy streets of Rome en route to the various religious destinations was noticeably void of the oasis of peace we had found in Medjugorje. For a tourist mingling amidst an ever-growing faithless society worldwide, malice can sometimes abound. Crammed like sardines onto the crowded subways, I was able to dodge the first assault of a man attempting to rip the gold crucifix and tiny miraculous medal from my neck. Turning to avoid the attack, I saw in his eyes the darkness of evil. On a separate occasion in boarding the train, our tour guide, Father Charles, was behind me as he suddenly began speaking very loudly in Italian. Turning around to see him scolding a woman, I asked, "Father, what's the matter?"

"She was trying to pickpocket your bag!" he replied.

In yet a third incident, as Rob and I squeezed together face to face on the jampacked subway en route back to the convent, I whispered, "Honey, I think the lady behind you is trying to steal something from your shoulder bag."

Having just purchased the canvas satchel to hold our souvenirs, it somehow had gotten pushed to the back of him as people crowded in. Trying to move it to the front, it didn't budge. Exiting the train, we were shocked to see a six-inch razor slice going across the middle of our shoulder bag, just big enough for her to slip her hand in and steal our purchases. But Our Lady was watching out for us. With the heavy stone statue of Mary in the "Pieta" positioned in the same spot as the bag had been cut, it prevented the woman from getting off with a thing!

I marveled on how the pedometer tallied up to nine miles of walking on one of our days over in Rome, yet I never suffered a single cramp! Before busing with our group for a day in Assisi, Father Charles celebrated a special Mass for us in The Divine Mercy Church. With my dedication of praying the Chaplet of Divine Mercy each day, as well as our frequenting The Chapel of Divine Mercy back home for Eucharistic adoration, I felt particularly blessed to be there. Tears ran down my face as Father read from Matthew's Gospel one of the same Scripture verses I meditated on before the Tabernacle each day. In the practice of *Lectio Divina*,[2] the prayerful meditation of Scripture, we never missed a day in picking up our Bibles to soak in God's word.

Heading down the highway toward Assisi, I looked up to notice Father Charles walking "with a purpose" toward the back where we were seated. Standing before me, he quizzed; "What was today's Gospel?"

"Matthew 11:28, 'Come to Me, all you who labor and are burdened and I will give you rest. Take My yoke upon you and learn from me, for I am meek and humble of heart. You will find rest, for my yoke is easy and my burden light,'" I paraphrased.

"How is it that you know this from memory?" he asked.

"Because, Father, I take Jesus at His word in this passage every day after Mass, laying all my troubles down before the Tabernacle to make the exchange."

Without inquiring as to what my troubles were, I didn't disclose to him of my failing kidneys. Sitting down in the empty seat across from where we were sitting, we conversed nearly the entire way to Assisi. Telling him of the quilt Jenelle had made for in honor of the late Pope John Paul II, I asked if he knew of a way it could get to Pope Benedict.

"Yes," he said. "Give it to me before you leave for the airport tomorrow and I'll personally bring it to the Vatican to pass off to the guards. They'll see to it that the pope receives it." Then, pulling out his little address book from his pocket, he asked, "Would you mind writing down your name and phone number for me to call you sometime?"

How wonderful was our time in Assisi, taking in the sites surrounding the lives and holy deaths of St. Francis and St. Clare!

Before arising in the early morning hours of our last day in Rome, I saw a vision of my dear Jenelle, who was walking directly toward me. Noticing her hair was trimmed, she looked very joyous in anticipation of our return home. I then was shown an image of Mary, followed by a vision of Jesus with His hands outstretched. Though I didn't see a cross, I knew within myself that He was hanging from the Cross. Then seeing several crosses in various sizes, I sensed that Jenelle had suffered many trials in our absence, taking consolation in knowing that Mary was helping her. How I longed to call her, but without a cell phone back then, my mind was put to ease in the joyful enthusiasm of our projected homecoming. Our mother-daughter relationship was close, and she'd become especially protective of me since the decline of my health.

Jenelle herself was no stranger to suffering, with her many food allergies, the chronic sports injuries, and the surgeries. Holes were drilled into the navicular bones of her feet as a means to correct the necrotic stress fractures which now caused her chronic pain. Notably, the pain in her feet was in the same area where Jesus' feet were nailed to the Cross. No longer could she do what she loved to do in playing basketball, volleyball, golf, or even go for a walk without the anguish of the stabbing pain. I wondered of the significance of the unseen cross from which I'd seen Jesus hanging. Was it Jenelle who was hanging on His Cross in the pain of her suffering?

With our luggage lining the sidewalks of the designated pickup point of the bus chartered to transport our group to the airport, we waited. As time continued to tick by, fearing we'd miss our flight, Joyce called out amongst our group, "Pray the rosary!" Quietly, we began to pray. Spotting our bus stopped in rush hour traffic some time later, it was still a block and a half away. Arriving at the airport past the scheduled departure time, we flew through check-in to find ourselves boarded on the plane for Vienna. Once settled, the pilot's voice came on the intercom, extending his sincere apologies for the late arrival that had resulted in the delay of our departure. For all intended purposes, we should have missed our flight, yet here we were on the receiving end of an apology! We said a prayer of thanksgiving.

Arriving early the next morning at the Vienna airport, we took our place at the end of the long check-in line to board our lengthy cross-Atlantic flight back to the States. In surrendering our seating arrangements into the hands of Mary, I was at peace. Getting singled out for a luggage check, the security guard pulled out three fist-sized rocks. Quite beautiful and uniquely shaped, I'd come across them when gathering stones on our first climb up Apparition Hill.

"Sir," I said pleadingly, as he confiscated the rocks, "I took them from a hill in Medjugorje where our Blessed Mother appears."

"I cannot let you take these on board," he said authoritatively. "These are weapons."

"Oh, I'm sorry," I replied. "I guess I didn't think of it that way. I only wanted them as a keepsake because they come from holy ground."

Looking around, the guard quickly tucked the rocks back into my luggage before closing it up.

"God bless you," I said to him. Nodding, he turned to walk away. Taking our seats in the aircraft, I had an aisle seat that allowed me to get up and walk without disturbing those around us. Two of the four vacant seats in the entire flight were right next to us, with collapsible arms allowing me to elevate my legs. "Thank you, Holy Mother," I prayed.

Two transfer flights later, I was elated to spot Jenelle standing in wait of our flight. Walking gleefully to meet her, I held her in my arms, saying, "Oh, I missed you so much!"

"You too," she replied.

On our drive home from the airport, I was thrilled to share with her some highlights of our trip. Asking how everything was for her while we were gone, she told me of the adversities she'd suffered in our twelve-day absence. Sharing with her what the Lord had shown to me before leaving Rome, I said gently, "It was Mary who helped you through." Piecing together in my mind the happiness I saw on her face at the airport as she walked toward me, it was the same joyful expression I'd seen in the vision. Thinking of how the majority of the thirty-three pilgrims had come down with a nasty respiratory infection on the trip, I thought also of how her trials coincided with the same time period that I'd been spared from getting sick or experiencing the adverse side effects of end-stage renal failure. Remembering a time when Jenelle had prayed to suffer in my place, I thought of the vision of Jesus' outstretched arms on the Cross, without actually seeing the Cross, wondering if she'd willingly taken my place on the cross of my sufferings.

Feeling the ill-effects of jetlag, I awoke from sleep at 3:00 a.m. feeling wide awake. Having had little more than four hours of sleep, I prayed the Chaplet of Divine Mercy for the sick and the dying. Still unable to sleep, I got up to begin the new day. Though Rob was starting to come down with the respiratory virus, he went into work nonetheless.

Returning from morning Mass, our friend Jerry called to ask if I'd be up to joining him and Dolores that same afternoon at the Shrine of Our Lady of Good Help to pray with a middle-aged man who was terminally ill. In spite of his grave condition, it was his utmost desire to go to the holy grounds where Our Lady appeared.

"Hearing that you were over in Medjugorje," Jerry told me, "he was really hoping you could be there."

Despite feeling tremendously fatigued, I found myself agreeing to come. Managing to locate the bag of rosaries that we brought to the apparition site to receive Mary's blessing, I reminisced of the joy I had felt in receiving the rosary brought back for me. Saying a little prayer, I asked Mary to help me select one for this suffering man who I never before met. I'll always remember the glow that emanated from Scott's eyes as we prayed with him down in the crypt below the church, and of his immense joy in receiving the rosary that held Our Lady's motherly blessing. In spite of the great difficulty of transporting him in the critical status of his health, his loved ones had honored his last wish before he passed. "Holy Mary, Mother of God, pray for us sinners now and at the hour of our death. Amen."[3]

Picking up right where I'd left off prior to leaving for Medjugorje in reading *Story of a Soul*, I found confirmation involving the mystical experience I had up on Mt. Podbrdo[4] concerning the statue of Mary. I read of an account of an acute illness that had threatened to take the life of St. Therese of Lisieux. Out of sheer desperation, her family brought into her room a statue of Our Lady to place before her sick bed. Gazing at it, St. Therese witnessed the statue of Mary smile at her and was soon healed of her affliction![5] As I reflected on what happened to me on Apparition Hill in relation to what had occurred to St. Therese, I recalled the advice given me in the confessional on our first day in Medjugorje, to bear my hardships in the example set by this beloved saint. It was near the time of her death the "Little Flower" wrote in a poem entitled, "Why I Love You, Mary" these words: "O you who came to smile on me, at the dawn of life's beginning; Come once again to smile on me...Mother!⁶ (St. Therese).

Playing a CD given to me by one of the pilgrims from our group, it was a recording of a duet done by our tour guide, Miki Musa and David Parks from Ireland. As I listened to the upbeat tune of the first stanza being sung over and over, "*Gospa Majka Moja Kraljica Mira*,"⁷ though I had no idea of the meaning behind the Croatian words, my heart overflowed with joy nonetheless. Then, upon hearing Miki sing solo another verse in English, I not only understood the words, but they confirmed to me the beautiful encounter I had with Mary up on Apparition Hill. "In the sunlight, I can see your face, smiling to me, my Mother!"⁸ It was there in the bright sunlight of the mountain's summit in Medjugorje on the very spot where Our Lady first appeared to the visionaries that I had seen the smiling face of my Mother. As the dispenser of all God's grace, I knew it had been by grace alone that my legs were able to make the climb up Apparition Hill.

Driving home from picking up the developed pictures from our trip, I could hardly wait to view them as I began paging through the envelopes while Rob drove. One picture in particular caught my eye. It had been a spur-of-the-moment snapshot taken by one of the pilgrims, who suggested we stand in front of the Holy Doors of Saint Peter's Basilica.

"Look at this!" I said to Rob, holding it up for him to take a quick glance. On the snapshot of us standing before the three-dimensional image on the Holy Doors, Jesus' left hand appeared to be placed directly behind my head, while His right arm looked as though it was wrapped around Rob's shoulder. Mary had her right arm extended out, appearing as though she was pointing at us. Stopping at a gas station to fuel up, I picked up my Bible.

Opening it randomly, I read: "His left hand is under my head/ and his right arm embraces me" (Song of Songs 2:6).

On most evenings after dinner, we'd hop in the car and drive the fifteen-minute jaunt over to the Chapel of Divine Mercy. What a great blessing it had been for us since the start of perpetual adoration at St. Pius to be able to frequent Eucharistic adoration at will. It was there that we were able to be still and listen to God speak in the innermost recesses of our hearts. Being in Jesus' true presence means also to be in the presence of God the Father and the Holy Spirit, as together they are three in One in the mystery of the Holy Trinity.

There was a certain woman we started seeing in the Chapel of Divine Mercy during the times we frequented the chapel. On one particular evening when she stopped in for Eucharistic adoration, Rob received a word of knowledge that we were to intercede in prayer for her. Interiorly, he was shown visions in relation to the specific areas of healing we were to pray for.

On a day off of work, Rob and I attended the noon Mass together. Going up to kneel before the Tabernacle afterward, the same woman we'd been praying for everyday for two months came and knelt down alongside us. Getting up to leave, she politely asked if we had some time to talk with her out in the narthex area of the church. Confiding with us some of the things the Lord had already laid on Rob's heart for us to pray for, we told her we'd already been holding her close in prayer.

"Thank you!" she said joyfully. "I need prayer!"

Having been purposefully placed in our lives for prayer, it was revealed to Rob a short time later that we were to embrace the woman as our spiritual daughter. It meant we were to cover her in prayer as we did our own children. Honored to accept what the Lord asked of us, she was the first of the "spiritual children" entrusted to our prayers.

On another day after the Mass at St. Joe's, I went up to the Marian Grotto to light a candle and pray my rosary. Halfway through, an elderly man walked up to the statue of Mary. I was moved at the tender love he displayed toward our Blessed Mother, as he touched her hand and said, "I'll be back later." Finishing my rosary, I went before Jesus in the Tabernacle. Leaving the church at nearly half past two, I saw the man kneeling in the same pew he always sat in at Mass.

As I was walking by, he looked up and introduced himself as Jake. "I'm eighty years old," he said, and after making a little small talk, he asked, "Can I tell you of an experience I had the year after my wife's passing?" He began by telling me that since her death, it had become his daily routine to rise early and drive to the park after breakfast. There, he'd walk and pray in the beauty of God's nature. "I spent time in the seminary discerning the priesthood before deciding to enter into married life," he told me. Returning back home around midmorning, he'd catch a nap before heading out to the noon Mass at St. Joe's. Afterward, he went to a local restaurant for a bowl of soup before going back to the park again to pray. Then, he'd stop by at church one more time before returning home. "I'm in bed every night by seven," he said. "But rain or shine, I get up every morning to the same routine." With his head dropping, he confessed, "In my prayers, I used to beg the Lord to take me home to be reunited with my wife."

One year after his wife's death, Jake awakened from his morning nap to get ready to leave for Mass. Feeling as though he was paralyzed, he told me that he was unable to move from the couch. "That's when I saw Jesus standing there, with Mary slightly behind Him and off to the side. She looked beautiful, and humble," he said affectionately, "She never uttered a sound. Jesus said to me, 'Jake, do not pray for Me to take you home. You remain here for a purpose, to pray for the holy souls in purgatory. When it's your time, I will call you home.'"

Jake told me that a few years prior he had lost his sense of taste and smell, and how he'd longed ever since to be able to taste the food he was eating. "But now, I never pray to die, and I'm thankful for my infirmities. I have diabetes, heart problems, and I'm losing my eyesight, but I offer everything up for the Holy Souls." "When man, after applying the remedy for his suffering, patiently bears for love of Me that which he is unable to cure, he gains a glorious prize" (Words of Our Lord to St. Gertrude the Great on suffering).[9]

Jake and I soon became buddies. One day as I was kneeling at the Marian Grotto, he told me that the rosary hanging from Mary's hand was a rosary he'd gotten from Lourdes. "It was my only rosary," he said."

Confused at his comment, I asked, "What rosary do you use to pray on then?"

"I don't pray the rosary," he answered. "I tend to lose concentration and feel like its wasted prayer," he said matter-of-factly.

"Jake," I said gently. "Your ardent love for Our Blessed Mother is apparent. It was Mary who requested we pray the rosary. The opponent of salvation would love for you to think that it's wasted prayer, because aside from the Mass, it's the most powerful prayer of all! It's the prayer that keeps the devil at bay, defeating the forces of evil. What helps me stay focused is to lose myself in each mystery by bringing myself right there with Jesus and Mary spiritually."

I gave him a rosary from Medjugorje, which he placed around his neck, saying, "I'll always know right where it is for my strolls in the park, and I'll use it to pray for the holy souls in purgatory!"

Seeing Jake back in his pew as I was leaving church one afternoon, he said, "Hi, Sue. I saw you praying up at the Tabernacle when I came back to pay my afternoon visit to Mary. I told the Lord that whatever it is that you pray so passionately for each day, from now on, the fourth mystery of my daily rosary is for your intentions."

Humbled, I sat down in the pew behind him and told him that my kidneys were functioning at only 10 percent. "I'm counting on God's promises in Holy Scripture," I assured him.

"Reading His word brings me so much hope that I often cry tears of joy." Seeing sadness in his eyes, I said, "If our lives are as perfect as we'd like them to be, then how would we ever feel the need for God? How would we appreciate anything if we already had everything, right?"

It was some time later that I received an e-mail of the twelve promises of the Sacred Heart as given by Jesus to St. Margaret Mary of Alocoque.[10] I marveled at the blessings offered to those who venerate the image of Jesus' Most Sacred Heart. "I will bless the homes where an image of My Heart shall be exposed and honored."[11] Having felt the love and solace of Jesus' Heart in the vision shown to me following the death of Pope John II, I felt an instant desire to practice the devotion. Saying a little prayer, I asked Jesus to help me find a beautiful picture of His Sacred Heart to place in a prominent place in my home to venerate each day.

Following Mass that same afternoon, Jake came up to me with a man of his same age. Introducing me to his longtime friend, he said, "This is the woman who taught me how to pray the rosary!" Humbled at his remark, he then handed me a box.

"What's this?" I asked.

"Well, I stopped by St. Patrick's Book Store this morning, and the only thing I was inspired to buy was this. It's for you." Staring down at the white box in my hands, I didn't know what to say. "Open it!" he said eagerly.

"Okay," I said. To my delight, I took out a beautiful picture of The Sacred Heart of Jesus! Knowing that I'd never discussed anything to do with the Sacred Heart with him, I was absolutely amazed at what had transpired only hours before. "This is lovely," I said. "Thank you so much!"

Turning to go have lunch, he smiled, saying, "You're welcome!"

Returning home, I placed the beautiful image on our fireplace mantle. Saying a prayer of thanksgiving, I then sat down to write out a card to Jake. Telling him of the pledge I'd made to Jesus that same morning, I told him how I'd asked for Jesus' help in finding a picture of His Sacred Heart. Approaching me after Mass a few days later, Jake said the note touched his heart so much that he had it out on his desktop to read again and again.

Sacred Heart of Jesus image

My first memory of devotion to the Sacred Heart stems back to my childhood. Walking with my dad uptown after dinner one evening, he purchased the hand-painted images of the Two Hearts of Jesus and Mary. With a family of ten to support, how patiently he had waited to have money enough to buy them. Years after his death, I asked my mom if she still had them. "Yes, but I'm afraid they're chipped up pretty bad," she told me. Hammering off the damaged plaster backing behind the images, the 3D wall plaques were simply beautiful! Now hanging in our bedroom, they're in close proximity to where we kneel to pray the Efficacious Novena to the Sacred Heart of Jesus each night.

A few weeks had passed by when I received a phone call from the National Coordinator of the World Apostolate of Our Lady of Fatima. Telling me he received my name from a woman who was on our Medjugorje pilgrimage, before hanging up he asked, "Would you like me to e-mail you an ongoing list of the CM Digest prayer requests?"

"Sure," I responded. "So you know about our prayer group then?"

"No," he replied inquisitively. "Tell me about it."

Because we were already fulfilling most of the requirements of becoming associate members of Mary's Blue Army,[12] Deacon Bob suggested the possibility of Intercessors of Light becoming a Fatima prayer cell. Having already entrusted Mary as the leader of the prayer group since it first began, he came to our home to discuss the World Apostolate of Our Lady of Fatima in further detail. Attending one of our prayer sessions to introduce the apostolate to the IOL members, he came back a third time to consecrate our home to the Sacred and Immaculate Hearts of Jesus and Mary. Ordering the corresponding picture of the Immaculate Heart of Mary to the one I received from Jake, what a blessed day of enthronement it was! To Lucia at Fatima Our Lady said, "Jesus wants to make use of you to make me known and loved. He wants to establish in the world devotion to my Immaculate Heart."[13]

With hundreds of prayer needs coming in each week, Rob and I were sometimes called on to pray with the sick. Having promised Ginny on our flight over to Medjugorje to pray for her friend, we brought the matter before Jesus in the Blessed Sacrament. Never having met Kristin, Rob was shown two separate visions of embryos in the womb concerning her. Interiorly, he received the knowledge that both pregnancies had resulted in miscarriages, causing her tremendous pain.

Contacting Ginny, we made arrangements to pray with Kristin in her hospital room. Though only in her forties, because of the complications of her disease the room had become her "home away from home." The blood thinners she needed to prevent life-threatening embolisms from forming in her lungs put her at a dangerously high risk of internal bleeding. On one occasion, her legs filled up with blood so quickly that before she could be rushed into surgery, they split wide open along the length of her shins from the intense pressure the internal bleeding had caused. With open wounds unable to heal, they were a constant source of ominous infections.

Kristin shared with us how she'd lamented the loss of two babies through miscarriage. Confirming the prophetic vision, we expressed to her our deepest sorrow.

"God the Father knit your precious little babies in your womb with good purpose," I said softly. "Had they never been created, they would never have had the opportunity to become beautiful little saints. One day, you'll reunite with them in heaven for all of eternity!" "Before I formed you in the womb I knew you" (Jeremiah 1:5).

"Yes," she said, smiling. "Thank you for reminding me." Pausing momentarily, she continued, "I really need to think of it that way, to thank the Creator of all life for creating my children, not only the two that are living, but also the two that are already with Him in paradise."

Another time after praying with Kristin, she told us that when Rob prayed in tongues, she understood the interpretation of what he was saying. Visibly moved, she revealed what Jesus asked of her: "Will you be a conduit of My love?" She understood that it was through her suffering that she would become a vessel of God's love. Asking if she could tell us of an experience she had years ago, she shared, "Once, when I was alone in my hospital bed, in my brokenness, I looked up and uttered, 'Perhaps I don't love You enough, Lord.' That's when the Sacred Heart of Jesus appeared to me." Pointing to the right hand corner of the room, she continued, "He was standing right over there, and I could feel love and peace radiating from His Heart."

It was on one of the few times we went to Kristin's home to pray with her that she pointed out a beautiful painting of the Sacred Heart of Jesus. Hanging beneath the skylight in her bedroom, it was positioned where she could see it in full view from her bed. "That's what Jesus looked like when He appeared in my hospital room years ago," she told us. Handing me a book entitled *Divine Intimacy*,[14] she said, "I want you to have this." Intending to read it herself, she'd been unable to focus on reading it or to realize her goal of becoming a third-order Carmelite. Just as with the other books given to us through God's providence, it was a most treasured gift. Reading it before the Blessed Sacrament twice through, the book served to bring Rob ever more deeply into the state of contemplative prayer.[15] To pray with Kristin was to pray with a living and breathing saint. She told us of an unexpected visit she had one morning after the Bishop learned of her immense sufferings. Standing next to her, he said, "I do not see the face of a suffering woman. I see only the face of Christ." In the gravity of her health, Kristin would sometimes call us at home for prayer. We received a card she handmade from her hospital bed, which read:

> Dearest Sue & Rob,
>
> I can scarcely find the words to thank you for all you've done for me and my family. You have renewed my hope when my spirit was lagging, and have opened my ears to the Holy Spirit.
>
> Love,
> Kristin

Telling us of a nine-year-old boy in desperate need of prayer, Tom and Mary asked if we'd be willing to pray with Andrew. The year prior, he'd been diagnosed with acute lymphoblastic leukemia. Going before Jesus in Eucharistic adoration the following evening, we lifted up the needs of the child and his family before the Lord. Receiving knowledge of specific areas of healing we were to pray for, we made plans to pray with the boy.

Turning onto the long driveway leading to their home, positioned on either side of the entrance were large imposing concrete angel statues. In contrast to what any parents' anguish would be concerning the well-being of a child, emanating out from their young son was the light of Christ. Feeling as though we were sitting in the presence of the Christ-child Himself, I thought of the frantic concern of Mary and Joseph when Jesus was lost in the temple, only to find their young Son sitting calmly in the midst of the teachers. "And all who heard him were astounded at his understanding and his answers" (Luke 2:47). Similar to the Bible story, Andrew sat peacefully amongst the adults in childlike innocence, exemplifying how one is to walk with Jesus in the midst of great trial.

Picking up his guitar, chills ran down my spine as he began to sing with the voice of an angel. Having won an audition to sing for President George Bush, among other accolades, the words of his songs echoed out the hope and trust they had in God. Making his CD recordings was an area that wouldn't be comprised, donating all of the proceeds toward a cure for leukemia. Gaining permanent access into our hearts, we prayed for Andrew and his family every day.

We received an urgent call for prayer one day, for a young adult named Timothy who'd been seriously injured in a motorcycle accident. In a comatose state, he was thrown thirty feet from his bike. Clinging to life by a thread, should he survive, it was feared he'd be paralyzed and suffer permanent brain damage. Praying for him in Eucharistic adoration that same evening, Rob was shown a vision of Timothy's legs from below the knees. Seeing his toes begin to wiggle, he was then shown a second vision of him and me standing over the man's hospital bed with our hands extended over his motionless body in prayer. Within his heart, he was told that Timothy would recover from his injuries.

Though we couldn't physically go to pray over the man, we faithfully prayed for him every day. Several months later, we received a letter from him saying that, with the exception of a lingering eye injury, which was hoped would heal over time, he had made a full recovery. Reading the police report of injuries thought to be fatal, Timothy thanked God for having spared his life.

It was the feast day of St. John of the Cross, and reading his collected works and those of St. Theresa of Avila, Rob and I better understood the mysticism we were experiencing. It was so nice to have Jenelle accompany me to Mass, and making our way up to the grotto afterward to pray our St. Andrew Advent Prayer,[16] I ran into Clare Marie. In the circumstances surrounding the first time we met, it was in God's providence that we found ourselves kneeling before the Tabernacle at 3:00 p.m. with two other women, singing together the Chaplet of Divine Mercy.

Introducing her to my daughter, Jenelle continued on to the grotto, while Clare-Marie stopped to share highlights of her recent trip to Assisi. Having returned from Assisi less than two months prior, I shared in the enthusiasm of her words. Though I hadn't known her for all that long, spiritually speaking, it was as though we'd known each other all our lives. Her attentiveness to the workings of the Holy Spirit in her life was apparent, and we were able to share openly our spirituality.

"Sue," she said, "I know that you want to go up to the grotto to pray with your daughter, but would you mind if I went up there with you?"

"Of course not," I assured. Before kneeling down before the statue of our Blessed Mother to pray, I was astonished to learn that she was praying the same Advent prayer as us, which honors the very hour and moment the Son of God was born. "At midnight, in Bethlehem, in the piercing cold."[17]

It had become tradition for us to bundle ourselves up on Christmas Eve to pray the final prayers right at midnight, outside in the piercing cold of the Wisconsin winter air. With blessed candles in hand, we get down on our knees at the very hour and moment in which the Christ-child was born! "In that hour vouchsafe, O my God, to hear my prayers and grant my desires; through the merits of Our Lord Jesus Christ and of His Blessed Mother. Amen."[18]

Talking with Clare-Marie as we were walking out together, I sensed somehow that she had more she wanted to say. Caught by surprise, we were greeted by a winter snowstorm. With near blizzard-like conditions, we quickly said our good-byes as we made a mad dash toward our vehicles.

"Get in, Mom," Jenelle said as we approached the car. "I'll clean off the snow."

Opening the door, I could faintly hear my name being called out through the sound of the wind. Looking up, I saw Clare-Marie running toward us in the blowing snow.

"Sue," she called, half out of breath, "could I please have just a few more minutes of your time? When we were praying before Mary, I could feel how much she loved us, and of how pleased she was that we were praying together as her daughters." Continuing, she said, "I felt inspired to sing to you a song I recently wrote, but I held back on doing it. Would you mind if I sang it to you?"

"I'd love to hear a song you were inspired to sing to me!" I replied. "Let's get in the car where it's warm!"

Finished brushing off the snow, Jenelle got in to hear her sing her song entitled "See How Much I Love You." Tears formed in my eyes as Jesus spoke to me through the words of her song. "See how much I love you. See how much I care. I stay with you always, in Holy Communion. Always see Me there."[19] Since having discovered more fully the true presence of Jesus in the Eucharist, I was drawn to Mass every day to receive Him there. "See how much I love you. See how much I care. I gave you My mother, to pray for you always. Always see her there."[20] Not a day went by that I didn't ask Mary if I could receive Jesus within her Immaculate Heart, or that I didn't go before His Holy Mother to seek her intercession. "See how much I love you. See how much I care. I gave you the sun, the moon and the stars; Always see Me there."[21] My thoughts traveled back to strolling with Rob along the shores of Lake Michigan, when my eyes were opened to see God's presence in all my surroundings.

Driving out of the snowy parking lot, Jenelle asked, "Mom, how many times in your life did you ever have someone tell you they were inspired to sing you a song?"

Smiling, I responded, "Before today, never."

In her gentle nature, she then shared with me what transpired as she prayed alone at the grotto during the time that Clare Marie and I were talking.

"I lit a candle for you before kneeling down to pray my St. Andrew prayer, when I suddenly found myself asking Mary straight out when you were going to be healed. Within my heart, I heard very distinctly the word 'Angels.' And so I asked Mary, 'What about angels?' Instantly, I heard the words, 'Angels will sing!' Asking Mary if she'd confirm her answer, ten minutes later there was a lady in the back seat of our car singing of how much God loves you!"

Smiling again at her summation, we marveled at the magnificent ways that God brings hope to the suffering through others! Yes, my kidneys were still failing. But in the uncertainty of my health, God was showing me the certainty of His love. Faith without seeing is the childlike trust He asks of us. Without affliction, how would we know of the magnitude of what Jesus suffered for us? Without struggles of our own, how would we be able to offer compassion toward enduring hardship? Without challenges, how would we learn that it's only in looking to God that we can rise above them? "Accordingly, we ourselves boast of you in the churches of God regarding your endurance and faith in all your persecutions and the afflictions you endure" (2 Thessalonians 1:4).

Feeling the tranquil blessing of inner peace in contrast to the sudden flurry of wintery weather, we received the assurance of God's abiding love in answer to a daughter's heartfelt plea to her Heavenly Mother. "When will my mom be healed?" she asked. "Angels will sing!" was the answer received. We knew all we needed to know. Placing the unknown back into the stainless hands of Mary to bring to her Son, there was quietude within our hearts and a renewed trust in the mercy of God. "Jesus said to them in reply, 'Have faith in God'" (Mark 11:22).

By the cross with you to stay,
There with you to weep and pray,
  Is all I ask of you to give.

—Stabat Mater

Trials and tribulations offer us a chance to make reparation for our past faults and sins. On such occasions the Lord comes to us like a physician to heal the wounds left by our sins. Tribulation is the divine medicine.[22]

—Saint Augustine of Hippo

Stations of the Cross

Eleventh Station
Jesus Is Nailed to the Cross

Only Jesus can understand what I suffer, as I prepare for the sorrowful scene of Calvary. Nobody can understand either what relief Jesus has when someone not merely shares His sufferings, but when a soul, for love of Him, does not ask for consolation but rather to share in these same sufferings.

—Padre Pio

Four Calling Birds

While we were in Medjugorje, I had wanted to find just the right thing to bring back for my mother. The minute I saw it, I knew it was for her! A beautiful incandescent sterling silver rosary bracelet; each of its beads were mounted in a variety of multicolored sparkling crystal gems. Hanging near the clasp was a small miraculous medal. Telling her it had received Mary's Motherly blessing, the bracelet never left her wrist.

With Christmas nearing, so too was the three-year mark of me having made the pledge to God that I would read Scripture to my mom every day if she survived the bout of pneumonia threatening to take her life. It was a promise I'd never broken. Prior to our pilgrimage, I made sure to prearrange with my sister to read the Bible stories in proxy for me.

It was while adoring the Eucharistic Jesus just a couple of months after I had first started reading God's word to my mom that Rob was shown a vision concerning her. In it, she was sitting in a dark room. The only light illuminating it was coming from her television set. The knowledge given was that the dark room symbolized the overshadowing source from which the light of Christ is concealed when one constantly occupies their minds with TV, headphones, the internet, etc. In doing so, one risks blocking out the ever-still voice of God. Interiorly, he also received a message that we were to bring my mother Holy Communion every Sunday.

How thankful we were for what God made known to us! From that day on, we brought her the Eucharist every Sunday and oftentimes in between. On the days we didn't physically administer the Eucharist to her, I began spiritually sharing my Communion with my mom at daily Mass, asking Jesus to be with her. I prayed continuously to the Holy Spirit, begging for His guidance in helping me assist my mother to gain all the spiritual merit possible during the time she was still with us. Stopping by to visit her nearly every day, before leaving, I'd turn on the five-disc CD player filled with recordings of the rosary, the Divine Mercy Chaplet, and a medley of other inspirational songs. When I came over to cut and fix her hair each month, I'd tear up in listening to her sing out loud tunes such as "How Great Thou Art." Whenever Rob and I would stumble upon a good movie playing on EWTN depicting the lives of saints, I'd quickly call her to have her tune in to watch it as well. I didn't want to miss out on a single opportunity to bring her closer to God, and how greatly she enjoyed them!

It wasn't long before we started seeing the fruit of our labors in witnessing her growing in the virtues. Despite the constant struggle she had simply in breathing, her countenance was of peace and joy. Constantly, I sought to comfort her that the Will of God would never take her to a place where His grace wouldn't uphold her. "Jesus is walking with you and will give you the fortitude to endure the path chosen especially for you," I'd encourage. "Even when I walk through a dark valley,/ I fear no harm for you are at my side;/ your rod and staff give me courage" (Psalm 23:4).

During the course of just under three years, I had read to my mother the entire New Testament, as well as numerous Proverbs and Psalms. Each night, I now went back to read again her favorite stories from the gospels of Matthew, Mark, Luke, and John. Never did she tire of hearing the word of God read to her and the comfort and hope it offered.

In the unrelenting progression of her COPD, she was placed on oxygen around the clock. Having become almost completely immobile, her legs were elevated in her recliner nearly twenty-four hours a day. In addition to the complications of her lung disease and of the chronic bronchitis and pneumonia that accompanied it, my mother was also diagnosed with congestive heart failure. One problem seemed to lead to another. Because of the constant sitting position and improper back support from her recliner, she began to experience horrific pain in the lumbar and thoracic areas of her spine.

Having brought Jenelle with me on frequent visits to see her great-grandmother, grandmother, and godmother throughout her childhood, she'd developed a close bond of love for all three. During the times she was home on college break, we'd often bike to the neighboring town to visit with Grandma Van, as we called her. Closing in on her 104th birthday, it was on one of these visits that, as I was bending down to give her a kiss before leaving, I said, "Jesus loves you, Grandma."

In a matter-of-fact tone, she replied, "I know, He's standing right here alongside me."

Never having heard her make a remark like that before, a chill ran down my spine. A short time later, Our Lord called her home.

On the occasions Jenelle would suggest we go to visit my mom, though most often I had already been there, I'd go back again. How she always perked up at the sight of us walking into her room! One thing about my mother, she loved flowers. Being especially fond of the beauty and scent of the rose, we loved to sit with her and reminisce of the sweet fragrance of memories past. With roses, however, come thorns. "Therefore, that I might not become too elated, a thorn in the flesh was given to me…Three times I begged the Lord about this, that it might leave me, but he said to me, 'My grace is sufficient for you, for power is made perfect in weakness'" (2 Corinthians 12:7–9). Feeling sad to see her grandmother undergoing such "thorny times" in the ongoing deterioration of her health, Jenelle was motivated to make for her a bright and beautiful lap quilt. As thrilled as she was to take on the project, she was equally as excited at the prospect of lifting up her grandmother's spirits. Bearing in mind the practicality of the warmth it would provide, she sewed a bright gold plush fleece on the backside of the quilt for her grandma to snuggle up in.

Completely taken aback at its loveliness and even more so at the inspired meaning behind her design, my eyes filled with tears when I saw the completed quilt for the first time. Within its center were two hearts.

"I don't know why," Jenelle explained, "but for some reason, I had to put two hearts on the quilt instead of only one as I planned."

I couldn't help but think of the deeper meaning behind her inspiration to incorporate two hearts in the design, not only in its implication of the love that flowed from her heart to the heart of her grandmother, but also in the significance of the Two Hearts of Jesus and Mary. The thorns that pierced Jesus' most Sacred Heart and those that lay hidden beneath the roses encircling the Immaculate Heart of Mary had been wounded out of love for us. Had it not been for the thorns allowed my mother, how would she have been able to grow closer to God as her life drew close to an end, if not by calling out to Him in her pain? Had she not been allowed to walk with Jesus along the Way of the Cross, how would she have been able to thank Him for the showers of graces being lavished upon her to help her through?

Along with Scripture, I'd sometimes read to my mom excerpts from *The Daily Pilgrimage to Purgatory*.[1] The writings of St. Margaret Mary offers encouragement of how doing simple acts of mortification while still here on earth can serve to replace the much more painful sufferings one would otherwise have to endure in purgatory for the purification of their soul after death.

Visiting my mother one day, I noticed her scapular[2] was no longer around her neck. Having become tattered and broken after accidently going through the washing machine, I felt an urgency to get her a replacement. Symbolizing our dedication to conform our lives after God's own Mother, the scapular reminds us also to trust in her Son. Placing my mom beneath the refuge of Mary's protective mantle, I was constant in summoning the Blessed Virgin Mary to be with her at the hour of her death, the same as I had perceived in my dad's passing.

At a family gathering the next day, my sister-in-law asked, "Sue, how's your mom doing?"

Telling her of the decline of her health and of my intent to replace her scapular, she said, "Oh, hang on a minute." Leaving the room momentarily, she came back saying, "Would you like this scapular to give to your mother? It's been blessed by Pope John Paul II."

Wow! Draping from her hands, she held up a brown scapular[3] she'd bought back from Europe. "I'd love it!" I replied as she handed it off to me in exchange for a hug. My heart imploded in the delight of having received once again the desires of my heart!

Jenelle entered the computer room as I was writing down the names of prayer requests into the Intercessors of Light book.

"Mom," she asked softly, "do you have a minute?"

"Sure," I said. "What's up?"

Seeming somewhat reluctant at first, she began, "You know that song 'I Can Only Imagine'?"

"Yes, I really like it," I responded.

In the song, the artist imagines what it would be like in heaven. The refrain goes like this: "Surrounded by Your Glory, what will my heart feel? Will I dance for You Jesus, or in awe of You be still? Will I stand in Your presence, or to my knees will I fall? Will I sing halleluiah; will I be able to speak at all? I Can Only Imagine, yeah-ah, I can only imagine"[4] (Mercy Me).

"Well," she continued, "I was listening to the song, and the moment I heard the words 'Or to my knees will I fall,' I saw inside my heart an image of grandma. She was down on her knees before the Throne of God. Then, as the song went on playing and the refrain was sung a second time, I saw the same image of her kneeling before the Heavenly Throne. On the third and final refrain, as they sang, 'Or to my knees will I fall,' I saw the image of grandma once more." Sitting quietly for a moment as I took in what she shared, she gently added, "Mom, grandma wasn't in a wheelchair or sitting in her recliner on oxygen. She was down on her knees in adoration before God!"

Envisioning my mom worshipping God face to face, my eyes filled with tears. Getting up from my chair, Jenelle wrapped her arms around me to give me comfort in reversed roles, the same as I'd so often done with my mom. Tears of sorrow and joy began streaming down our faces, as we laughed and cried at the same time. How bitter was the knowledge of my mother's imminent death in contrast to the sweetness of the foreseen ecstasy the Lord had shown of her. "I am your Mother and Jesus is your great friend. Fear nothing in His presence. Give Him your heart. Tell Him of your sufferings from the bottom of your heart, for this way you will be strengthened in prayer. Your heart will be free, at peace and without fear" (Our Lady of Medjugorje).[5]

It was the start of Lent, and just as I'd experienced in the years past, I began suffering from an assortment of trials throughout its duration. I recorded them down in my journal—surface phlebitis, severe stomach pain, fever, nausea, excruciating leg cramps, loss of appetite, bouts of asthma, bronchitis, and so on. On our monthly visit, Father Kieran voiced, "Sue, you're enduring the redemptive sufferings of Christ." But the pain I suffered most was interior, taking an active part in my mother's courageous walk along the Way of the Cross.

Deciding to take a Friday off work to spend the day at Holy Hill during the holiest season of the year, Rob suggested we arrive early to allow time for confession before Mass. Weather permitting, we hoped to pray the Stations of the Cross outdoors.

Discovering there was Exposition of the Blessed Sacrament on the first Friday of the month, what a better way to end our spiritual day of renewal! Staring at Jesus in the Monstrance, my gaze eventually fixated upward on a sculpture positioned directly above. I marveled at the gorgeous image of the Virgin holding the Christ child in her arms. Arrayed in elegant garments of gold, it triggered my memory of the vision of me as a child in a gold dress. On impulse, I asked Jesus; "What about that gold dress?" Knowing that I was to strive for a childlike faith, I felt at times that I was falling under the weight of my cross. In the day-to-day effort of coaching and encouraging my dear mom in her sufferings, though it tore at my heart to see her in such a state, my heart melted just the same in witnessing the courageous way she was embracing her cross. Closing my eyes, I laid all my concerns upon the altar of the Lord. I asked the Father for the Blood of His Son to be poured out upon each of my needs, in particular, that of my mother's ill-health. It was 3:00 p.m., and before departing for home, we prayed the Chaplet of Divine Mercy. "Jesus, I trust in You!"[6] (*Diary*, 47).

On the following evening, leaving the Chapel of Divine Mercy, Rob told me he'd been shown a vision for me.

"I saw you standing in your tan quilted jacket, holding hands with your mother. I could sense the mutual love you shared for each other, and I was made aware of how pleased God is in the way you minister to her each day." Unable to speak, tears of happiness filled my eyes. "Oh," he said in driving off, "I almost forgot. I was also given two words for you."

"What were they?" I questioned.

"Gold slippers," he replied. "The Lord has awarded you gold slippers to go with your little gold dress."

Instantly remembering my spontaneous prayer before the Eucharistic Jesus at Holy Hill, I had not shared with Rob the spontaneous supplication that had flowed from my heart. Heavily laden with concern for my mom, what I had asked, in essence, concerning my little gold dress, was whether or not I was growing in childlike faith. Joyful tears filled my eyes. "Amen, I say to you, whoever does not accept the kingdom of God like a child will not enter it." Then he embraced them and blessed them, placing his hands on them (Mark 10:15–16).

Over the span of twenty years, there'd been numerous times that I rushed off in the middle of the night to meet my mother in the ER, pleading for God's mercy. Once there, as relieved as she was to see me, I was thankful to see her alive. With flu season in full swing, a number of the residents at my mom's assisted living home were coming down with the respiratory virus. In her already weakened condition, her immune system ultimately gave way in succumbing to the flu. Struggling to breathe, she was transported by ambulance to the hospital in the wee hours of the morning.

This time, she was not treated and released as usual, but was admitted into the hospital. Deep in my heart, I had a foreboding sense that my mother's life hung in the balance. After calling a few of my siblings to spread the word, I sensed very strongly that I should call for a priest. Later that same day, my mom opened her eyes to receive Communion before Father Patrick anointed her with the powerful healing oils of the Sacrament of the Sick.

Walking into her hospital room the next morning, I was delighted to see the nurses preparing for her release! "Magnify the LORD with me;/ let us exalt his name together" (Psalm 34:4). Thrilled at her sudden improvement, I called Father Patrick to tell him the great news. Expressing his joy, he added, "Don't hesitate to call back should it be necessary for me to anoint your mother again."

"Thank you, Father!" I said heartily. "How much time should elapse in between?"

Reassuringly, he offered, "I could come again in a couple of weeks if need be."

In the days following her first hospitalization, two of my sisters stopped by to visit my mom when I was there. Asking if they'd be willing to kneel down at her bedside to pray, I opened my little blue Pieta Book. Praying out loud the three beautiful prayers for the dying, they were honored to partake. Telling them of a "Devotion to the Drops of Blood Lost by Our Lord Jesus Christ,"[7] I retrieved the holy card from my Bible to show them of the splendid graces of saying it. Joining hands with our mother, we prayed the devotion together, suggesting to them afterward, "On days you can't be here to pray it with Mom, you could pray it in proxy for her."

On Good Friday, I began the Novena of Divine Mercy. Feeling the triumphant joy of Easter Sunday two days later, I articulated to Rob how deeply I longed for my mom to be able to see the beautiful flowers on the altar and to partake in the celebration of Mass. Deciding to stop off at the Chapel of Divine Mercy before bringing her Communion, Rob handed me something off of the shelf. In my hand was a glorious picture of the Easter Altar that I desired my mother could see! "Find your delight in the LORD/ who will give you your heart's desire" (Psalm 37:4).

The next morning, I was awakened early by the phone.

"Sue, it's about your mom," the caretaker said on the other end of the line. "She's having great difficulty in breathing."

"Please tell her I'll meet her at the hospital," I voiced. With her recent bout of the flu, even the smallest flicker of lingering infection had the potential to start aflame a fire even more devastating than the first. Walking into her room in the ER, I noticed right away how flushed her face was. Looking up, she offered a weak smile. Taking hold of her hand, I asked, "How are you doing, Mom?"

"Not too good," she said softly. Admitted into the intensive care unit, she was placed on a ventilator.

My mom was a fighter. Never giving up in the struggles of COPD, despite the severity of the episode she now suffered, by day two she was bouncing back enough to be moved out of the ICU. Happy to have her family gathered at her side, the same ventilator that had been such a welcomed relief to her the day before had now become more of a hindrance in preventing her from joining in on the conversation. At her request, the nurse released the tight suction of the mask from her face. Content in being able to join in on the chitchat, it wasn't before long that her cheerful nature and lighthearted wit had us all laughing.

Throughout the evening, the two nurses assigned to my mother's care seemed to take pleasure in the gala surrounding her. But as the evening drew on, I noticed a somewhat disgruntled manner forming between the two, seemingly trying to conceal whatever irritated them. At first, I discarded it as something unrelated to my mother, but as I continued to pick up on their dispiritedness, I grew concerned. As they walked out into the hallway, I went to catch up to them.

"Thanks for taking such good care of my mom," I said. "But I wanted to ask you, is something wrong?" Caught completely off guard, it appeared as though they didn't want to say too much. "Can you tell me what's wrong?" I asked politely.

With a heavy spirit, one of the nurses said, "I'm really sorry, but something is terribly wrong."

Somberly, they reported that after my mother was already responding to treatment, the doctor assigned to her care when she was admitted wrote the order to rescind from her the vital and necessary medical treatment conducive to life. Other than the IV drip consisting only of water, it contained no nourishment of any kind to sustain her life or the antibiotic necessary to recover from the infection. Essentially, the doctor put into motion my mother's death. Being witness to her improved condition and jubilant interaction with her family, the compassionate nurses were angered over the doctor's decision of death over life. Stunned at what they divulged, I was speechless. Reaching out to squeeze my hand, they returned to their duties.

I well understood that my mom was nearing the end of her pilgrimage here on earth. But I'd always thought it would be on the decree predestined by God, and not as a result of a decision made by a random doctor. As medical power of attorney, I spoke with my mom more than once of her wishes concerning her end-of-life healthcare. Considering that she was coherent and in a sound state of mind, it seemed preposterous that her doctor would make such a radical decision without first speaking to either of us. With her progressed lung disease, would my mom live another few months or perhaps until the next flu season? Only God knew the answer to that. But what was indisputable to me was that my mother still had within her the fight to live. Certain she would have opposed the orders that sealed her fate, as her advocate, I arranged to meet with her doctor as soon as possible. Learning she'd already left for the evening and was off the following day, I set up a time to meet with the doctor on Thursday.

My heart became heavy in recollecting the Terri Schiavo case.[8] With numerous prayers being lifted up by the faithful around the world, her parents' hands were tied in attempting to protect the life of their beloved daughter, who wanted to live. In the controversy surrounding it, Jenelle was moved to take up her drawing pad to sketch out an oversized "Ribbon of Life" quilt in her memory. Its design depicted the value of human life, not according to the designs of man, but of God's, to protect and promote the value of human life from the moment of conception to the natural ending of one's life. Mailing off her completed project to Fr. Frank Pavone, Terri's grieving family received the quilt she'd sewn her heart and soul into. In a letter of gratitude, they indicated that the banner quilt would hang at the Terri Schiavo Life & Hope Network in the office of Terri's mother.

"Ribbon of life" banner quilt, *Quilting Cause*

Visiting with my mother the following day, her body was beginning to succumb to the infections invading her system. Unable to meet with her doctor until the following day, I feared her health status was approaching the point of no return. Later that same evening as Rob and I prayed our nightly Efficacious Novena to the Sacred Heart of Jesus, he was shown a vision of an angel. In her hands, she held *The Book of Life*.

"In the book, I saw written your mother's name," he said.

Feeling my heart pierced, I asked, "Did you sense her death would be soon, or will be a ways off yet?"

"Soon," he replied softly. Inwardly, I'd already begun to grieve.

As I drove to Mass on Thursday morning, I began praying the "Peace Rosary"[9] as taught by Our Lady of Medjugorje to the visionaries. My troubled heart became settled in the understanding that nothing could be assailed against my mother, or anyone, unless the good Lord allowed it. That didn't validate a wrong as being right, nor implicate God as the assailer. But remembering Romans 8:28, it accentuated to me that good will come out of all things for those who trust in the Lord. Placing all of my trust in God, I implored for Mary and Joseph to be with my mom, asking that she have a holy and peaceful death. I prayed for Divine Wisdom in the decisions I would have to make concerning her. Feeling my inner peace return, I was learning that it is within God's Holy Will that lays hidden the peace that goes far beyond the perception of our understanding.

Receiving Jesus in Holy Communion, I surrendered my pain as I pled for His precious Blood to be poured out over my sweet mother. At the holy water fountain after Mass, a friend from church walked toward me and said, "Sue, I'd like you to meet Paz."

As my eyes fell upon the elderly little Filipino woman standing next to her, she looked up and said; "Hello. My name is Paz, and it means 'Peace.'" Sensing her deep spirituality, I found it interesting that after literally begging for God's peace, I'd actually be introduced to one of His faithful followers whose name literally means peace! "I will listen for the word of God; surely the LORD will proclaim peace To his people, to the faithful, to those who trust in Him (Psalm 85:9).

Before going back to the hospital to be with my mom, I stopped off at the Tabernacle to talk with Jesus. In heart-to-heart conversation, I surrendered to Him the way in which my mother's passing would unfold, asking Him to choose whether I or another sibling would be with her. "Please don't let her die alone," I prayed. Returning to my mom's side, she was drifting in and out of sleep. Wasting no time, I called Father Patrick to administer to her once again the anointing of the sick.

"I'll come this afternoon," he assured.

As God's providence would have it, just as my sisters and I were about to begin the Chaplet of Divine Mercy at my mother's bedside, Father Patrick walked into the room at exactly 3:00 p.m. Overjoyed, it was as though Jesus Himself had shown up in my mom's greatest need. Jesus had recommended to St. Faustina for the faithful to pray the Chaplet to aid the dying: "At the hour of their death, I defend as My own glory every soul that will say this Chaplet; or when others say it for a dying person, the pardon is the same"[10] (*Diary*, 811). As family members stopped in throughout the day, I'd initiate praying for my mom a rosary or chaplet, while other times, I'd simply pray silently to myself.

Later on that evening, I finally had the opportunity to meet with the doctor in charge of my mom's case. One on one, I spoke with her of the family's disheartenment involving the irreversible order given to terminate medical treatment and nourishment for my mother. I spoke with her of the conflict of interest her erroneous decision had made on my attempt to honor my mother's end-of-life wishes. Trying to talk with her sensibly about my views on the respect of life "from the womb to the tomb," it became unmistakably apparent that my words were falling on deaf ears.

Getting up suddenly, the doctor appeared to "walk with a purpose" into my mother's room. With most of my siblings gathered at the foot of her bed where she lay sleeping, she went directly up to my mother's face and said, "Gloria, can you hear me?"

Without delay, my mom opened her eyes and stared into the eyes of the doctor. In a clear-cut manner, the physician articulated to her that her COPD had progressed to the point that she was not going to make it. The doctor then asked if she'd like hospice to be called in to keep her comfortable until the end. It was at that precise moment that I saw in my mother's eyes a deep pain that emanated out from her anguished soul. I thought of "Jesus forsaken." Shaking her head no, the doctor turned abruptly, exiting the room.

Quickly stepping up to my mom's side, I stroked her hair. Telling her how very much I loved her, I reminded her that God was in control. "Jesus loves you," I whispered while kissing her forehead. Closing her eyes, my mother relinquished her fight to live in exchange for the promise of eternal glory. In witness of the bitter agony I'd seen stemming out from her soul, I knew that she was on the Cross with Jesus. "And at three o'clock Jesus cried out in a loud voice, '*Eloi, Eloi, lema sabachthani?*' which is translated, 'My God, my God, why have you forsaken me?'" (Mark 15:34).

During our prayers that evening, I surrendered the pain of my heart into the Sorrowful and Immaculate Heart of Mary, asking that she bring it to Jesus. All night long, my slumber was sweet and intermingled with prayer for my mom. The moment I awoke the following morning, the Lord showed to me a vision. I saw a very bright and luminous Host coming down from the heavens. As it traveled about two-thirds of the way downward to earth, it stopped. I then saw a beautiful white bird with light grey undertones beneath its wings fly out from the Host and begin to soar downward. Immediately following, I saw a second bird fly out from the Host, identical to the first, followed by a third and then a fourth. Single file, the birds continued in flight until, upon reaching the earth, all four turned swiftly in a boomerang-type movement as they flew back toward heaven. Seconds later, I was shown another vision of the number 4. It was lit up in red, looking somewhat like a digital number on an alarm clock.

Having no idea of the meaning behind the visions shown to me that Friday morning, I had the infused knowledge that they had to do with my mother. Turning over to look at the sculpted figures of the Sacred and Immaculate Hearts that hung from the wall, I prayed my morning offering while depositing all my joys and sorrow of the new day into the Two Hearts of Jesus and Mary. Pondering the events of the week gone by, I found myself longing for the chance to be with my mother alone, to read the Scripture promises she'd grown to love. My thoughts then turned to a woman who had shared with me of her call to pray for the dying. Suddenly, the desire welled up inside me to ask Theresa to pray for my mom. But it was much too early to call her, and setting the idea aside, I got out of bed. My main objective was to shower and get up to the hospital to be with my mom as soon as possible.

As I walked through the parking lot, I met up with my sister, who had offered to do the night watch.

"I'm so glad you're here," she said to me. "I have to leave and I didn't want mom to be alone."

Thanking her, I told Deb that I'd be staying until 11:45 a.m., when I planned to head across town to meet Jenelle for Mass. Making my way up to my mom's room, I thanked God along the way for granting the desires of my heart in having alone time with her.

Lying peacefully under the mask of the oxygen, she was unresponsive to my touch. Kissing her, I said "Mom, I'm here… mom." No response. Noticing her breathing had become shallow, I knew she had entered into the active process of dying. Bending down closely to her ear, I wrapped my arm around her as I began telling my sweet mother all that was on my heart to say. I thanked her for opening herself up to the plethora of God's grace in regard to the suffering she endured with Jesus. I spoke softly into her ear of the privilege it had been for me to help her embrace her cross. I whispered to her of the love I'll always feel for her, both as my mom and cherished friend.

Then, as I promised God I would do three years prior for all her remaining days of life on earth, I pulled up a chair right next to her bedside. Taking hold of her hand, I began reading to my mother for the very last time, the mighty word of God.

> "Of this you have already heard through the word of truth, the gospel, that has come to you. Just as in the whole world it is bearing fruit and growing, so also among you, from the day you heard it and came to know the grace of God in truth." (Colossians 1:5–6)

With impeccable timing, just shortly before it was time for me to leave for Mass, my aunt and uncle showed up unexpectedly. Seeing the graveness of her condition, I told them I'd been reading Scripture to her for most of the morning. In noticing my aunt's eyes light up, I said, "I have a few minutes before I have to leave. Would you like me to read more?"

"Oh, yes!" she replied, "I'd enjoy that."

Assuring my aunt that my sisters would be arriving shortly, I tenderly kissed my mom good-bye.

Spotting Jenelle in the last pew of the church, I knelt down alongside of her. Shaking my head, I whispered to her that her grandmother's life was quickly fading. Content to be in church, I petitioned for Jesus and Mary and hosts of angels to assist and defend my mom in the hour of death. Consumed in prayer, it wasn't until the start of the Mass that I noticed Theresa in the pew directly in front of us! My heart imploded with joy in the knowledge that the Lord had once again given to me the desires of my heart!

Turning around at the handshake of peace, I quickly whispered, "Theresa, I wanted to call you this morning to ask if you'd pray for my mother. She's dying."

In a loving and compassionate manner, she responded kindly by saying, "As soon as Mass is over, I'll go and spend an hour before the Blessed Sacrament for your mom."

Reaching out to hug her, I thanked her from the bottom of my heart. As I received Communion, I asked Jesus to be with my mother spiritually, and as the priest gave the blessing at the end of the Mass, I made the sign of the Cross as I prayed, "Sweet Jesus, please extend Your priestly blessing to my mother." Having offered our Masses in petition for her to have a holy death, Jenelle and I first walked over to the holy water fountain before going up to the Tabernacle to pray. Standing there was my friend Debbie, who rarely attended the noon Mass. Telling her of my mom's grave condition and of the agonizing pain I saw in her eyes the evening before, she asked, "Are you praying the Divine Mercy Novena?"

"Yes," I replied.

"Sue!" she exclaimed, "your mom was allowed to suffer the anguish of her impending death on the seventh day of the novena! That's the day Jesus asks us to pray for the souls who hope in His mercy through their suffering."

What great consolation I found in my friend's words. Hugging me, she promised to pray a rosary for my mom.

Going first to the Marian grotto to light a candle, Jenelle and I knelt side by side before Jesus in the Tabernacle. Removing my Divine Mercy Novena from inside my Bible cover, I prayed it before saying a rosary for my dear mom. Suddenly, my heart squeezed in sorrow, feeling within myself the urgent need to get back to the hospital.

"Jenelle," I whispered, "we have to leave."

Walking out of the church, I resisted the urge to run to the car to sooner get to my mother's side.

Surprised, in reaching her room we were greeted at the doorway by two of my sisters. Puzzled at their mutual expressions of joy, they stated, "Mom passed away about ten minutes ago." My heart sank. Going on, they explained, "We were standing on opposite sides of her bed and holding her hands. Praying out loud the 'Drops of Blood Devotion' you taught us, right as we said the final Amen of the last Glory Be, she breathed her last!" Hugging and comforting each other, we circled around her bedside to pray the Divine Mercy Chaplet. "In the midst of all afflictions and adversities they go forward, confident of Your mercy. These souls are united to Jesus and carry all mankind on their shoulders. These souls will not be judged severely, but Your mercy will embrace them as they depart from this life"[11] (*Diary*, 1225).

Overcome in awe of the marvelous ways our Lord had surrounded my mother with prayers of the faithful during the time of her passing, it all started with granting my heart's desire to read alone to her His promises in Scripture. In the gift of Theresa's Eucharistic holy hour for my mom during the hour of her death, in the blessing of my friend's encouragement and prayers, in the opportunity allowed Jenelle and me in offering our Mass and praying for my mom before Jesus in the Tabernacle, in the special grace of feeling my heart being squeezed at the time of her death, and in the intimate blessing of my mother expiring the moment my sisters finished praying "The Devotion to the Drops of Blood Lost by Our Lord on His Way to Calvary," she had been blessed! Eternally grateful for the wonderful grace of ministering to my precious mother during the three years I believed the Lord had extended her life, His desire was that she become holy.

In the sorrow of her passing, Rob and I invited the family to congregate at our home that evening. It had been a long day, and as we settled down before praying our night prayers, I suddenly remembered the visions shown to me earlier that morning regarding my mom.

"Hon," I said softly, "will you please pray with me for God's wisdom concerning the visions?"

"Sure," he answered sympathetically.

During our prayer time, he received an interior locution involving it. "The answer lies in the fourth day of 'The Twelve Days of Christmas' carol," he told me.

"I was shown the number four immediately following the vision of the four birds!" I said excitedly. "But I can't remember what 'my true love' brings on the fourth day!"

Together, we began chiming out as many verses as we could remember, seemingly all except the fourth day of Christmas!

Desperate to learn the meaning of the vision, I called Jenelle despite the late hour.

"Four calling birds!" she revealed.

The moment I received the knowledge behind the vision concerning my mom on the day of her passing, I felt a warm sensation wash over me. The song had been inspired somewhere prior to the 1800s, when Roman Catholics in England weren't permitted to openly practice their faith. For fear of persecution, someone during that era wrote "The Twelve Days of Christmas"[12] to catechize the youth. Each of the twelve days leading up to Christmas possessed a code word with a religious meaning behind it to help the children learn their faith. "On the fourth day of Christmas my true love gave to me, Four-Calling-Birds."[13] Learning that "my true Love" symbolized the Almighty God, how utterly amazed I was that the "four calling birds" represented the four Gospels of Matthew, Mark, Luke, and John!

Surviving her bout of pneumonia three years prior, I'd been faithful in keeping my promise to read Scripture to my mother every day. Beginning with the four Gospels of Matthew, Mark, Luke, and John, after reading her the entire New Testament, I read anew to her the "Good News" of the four Gospels! Four calling birds and four Gospels! Having honored God's request to bring my mother Communion every Sunday, to be shown a vision of Jesus descending down from heaven in the form of a Host on the morning of her death was, for me, an absolute testimony of His true presence in the Holy Eucharist! In the day-to-day witness of my mother's self-abandonment into God's Will, I was saturated in the blessed assurance of the victory she attained. Shouldering her cross with Christ, no greater peace did she possess than during the last three years of her life, when, as her cross grew heavier, her burden became lighter.

The "four calling birds" flying out from the center of the host as Jesus *came down* from heaven to *call* my mother home signified to me the transforming power of the Eucharist. "For the bread of God is that which comes down from heaven and gives life to the world" (John 6:33). Through it, Jesus was fulfilling His promise not to leave us as orphans, but to remain with us until the end of time. He remains with us not symbolically, but physically in His true presence. It was in receiving Jesus in Holy Communion and through hearing and believing in the Gospel that my mother secured her eternal resting place in His kingdom!

Friends and family gathered at the morning visitation to pay their respects. Marilyn, a woman from our neighborhood growing up, was available to sing one of my mother's favorite songs at her funeral, the "Ave Maria." With only fifteen minutes remaining until the start of Mass, the immediate family began filing up to view my mother for the last time before the closing of the casket. Standing last in line, Jenelle asked, "Mom, would it be okay for me to exchange my crystal rosary for Grandma's?" Looking up, the dress selected by her and my sister for my mother to be buried in glistened in mother-of-pearl sequins. Draped from her hands was the luminescent rosary she'd picked out on one of our daytrips, with the rosary bracelet from Medjugorje still on her wrist. Not visible to the eye was the scapular blessed by Pope John Paul II.

"She would be honored," I comforted.

Approaching the casket, the funeral attendant quickly stepped up to alert Jenelle there was five minutes remaining before the start of the 10:00 a.m. Mass. Kneeling down for a moment of prayer, she rose to gently make the rosary exchange. Conscious not to go over the time allotted her, she checked her watch. Stepping aside for the casket to be closed, it was 9:57 a.m. Throughout the Mass for my mother, my heart overflowed in thanksgiving of the graces our Lord had lavished upon her. Walking with Jesus in her sufferings, she would share also in His Resurrection. My tears were those of immense Easter joy! "I am not dying, I am entering into life" (St. Therese, the Little Flower).[14]

Following the burial ceremony at the cemetery, Jenelle discovered her watch had stopped ticking at 9:57 a.m., at the exact time she'd finished making the rosary exchange before the casket was closed.

"Mom, the quartz battery was almost brand new!" she said excitedly. Later placing it inside of her pewter trinket box, her watch held for her a sentimental value worth preserving, a memory when, for her and her dearly loved grandmother, time stood still.

That evening, Rob and I decided to seek out the tranquility of the Chapel of Divine Mercy. Surrendering my sorrow and heartache back to God, how grateful I was for the numerous consolations and blessings received along the way. On the drive home, Rob told me of a vision shown him. In it, he saw the two of us adoring Jesus in the same place where we were kneeling, in the center-front row before the Monstrance. With us, however, was my mother. Clothed in the same dress she'd been buried in just hours before, she was on her knees. Bending down toward the floor with her arms extended out, she was in worship before the Most Blessed Sacrament of the Altar. "But I can enter your house/ because of your great love./ I can worship in your holy temple/ because of my reverence for you, LORD" (Psalm 5:8).

How elated I was to envision my mother this way! No longer did we have to "imagine" what she would do upon finding herself surrounded by God's glory. How great was the solace of "knowing" that it was to her knees she fell in humble adoration before the Throne of God! In fulfillment of the prophetic vision shown to Jenelle, there was no more wheelchair, no more suffering, no more struggling to breathe.

> "Surrounded by Your Glory, what will my heart feel? Will I dance for You Jesus, or in awe of You be still? Will I stand in Your presence, or to my knees will I fall? Will I sing halleluiah; will I be able to speak at all? I Can Only Imagine, yeah-ah. I Can Only Imagine."[15]
>
> —Mercy Me

Virgin of all virgins blest!
Listen to my fond request:
  Let me share your grief divine.

—Stabat Mater

My Saviour! I cheerfully accept all the painful dispositions, in which it is Thy pleasure to place me. My wish is in all things to conform myself to Thy holy will. Whenever I kiss Thy Cross, it is to show that I submit perfectly to mine. Amen.

—Saint Margaret Mary of Alacoque[16]

Stations of the Cross

Twelfth Station
Jesus Dies on the Cross

Here at the foot of the Cross, souls are clothed in light and inflamed with love. Here souls receive wings that will carry them still higher. May this Cross be always for us our place of rest, our school of perfection, our beloved inheritance.

—Padre Pio

Hunger for Holiness

It was during Lent preceding my mother's death that we first began realizing the significance of the "Crown of Thorns" picture in our prayer room. Pointing to the framed image propped on a decorative floor easel across from where he was sitting, Rob questioned, "Do you see anything unusual in that picture?"

Examining it, I asked, "What do you mean?"

Without answering, he called Jenelle into the room, asking the same. Unable to make out what he was referring to, he then instructed us to focus our eyes directly below Jesus' beard. Then we saw it—a full-bodied image of a man standing within the center of the bodice of Christ.

"It looks like you!" Jenelle said to him. Truly, there was no denying that the image within the picture bore a strong resemblance to Rob. Further explaining, he said, "I noticed it while we were praying the rosary, receiving the interior knowledge that it was me."

Throughout the course of Lent, he'd discover other images within the picture as well. Next was a somewhat abstract figure of a woman who he claimed was me. Astonished to see the figure of a woman standing off to the right of where Rob's image was within the picture, her outline was made up of Jesus' left shoulder and the outer edge of His bodice. Holding up a candle in each hand, her head was bowed before the pierced head of Jesus and angled slightly in the direction of where Rob was depicted.

"That can't be me," I objected. "That person looks holy."

"It is you!" Rob persuaded. "I received the knowledge that it's you."

Yet another occasion as we were praying the rosary, glancing up at the picture of the Sacred Head so wounded for the prideful sins of mankind, Rob identified Jenelle within the print. "Look to the left of where I am on the picture, and you'll see where she's kneeling," he instructed. Sure enough, off to the right of Jesus' bodice and facing in Rob's direction was a young woman kneeling with a veil on her head. Instantly, it reminded me of a side portrayal of St. Bernadette.

"That's Jenelle?" I asked.

"Yes," he affirmed.

"Why do we look so saintly while you look like a regular person positioned in between?" I questioned.

"Because it will be through your prayers that I'll remain grounded in faith." Seemingly already well-grounded in faith to me, I wondered just what it all meant.

Awaking to the first anniversary of the passing of Pope John Paul II, I put on a pot of coffee before joining Rob in our prayer room to say our Sunday morning rosary. Ever since receiving the late pope's intended "message of love" following the St. Therese novena I prayed for him in the days surrounding his death, I felt a special closeness with him. Now, one year later, I'd just finished praying a novena honoring his special date of commemoration. As we were praying, Rob received within his heart a message beckoning us to come to the Chapel of Divine Mercy that day at 3:00 p.m. Given that it was Pope John Paul II who established the feast of Divine Mercy Sunday, I was especially pleased with our summons to pray before the Blessed Sacrament right at the "The Hour of Mercy" on the anniversary of his birth into eternal life! How providential that our Lord would call him home on the vigil of such great a feast in which the unfathomable mercy of God is celebrated!

Later on that same afternoon, I began feeling the ravaging effects of my low iron resulting from my failing kidneys. Shivering cold, I felt tired and completely fatigued. Going to Rob, I asked,

"Hon, do you think it's imperative that we go to the chapel at 3:00 p.m.?"

"That was the message. Why?" he asked.

"Well, I'm so cold and exhausted that I'm not sure I can, but I really don't want to disobey God."

"Sue," he said reassuringly, "God knows our hearts. He already knows how much we were both looking forward to going to the chapel during the hour of mercy. We'll pray it from home, and if you're feeling up to it, we can do a holy hour either before or after Mass."

Regardless of the justifiable reason that I was unable to get to the chapel, as I lay in bed resting, my heart ached in not having been able to do as God had asked of us. Knowing in my head that our Lord did not hold against me the physical limitations of my disease, it was from the very depths of my heart that I prayed, "Jesus, You know how much I wanted to honor your request, and You also know how deeply saddened I now am for not being able to. If it would please You, I'd like to get up at 3:00 a.m. to pray the Chaplet of Divine Mercy on my knees. If so, please awaken me at that time."

Feeling somewhat rejuvenated, we left for Mass early to spend a Eucharistic holy hour in honor of John Paul II. Returning home, we were thrilled to find a movie playing on EWTN depicting his life! Afterward, as we were praying our nightly novena to the Sacred Heart of Jesus before going to sleep, Rob heard interiorly these words, "You will be hearing from John Paul II again." In his heart, he received the knowledge that the late pope was interceding on our behalf! At exactly three o'clock in the morning, I awoke from sleep. What a true blessing it was for me to kneel on the hardwood floor to pray the Chaplet of Divine Mercy as I had promised! "Thank you, sweet Jesus!" I prayed, before crawling back in bed.

How humbled I was for God to make known to us on the first anniversary of Pope John Paul II's passing that he was interceding for us! My mind traveled back to five months earlier in the treasured memory of kneeling before the closed casket of John Paul II in Rome. Having prayed for his intercession for my family and the ministry we'd been called to, I began piecing together special dates in my life that seemingly coincided with his. Elected pope on my twenty-fifth birthday, his pontificate lasted for twenty-five years. It was in the same year he was elected pope that I had first learned I had inherited PKD. Years later, on my forty-ninth birthday, and on the anniversary of his pontificate, I received the *dark* news that my kidneys were failing in contrast to the "Mysteries of Light"[1] that Pope John Paul II added to the rosary on the very same day!

Thinking of Jenelle's inspiration to design the elegant, handmade papal quilt both in the late pope's memory and in honor of the "Year of the Eucharist"[2] he had declared in celebration of God's greatest gift to the Church, it came to a close in the same month we went on pilgrimage to Europe. I wondered just how it would be that we'd "hear from John Paul II again."

Another day as we were praying a rosary in our prayer room, Rob was made aware of a fourth image within the "Crown of Thorns" picture. This disclosure would touch my heart most dramatically. In the face of Christ was the image of Pope John Paul II standing upright and clothed in pontificate attire. In his hands he held the Papal Cross. Amazingly, our three images fully made up the "Body of Christ," the Church, while the image of Pope John Paul II was within the "Head of Christ," as vicar of Jesus, the Head, stemming all the way back to His commission to St. Peter as the first pope in the one, true, apostolic Church.

In the plethora of graces being poured out on us, we discovered God's grace to be especially encompassing to those experiencing adversity. "But if by grace, it is no longer because of works; otherwise grace would no longer be grace" (Romans 11:6). No one goes through life completely unscathed of its afflictions, because to follow Jesus means also to walk with Him in the valleys of life. To link one's struggles to our Savior means to gain in His redemption! To fully rely on divine providence, means to blossom right where we are in all of life's circumstances to bear fruit for the kingdom.

Secular society neither understands the paradox of the cross nor of the irony and contradiction surrounding it. Failing to comprehend that Jesus' glory is directly connected to His suffering and death on the Cross, many are unmindful of the victory attained by walking with Jesus in times of tribulation. Unaware of the unfailing love of God or that there's no pain on earth that could equal the loss of heaven, they despise the cross. Wandering off from the faith, they go in search of an easier path, oftentimes resulting in rash decisions and further devastation. "For it was fitting that he, for whom and through whom all things exist, in bringing many children to glory, should make the leader to their salvation perfect through suffering" (Hebrews 2:10).

In a culture that opposes the cross, a life filled with difficulties and challenges is viewed as the course of demise. But in the spiritual life, the same obstacles despised in the eyes of the world are valued by God's righteous ones as a source through which they can ascend to higher levels of holiness. By persisting on using the struggles of everyday life as tools of instruction in learning how to become holy, one will gain a far greater insight into the value of uniting their trials with Jesus.

> "In this you rejoice, although now for a little while you may have to suffer through various trials, so that the genuineness of your faith, more precious than gold that is perishable even though tested by fire, may prove to be for praise, glory, and honor at the revelation of Jesus Christ."
>
> 1 Peter 1:6–7

Challenged with the daunting task of planning my meals with minimal amounts of protein, phosphorous, potassium, sodium, and calcium, I was extremely self-disciplined with the strict food limitations allowed me. In Eucharistic adoration, our Lord would often show Rob visions of various foods for me to consume—tuna, blueberries, raspberries, two ounces of red wine, red grapes, carrots, artichokes, tomatoes, specific herbal teas, and the like. Within his heart, he received an interior locution that I was to bless my kidneys each day with St. Raphael healing oil as well. Faithfully, I did the things the Lord instructed me to do.

On my monthly visit with my nephrologist, I reported to him that I'd been experiencing constant nausea for nearly the entire four weeks since my last visit. A symptom of uremia, in which the kidneys not only deplete valuable nutrients but fail in excreting poisonous toxins from the blood, he offered me no relief other than to say it was to be expected. But because I was meticulously keeping my blood minerals in check, I suggested to Rob that we stop off at the Chapel of Divine Mercy to ask the Divine Physician His advice concerning it. In the state of contemplative prayer, he was shown a vision of a scrumptious looking donut for me.

Smiling, I asked, "I get to have a donut?"

Typically shown foods of a much healthier nature, in our weekday fast, we were in the habit of denying ourselves sweets. Amazingly, within a half hour of eating the donut, my queasiness was gone. Having voiced concern to my doctor the month before in noting that my blood sugars were below the normal range, it was simply by adding more complex carbs to my diet that my nausea completely vanished.

As I was praying one day, I was inspired to begin a monthly novena to Jesus in the Most Blessed Sacrament of the Altar.

Composing a prayer from my heart, it was with great zeal that I promised the King of all kings to come before Him in worship for nine consecutive days each month. But on the first day of my Eucharistic novena, for three months in a row, I came under strong diabolical attack. Ever since being called into intercessory prayer, which included praying fervently for the salvation of souls, we were no strangers to intermittent assaults from the forces of darkness. "Put on the armor of God so that you may be able to stand firm against the tactics of the devil" (Ephesians 6:11).

Seeking God's protection, we went to the Chapel of Divine Mercy. In prayer, Rob was shown a vision of him and me sitting in the back of what looked to be a WWII army truck with a canvas top. Positioned right in between the two benches that were lined with soldiers, he received the interior knowledge that they were praying for us. Waging war against the principalities of evil in the spiritual battle for souls, the soldiers represented God's righteous ones who, as "soldiers of the faith," intercede in prayer for His people. "Then war broke out in heaven; Michael and his angels battled against the dragon. The dragon and its angels fought back, but they did not prevail and there was no longer any place for them in heaven" (Revelation 12:7–8).

To be reflections of God's light in our darkened world, we must first hunger for holiness within ourselves. Only then will we be able to lead others onto the path of holiness through the exemplary standard in which we lead our daily lives. To combat the idea of thinking it unlikely for us to become holy, we must remember that in surrendering one's life to God, He will take us from where we are to where we need to be. The more that Rob and I brought ourselves closer to Jesus, the closer He came to us.

A day no longer went by that we didn't receive the encouragement and hope He offered.

With the severity of the leg cramps I was suffering, the nephrologist's assistant noticed my sodium level was hovering around the low-normal range.

"How much water do you drink a day?" she asked.

Quick to answer, it had been over a year that I'd been faithfully drinking exactly six bottles of water a day according to the revelation Rob received in Eucharistic adoration for me to do.

"Six bottles," I said.

"I'll tell you what," she surmised, "why don't you try drinking less water each day."

Hearing her words, my heart sank. Since the amount of water I was drinking was in direct correlation to what the Lord indicated I drink, her suggestion left me unsettled. Heading over to the Chapel of Divine Mercy, we decided to seek once again, the guidance of the Divine Physician.

From my heart, I prayed, "Jesus, because You instructed me to drink six bottles of water each day, I don't plan on changing it unless You direct me otherwise. How many bottles of water am I to drink?"

While adoring Jesus, the problem at hand was completely drowned out in the overwhelming presence of the Lord. Right as we bowed down on the floor in reverence prior to leaving, Rob received interiorly this message: "The number of bottles of water is the same as the number of jugs of water turned into wine at the Wedding Feast at Cana."

Ecstatic to have received an answer, "The Wedding Feast at Cana" was where Jesus performed His first miracle on earth, and the mystery of the rosary that I offered for priests in the changing of bread and wine into the Body and Blood of Christ!

"Were there seven jugs?" I asked Rob.

"I'm thinking there were only five," he replied.

Reaching to get my Bible, I couldn't turn the pages fast enough to read. "His mother said to the servers, 'Do whatever he tells you.' Now there were six stone water jars there" (John 2:5-6). How moved I was that our Lord would confirm that I was to continue doing exactly as He had instructed to keep my kidneys hydrated. My heart smiled in viewing my lab results on the following month, which indicated my sodium level had raised well within normal limits.

While in Eucharistic adoration one evening, Rob was shown a vision of the two of us kneeling inside a small room consisting of only three walls. Noting that we were before the Blessed Sacrament, he then saw Jesus off to the right, who was a third of the way up in mortaring the rocks of the fourth wall around us. Interiorly, Rob heard the words, "Get My sandals, we're getting ready to go."

Jesus, the Master Builder, calls each of us to strengthen the foundation of our faith in the trials we suffer. The mortar signified the seal of our commitment of coming before His true presence in the Blessed Sacrament. The stones He was using were taken directly from the rocky path of carrying our crosses with Him. Rebuilding us spiritually, Jesus was closing us in as His very own. "Come to him, a living stone, rejected by human beings but chosen and precious in the sight of God, and, like living stones, let yourselves be built into a spiritual house to be a holy priesthood to offer spiritual sacrifices acceptable to God through Jesus Christ" (1 Peter 2:4—5).

Under the weight of life's crosses in the pressures of the world, it's important to endure all things in hope. On our frequent visits to the Chapel of Divine Mercy, Our Lord would sometimes allow me to see images within the Host of His Holy Face and that of His Holy Mother. During the season of Lent, I'd often see within the Eucharist the three crosses of Calvary, or of Jesus carrying His Cross.

While in contemplative prayer before the Blessed Sacrament, Rob was shown a vision of a long banquet table draped in a spotless white cloth. Seated around the table were the devoted members of the Intercessors of Light prayer group. Noticing that one chair was empty, he wondered who was missing. Interiorly, he received God's wisdom that the empty chair didn't represent someone's absence, but that in praying for the needs of others, it signified that there's always room for one more.

Late afternoon on a day off work, we decided to lie on our king-sized bed to pray a rosary. Upon finishing, Rob suggested we also pray our scripture verses together. Having already read all of the passages tagged in my Bible, I offered to recite them out loud from memory in order to remain in an atmosphere favorable to meditation. Switching positions to lie on my back, Rob turned on his side facing the wall. Closing my eyes, I began praying softly the many Scripture verses that were ground in my memory from daily recitation. All at once, I had a sense that someone very holy was standing next to me. Feeling the sensation of a hand being placed gently on top of my head, a deep peace came over me. After finishing all the Scripture I could recall, Rob turned toward me and said, "Hon, while you were reciting God's word, I was made aware that Jesus was standing alongside of you."

Immediately becoming choked up, I paused before responding, "I perceived that someone of great holiness was standing at my side, but I didn't know it was Jesus." With a quivering voice, I shared with Rob the gentle touch of His hand I'd felt placed atop of my head. "Tremble before God, all the earth" (Psalm 96:9).

Conscientious in praying my monthly Novena to the Blessed Sacrament, I traveled across town to the Chapel of Divine Mercy after the noon Mass on the two days of the week we were involved with evening prayer groups. Leaving the chapel one afternoon, a woman followed me out. Asking if I'd consider being a small group leader in the upcoming Life in the Spirit seminar at their church, I promised to prayerfully consider it.

But realizing on my drive home that the dates of the St. Pius seminar conflicted with the same time period that the Cross and Crown prayer group hosted their annual Life in the Spirit seminar, I quickly decided that it wouldn't work out. Most often, we'd be involved in some way by leading a small group or in giving a witness talk, and with Rob telling me he'd already been asked to participate, that clinched it. I'd attend with Rob at the Cross and Crown seminar. But then I remembered of giving the woman my word to pray about it, and as of yet, I had not done that. With a quick prayer, I planned on attending the seminar with Rob unless it was God's Will for me to do otherwise.

Approached by the same woman the following Monday after finishing up my Novena to the Blessed Sacrament, I told her of the conflict and that it would not work out for me to help at the seminar. Gracious in thanking me, we parted ways. On my drive home, I had a disquieted feeling inside of me. Trying to discern if the Spirit was calling me to serve at the St. Pius Life in the Spirit Seminar, I struggled with the idea of Rob and me assisting at two separate churches apart from each other.

Four days following the first night of the seminar at St. Pius, I sat with Rob in the introductory night of the Life in the Spirit Seminar at St. Paul's. From the time it first began, my spirit was disconcerted and my heart heavy. That's when it dawned on me that I'd chosen my free will over God's Will for me. Feeling just awful for not having listened to the promptings of my heart, I prayed, "Lord, please forgive me. I promise to help out with the seminar at St. Pius if they're still in need of assistance."

As the seminar came to a close, Rob bent down and whispered, "We need to leave."

Puzzled at his statement, I asked, "Aren't you feeling well?"

"It's not that," he replied. "The Lord has put it on my heart that we're not where we're supposed to be."

I couldn't believe my ears. "Where are we supposed to be?" I questioned.

"I don't know. I just know that it's not here."

"I do know where God is calling us," I responded.

Taken by surprise, he asked, "Where?"

Telling him of the heaviness that had also weighed me down throughout the evening, I said, "We're called to serve at the St. Pius Seminar."

With an uplifted spirit, he asked, "Can you call tomorrow to see if there's an opening for both of us?"

"Yes," I assured, "but their seminar has already started and now we need to pray for God to open up two spots for us!"

Calling the church office early the next morning, I received the phone number of the woman I'd spoken to outside of the chapel. I was amazed to learn she had just received a call previous to mine from a married couple who chose to back out of their commitment. Now they were in need of one man and one woman as small group leaders!

"Thank You, Jesus!" I prayed.

Relieved, Rob quickly found a replacement to lead the small group with our dear friends at the Cross and Crown.

Over the course of the weeks to follow, there was one woman in my small group that I felt a special need to pray for. As I became more familiar with the candidates, I voiced to her one evening that I felt prompted to pray for her every day.

"Oh," she said. "That's probably because, in a way, I'm serving two gods."

"What do you mean?" I asked.

She went on to explain that she was raised Anglican, but with her job, she traveled around the country teaching a non-Christian religion. Her mother had been so distraught over what she was doing that it had caused a wedge in their relationship. Sadly, before it was resolved, her mother passed away. I could see the pain emanating from the eyes of this beautifully articulate woman, and though I didn't know how it came to be that she was attending the seminar, I knew she was in the right place.

"I'm so sorry to hear that," I comforted. "I'll continue to keep you close in prayer."

Writing her name under multiple categories of prayer in the large three-ring binder for the Intercessors of Light, I prayed not only for her emotional healing, but also for her spiritual guidance and direction. In combination with the wonderful stories Rob was telling me of things taking place in his small group, I began to understand the lessons God was teaching us. Though I'd heard God's call, it wasn't until I finally gave my unequivocal *yes* that Rob was inspired to do the same. I learned that the devil even prefers steering good-hearted Christians in the direction of "other good things" if it means that he can keep them from doing God's Will, because it is within the Will of God that one will bear the most fruit.

At the reception following the last night of the seminar, a young woman approached me. Though I didn't know her name or anything about her, it was two months earlier that I was inspired to pray for her. Seeing her frequent the chapel, I had sensed within myself that I was to pray for her in regard to discerning religious life. Introducing herself, she asked if Rob and I would be willing to pray for her.

"Yes," I said happily. "Did someone tell you of our intercessory prayer group?"

"No," she replied. "I didn't know about that. I just felt in my heart that I could come to you for prayer. I'm discerning on becoming a sister and haven't yet told my family." Telling her that I'd already been praying for the very intention she just articulated, she said very sincerely, "Thank you so much."

Weeks later, the woman came up to me following the noon Mass at St. Joe's. Not having seen her at that particular Mass before, she told me she came on her lunch hour in the hope that I'd be there. "You know that prayer group you mentioned when I asked you for prayer?"

"Yes," I replied. "We entrust the Holy Spirit to tag the hearts of those who are called to be intercessors."

"I'd like to come," she said.

Another evening, as we were exiting the Chapel of Divine Mercy, Rob told me of an interesting vision shown to him. It was of him and me wearing tall hats that are worn in a particular order of sisters. "Outstretched before you and I was the hand of God, anointing us into ministry," he told me. Having no idea as to the meaning behind the hats, we contacted Father Kieran ahead of our scheduled meeting to help discern what it meant. He informed us that the nuns who wear that habit are of the order of the Sisters of Charity. Stating their main ministry is in healthcare, how humbling it was to receive God's anointing on our healing ministry. "But, as he who called you is holy, be holy yourselves in every aspect of your conduct" (1 Peter 1:15).

Just before opening my eyes on the morning of February 21, I was shown a vision of a woman with long hair. She was inside a deep hole in the ground. In the middle of the trench, I could see a round disc-like swing with a rope attached to it, as though it was lowered down from heaven. From the back, I saw the woman take hold of the rope as she sat on the swing. Above her hands were burning flames of fire, symbolic of the Holy Spirit. Interiorly, I received the knowledge that the woman was to be lifted out of the pit through our prayers. Within my heart, I heard her name repeated three times.

Having first met her at a Life in the Spirit seminar a few years prior, she was a Spirit-filled woman. Living in different towns and completely unaware of what was going on in her life, I hadn't talked to her for over a year. Writing her name down into the Intercessors of Light prayer binder, we began also to pray for Kayla in our daily prayers. Months later, I was happily surprised to see her sitting several seats ahead of us at Saturday morning Mass.

Coming up to us afterward, she opened her arms and gave me a big hug.

"How are you doing?" I asked.

Dropping her head, a look of sadness came over her.

"Kayla," I said softly. "The Holy Spirit prompted us to pray to help lift you out of what seemed to be a despairing situation, and we've been praying for you ever since."

Telling her the date of the vision shown to me, she started laughing and crying at the same time. She relayed that it was in that same time period she was spiraling down into a dark pit of depression. With tears flowing, she then told us that shortly after her grandmother had passed away, her brother had been tragically electrocuted, leaving behind a wife and young children. "Thank you so much for your prayers," she said as she stood up, wiping the tears from her eyes. "It's getting much better. But please pray for my mom," she added. "She's still having a hard time dealing with the grief of losing both her mother and son."

One night as we prayed before the Blessed Sacrament, Rob was shown a vision of people who were leaving the Catholic Church. Extending his broad shoulders outward in grabbing hold of the sides of the doorway to block their way, his attempt was futile. Interiorly, he received a message that through steadfast prayer, the faith of those who'd otherwise leave the Church would be renewed, and through the same committed prayer others would return.

That same evening, I was shown an image of Rob and myself traveling along a narrow path. Off to the left of us were people we stopped to minister to. Handing them a wreath, it lit up very brightly in the hands of those whose hearts were open to receive the encircling light of God's love. I then noticed one man for whom the wreath did not light up. Gazing in the direction off to the right of the narrow path, I turned to see what he was looking at. There, I observed other fallen souls who served to tempt him in the vices he was most vulnerable.

With greater zeal we prayed for those who had strayed from the path of life onto the foreboding path of perdition. Seeing this, I understood that it's in our weakness that sin will enter in. To become holy means to turn from sin and to live for righteousness. It means to have God in the first place of our lives, and requires us to align our free will perfectly in line with the Will of God until they become one. Holiness necessitates dying to ourselves in our earthly desires in exchange for what God, in His infinite wisdom and knowledge, aspires for us.

Called into a life of prayer and fasting, the Lord unveiled to us a great awareness of our own sinfulness. Leaving the distractions of the world behind, He was able to reshape our hearts.

> Dear children! I rejoice because of all of you who are on the road to holiness and I beseech you, by your own testimony help those who do not know how to live in holiness. Therefore, dear children, let your family be a place where holiness is birthed. Help everyone to live in holiness, but especially your own family.[3]
>
> —Our Lady of Medjugorje

Jesus awaits us in the innermost center of our souls. To journey with Him inwardly means allowing Jesus to live His life in us and through us. It means taking up our cross to follow Him. We must long for heaven and strive to be holy in everything we do. Not in going through the motions, but by striving to have a heart so pure that everything we do reflects God's love. But in order to live holiness as walking and talking images of Christ, any remaining walls of division that have been built up against anyone, living or dead, must first be torn down. This applies not only to individual relationships, but also to racial prejudices and social injustices.

There's only one thing strong enough to break down the barriers of anger and hatred—love. God is love. For those who hunger for holiness, He will provide for them the grace sufficient to be filled to overflowing. "When he saw the crowds, he went up the mountain, and after he had sat down, his disciples came to him. He began to teach them, saying:/ 'Blessed are they who hunger and thirst for righteousness,/ for they will be satisfied'" (Matthew 5:1–2, 6).

Wounded with his every wound,
Steep my soul till it has swooned
  In his very Blood away.

—Stabat Mater

I always want to see you behaving like a brave soldier who does not complain about his own suffering but takes his comrades' wounds seriously and treats his own as nothing but scratches.

—Saint Therese of Lisieux, to her novices[4]

Stations of the Cross

Thirteenth Station
Jesus Is Taken Down from the Cross

Our Lady of Sorrows loves us. She gave birth to us in suffering and love. May you never forget her, and may her sufferings be engraved in your heart. May she inflame your heart with greater love for her Divine Son.

—Padre Pio

Celestial Choirs

As we were leaving the Chapel of Divine Mercy, Rob shared with me a vision the Lord had shown him.

"It was in regard to you," he said. "You were removing two pair of slacks from your closet shelf. One of them was grey and the other one was blue. Interiorly, I heard the words, 'She won't be needing them anymore.'"

Immediately, I knew exactly the slacks he was talking about. Having just laundered them that same day, I'd placed them back onto my closet shelf. Though Rob didn't understand the message given to him, I knew precisely what it meant. Made out of a lightweight microfleece material, the slacks had an elasticized waist and were much more comfortable around my stomach than my zip-up jeans with no flexibility. With my polycystic kidneys measuring three times the normal size, I'd resorted to wearing them around the house, thinking of them as my "kidney pants."

As an act of faith, as soon as we returned home I removed the slacks from my closet shelf to place in storage. After our night prayers, my mind wandered back to nearly four and a half years prior when I received the news that my kidneys were failing. Who knew that something so devastating would turn out to be the powerful means by which my mind would be opened to understand the potential that adversity has to bring glory to God! Learning to believe in what I couldn't see, I was filled with peace and my soul overflowed with grace. Through His promises in Holy Scripture, my despair was replaced with hope.

While in Eucharistic adoration, Rob saw the hand of God in a white glove.

"It was Jesus reaching for a book on a shelf to give to you," he told me. "It was titled *Surrender*."

I knew what the Lord was asking of me. Constantly striving to surrender myself into His Holy Will, I struggled in turning over the last 10 percent. Giving Him full reign over my life meant relinquishing entirely my free will. Our Lord had taught me that offering the storms of my life over to Him didn't always mean escaping the turbulent waters that swirled about, but it did mean that I'd receive His peace in the midst of them. Jesus now beckoned me to walk with Him on water. Without the faith of a child, I'd sink. He was calling me to let go of my own wants and inhibitions in trust that He was in control: to fully rely on His sure and steady hand to help me step out in faith, to help me to grow in holiness. In order for my hardships to serve as the means in which my heart would be transformed into the Heart of Christ, my will needed to be one with His. "This is the will of God, your holiness" (1 Thessalonians 4:3).

On one of our regular visits at the Chapel of Divine Mercy, Rob was shown a vision of a tall crucifix mounted on a black structure of some sort. While the body of Jesus crucified was facing in one direction, he could see that he and I were facing in the opposite direction, with our backs directly behind the crucifix.

Instantly becoming concerned with the image he described to me, I asked, "Do you think we've somehow turned our backs on Jesus?"

"No, that's not the case," he said reassuringly. "I don't know why we were positioned that way, but I definitely had a sense we were doing something that was good and pleasing to God."

Two weeks later as I stood cutting Rob's hair, I suddenly felt within myself a strong desire for us to attend a monthly Prayer Cenacle for Priests[1] that I learned was taking place at a neighboring church. I had no idea it was connected to the same prayer cenacle I'd recently read about in the book *To the Priests, Our Lady's Beloved Sons*.[2] It revealed the interior locutions of Fr.

Stefano Gobbi, a priest from Milan, resulting in numerous prayer cenacles being formed on all five continents. Telling Rob about it, I asked, "Do you think we could attend the prayer cenacle this weekend?"

Pausing for a moment, he responded, "Sure, I don't know why not."

Just in thinking of how the apostles had gathered in a prayer cenacle with Mary in the upper room following the death of Jesus, the Great High Priest, my spirit was stirred up to pray for priests. "Therefore, since we have a great high priest who has passed through the heavens, Jesus, the Son of God" (Hebrews 4:14).

Processing with the group from the narthex to the inside of the church where the Blessed Sacrament was exposed, we filed into the seats lined up before the Tabernacle. Soon after taking our place in the center seats of the back row, Rob nudged me. Turning around, he pointed up at the large crucifix erected just inches from the back of our chairs.

"Look," he whispered. "My vision."

The same as was shown in the prophetic vision, we found ourselves sitting with our backs to the large crucifix positioned behind the altar. With the Crucifix facing outward to where the congregation gathered for Mass, we were seated in the opposite direction facing the Tabernacle. Summoned by God to pray for His priests, we were pleased to accept!

"Ouch," I said out loud as I placed my feet onto the floor to get out of bed. They were especially sore in the aftermath of the horrific cramps from two nights prior. Hobbling around the house in an attempt to do my daily routine, I was forced to forego my morning walk, which was key in getting my iron-poor blood circulating. Shivering cold and barely able to pick up my feet to walk, I decided to sit down and read *Thank God Ahead of Time*,[3] a book given to me on the life of the Venerable Solanus Casey.[4] The more I read of this humble and suffering priest, the more I couldn't help but love him. "I'm offering my sufferings that all might be one. If only I could see the conversion of the whole world" (words of Fr. Solanus).[5]

Happy tears filled my eyes as I began to see the pain in my feet as another opportunity to bring glory to God. Father Solanus' healing prayers were sought out by the droves of people who came from all over, many receiving miraculous healings. Having himself read the four-volume set of *The Mystical City of God*,[6] he strongly encouraged those who came to him to read the book and to enroll in the Seraphic Mass Association.[7] Reading this, I suddenly felt a great longing to be enrolled in the SMA myself, as well as to acquire the set of books the holy priest read three times on his knees!

I was amazed to learn that Farther Solanus died on July 31, 1957, on the same date he celebrated his first Mass fifty-three years prior. More fascinating to me was that it was offered at St. Joseph's Church in Appleton where I attended noon Mass each day. Checking the mail before getting ready to leave for Mass, I received a card from two sisters I'd met on our Medjugorje pilgrimage a year and a half prior. Opening it, I was astonished to see that they had enrolled me into the SMA!

Jesus stands at the door of every heart, waiting to be invited in. He knows all our faults and failures, our struggles and our concerns, and He longs to console those who are drowning in the agony of life's sorrows. Brought into the state of contemplative prayer before the Blessed Sacrament, Rob was shown a vision of the chapel wall he was kneeling next to. But instead of being made of plaster, the entire wall was glass, with a door leading outside. Interiorly, he received the knowledge that the world is blinded from seeing the door that will open for them a personal relationship with Jesus in His true presence. Those who can see, on the other hand, are not to waste a precious moment in bearing fruit for the kingdom by bringing souls to Jesus.

As we lay on our bed praying the Chaplet of Divine Mercy one Sunday afternoon, Rob was shown a vision of him and me standing directly below a towering marble wall. Very smooth and shiny in surface, the wall was symbolic of spiritual perfection. Looking up, he saw numerous saints hovering above the beautiful marble structure that gleamed with light. They beckoned to assist us in our ascent toward holiness. A feat impossible to climb on our own, it's through the grace of God and in seeking the aid of Mary and the saints that one can achieve spiritual perfection. "Dear children, you know that I wish to lead you on the way of holiness, but I cannot compel you to be saints by force. I desire that each of you by your own little self-denials help yourself and me so I can lead you from day to day closer to holiness" (Our Lady of Medjugorje).[8]

When purification by Way of the Cross becomes too difficult a path to follow, it's in submitting oneself into God's Will that they will find peace. Amidst life's obstacles and challenges, it's vital to place our trust entirely within the merciful Heart of Christ. As I was undergoing a particular trial one day, it was in taking time out to pray the chaplet at 3:00 p.m. that I received sweet consolation. Interiorly, Rob saw Jesus lying in between the two of us, holding our hands. With Christ in the center, there were angels suspended above as we prayed together the Chaplet of Divine Mercy. When he shared this with me, I was reminded of how our adversity was what helped us in becoming Christ-centered, placing Him in the centermost part of our lives.

During Eucharistic adoration, Rob was periodically shown visions of saints who were interceding on my behalf. Oftentimes they were of priests and nuns who were dressed in the same attire they wore in the various religious orders they had belonged. Some he recognized or was given interior knowledge as to who they were, on one occasion, seeing St. Dominic standing next to Mary in prayer for me. Humbled at the consolations being lavished upon me, the sweetness that comes from walking with Jesus in suffering far outweighs the crosses that one is called to shoulder. I was constantly praying novenas for the intercession of various saints. In another such vision, he was shown a Franciscan priest with a beard who was holding my hand and sitting alongside me on a cement step, noting that it didn't resemble modern-age concrete but that of a time long ago. Another time, he saw a saint who was carrying a bag. In it, he was collecting our prayers as well as prayers of the faithful that were being said on my behalf to present before God. What comfort I took in the scenes shown him, knowing the same is true for all who call upon the aid of Mary and the saints to help them through difficult times. "But rejoice to the extent that you share in the sufferings of Christ, so that when his glory is revealed you may also rejoice exultantly" (1 Peter 4:13).

Returning home from Chistmas Eve Mass, I began preparing hor d'oeuvres. Since my mother's passing, we decided to forego hosting a family gathering in our home in favor of an intimate celebration with Jenelle, bundling ourselves up at midnight to carry out the tradition of our St. Andrew Christmas Novena. Our son and his family would be arriving on Christmas day.

"Hon, I'm going into the bedroom to pray for a while," Rob told me.

While in meditation, he was shown the images of two saints hovering on either side of the fireplace in our prayer room where our home had been enthroned to the Two Hearts. Both of them had beards and were fully clad in brown hooded gowns. Interiorly, Rob received the knowledge that they were praying for both of us. One of them was Father Solanus Casey. I found it interesting that he'd receive a vision of Solanus on Christmas Eve, since it had been on Christmas Eve back in 1896 that he'd traveled to St. Bonaventure Monastery in Detroit, Michigan following a novena to Mary in discernment of his vocation. On the ninth day, he received the message, "Go to Detroit."[9] At the midnight Mass on Christmas Eve, Father Solanus Casey knew exactly where God wanted him to be.

As to the identity of the other saint, Rob did not yet know. "He was wearing the hood of his garment up, and I saw a glowing light around him and streaming out from his eyes," he said. A few days later, we attended the evening Mass at Sacred Heart Church with two other couples before going to the home of Andrew's parents. On the way there, Mary began telling me of a special monthly devotion to St. Charbel that she and Tom were planning to start up. Unfamiliar with that particular saint, when I told her of the raised hood and vivid beams of light shining out from the "mystery saint" from Rob's Christmas Eve vision, Mary's jaw dropped wide open.

"What?" I questioned.

"It sounds just like you're describing St. Charbel!" she said in astonishment. "There was even light seen coming out from his gravesite!"

Giving us a book on the life of St. Charbel Makhlouf, we read of this holy Lebanese hermit who had endured great amounts of suffering and self-mortification for the love of God. Even more astounding to us in relation to his image being shown to Rob on Christmas Eve, was in learning he had died on Christmas Eve while saying his last Mass during the elevation of the Host and chalice. In the various images of St. Charbel, he was pictured with his hood up and rays of light extending out from his body, just as Rob had seen him hovering above our mantle in prayer. People traveled from great distances for St. Charbel's prayers, and the same as was true with Solanus Casey, many were healed.

Reading the book prior to Rob, I was astonished to see pictured in it a cedar of Lebanon. Recognizing its characteristics to be similar to a tree shown to Rob in a vision awhile back, I held up the book and asked, "Does this look like the tree you were shown in that vision?"

"Yes, it sure does," he answered. Having drawn a picture of it in his journal, it was a cedar of Lebanon the Lord had shown him.

> "The just shall flourish like the palm tree,/ shall grow like a cedar of Lebanon./ Planted in the house of the LORD,/ they shall flourish in the courts of our God./ They shall bear fruit even in old age,/ always vigorous and sturdy,/ As they proclaim: 'The LORD is just;/ our rock, in whom there is no wrong.'" (Psalm 92:13–16)

It was with a grateful heart that I had retrieved the statue from the St. Joseph Oratory that I had purchased as an act of faith for our future daughter-in-law and first grandchild. Soon after the birth of our grandson, Rob and I brought him with us to Mass one day. Holding him up before the Tabernacle, we gave thanksgiving to God as we prayed together Hannah's prayer: "I prayed for this child, and the LORD granted my request. Now I, in turn, give him to the LORD; as long as he lives, he shall be dedicated to the LORD" (1 Samuel 1:27–28). Having prayed for St. Joseph's intercession for our son to be a good leader of his own "holy" family, already expecting their second child, we gifted to his growing family an outdoor statue of the Holy Family.

While caring for our grandson one day, though I'd usually crank up the volume on the CD player to sing the Divine Mercy Chaplet at 3:00 p.m., my precious baby boy laid sound asleep. Feeling under the weather from a bout of asthma, I was wheezing, and my lungs felt achy. Combined with the steady decline of my kidney function, the chronic leg cramps, and fatigue, I decided to lie on my bed to pray the chaplet quietly to myself.

I was definitely feeling the weight of my cross, and I found myself questioning how I'd possibly be able to keep up with all I was doing—receiving prayer requests each week sometimes tallying into the hundreds, the phone calls, hosting the intercessory prayer group each week, praying with the sick, going out most every evening with Rob to various religious events and such. Spontaneously, I began praying, "Heavenly Father, please help me to recognize my crosses as opportunities to grow in holiness. Provide me the strength to carry out Your Will, and help me to believe without seeing." After reciting the chaplet that day, I experienced God's presence in a tangible way. The mystical encounter left lingering in my soul an extraordinary sense of peace. More than ever before, I understood that it wasn't my own resilience that would take me through life's valleys, but the love and mercy of Jesus Christ.

That same evening in the Chapel of Divine Mercy, I knelt down next to where the first class relic of St. Faustina was mounted on the wall. On impulse, I asked if she'd be willing to stay at my side all the way through to the date of my next blood draw. Petitioning for the fortitude necessary for me to persevere, I asked St. Faustina if she'd somehow confirm to me her acceptance of my appeal.

Leaving the chapel, Rob relayed to me a vision he'd been shown. "The two of us were freefalling from the sky, as if from an airplane," he said. "Facing each other, we were holding hands with our arms extended out, forming the shape of a diamond." Viewing the scene from above, he noticed within the center of the diamond shape was the Cross of Christ, and that we were holding on tightly to its outer beams. Interiorly, he gained the wisdom that it's in uniting life's hardships with the sufferings of Jesus that we're able to "hold on" in our sufferings, and when we surrender our struggles into God's Will, it serves as the parachute that will safely land us in the freefall of adversity.

Awakened from a sound sleep in the middle of the night, I glanced over to see that it was almost 3:00 a.m. Reaching over to retrieve my rosary from the nightstand to pray the Divine Mercy Chaplet, Rob turned over and asked, "Are you getting leg cramps?"

"No," I replied. "I'm about to pray a chaplet for the sick and the dying. Do you want to pray it with me?"

Happy to join in, upon finishing he shared with me of a vision he'd been shown. "St. Faustina was standing right alongside of the bed where you're lying, and she was holding out a white piece of paper with a message for you, a message from Jesus."

"What's the message?" I asked.

"I don't know," he answered.

Then I suddenly remembered my query to St. Faustina the night before in the chapel, both in my request for her to remain at my side, and of asking for confirmation. Feeling blessed in knowing she had accepted my plea, I wondered what was in the message from Jesus.

How pleased I was to have Jenelle accompany us to the Chapel of Divine Mercy that Saturday evening for our committed hour of adoration. Kneeling before Jesus in the Blessed Sacrament, I prayed for wisdom concerning the message He wished to convey to me through St. Faustina. Getting into the car for our drive back home, Rob told us of a vision he'd been shown while in contemplative prayer.

"I saw the hand of God holding out a notebook, and I heard interiorly these words, 'Message for Sue.'"

From the back seat Jenelle spoke out, saying, "As I was reading St. Faustina's book *Diary*[10] in the chapel tonight, I had a sense that a specific paragraph was intended for you, Mom. I marked the page in her third notebook for you to read." Being that neither Rob nor I had yet read St. Faustina's diary, the first thing that struck me was in the commonality of the word "notebook," used both in the message Rob had just articulated to me and now in the same terminology used by Jenelle.

"What do you mean notebook?" I asked.

She explained to us that St. Faustina wrote her *Diary* not in chapters, but in six separate notebooks. My interest instantly heightened. Handing her book up to the front, she pointed to the paragraph for me to read.

I read out loud the message given to me by Jesus through the words of St. Faustina:

> On April 14, I felt so bad I barely managed to get up to assist at Holy Mass. I felt much worse than I did at the time they sent me for treatment. There was wheezing, and there was rattling noises in my lungs and strange pains. When I received Holy Communion, I don't know why, but it was as if something were urging me to this prayer and I began to pray in this manner: "Jesus, may Your pure and healthy blood circulate in my ailing organism, and may Your pure and healthy body transform my weak body, and may a healthy and vigorous life throb within me, if it is truly Your holy will that I should set about the work in question: and this will be a clear sign of Your holy will for me." As I was praying this way, I suddenly felt as if something were jolting my whole organism and, in an instant, I felt completely well. My breath is clear as if there had never been anything the matter with my lungs, and I feel no pain, and this is a sign for me that I should set about the work.[11]
>
> —*Diary*, 1089

It was in praying the Divine Mercy Chaplet that I had abandoned the burden of my declining health back to God. Concerned, I didn't know how I could possibly keep up with our busy lifestyle and the mission of our ongoing healing ministry. To receive a message from Jesus in the same words that were spoken to Him by St. Faustina in regard to her state of health and involving her work in question, I was overcome in awe of our awesome God!

Our devotion of praying for the holy souls in purgatory began to flourish when our Lord started showing Rob numerous visions of suffering souls who, although they had gained eternal salvation, were still in need of atonement for their sins. It was in Eucharistic adoration that he saw scenes in which one, or multiple persons would approach him for prayer. Men and women of all ages and nationalities, he was often able to discern the timeline in which they lived by the hairstyles and clothing they wore.

> "For if he were not expecting the fallen to rise again, it would have been useless and foolish to pray for them in death. But if he did this with a view to the splendid reward that awaits those who had gone to rest in godliness, it was a holy and pious thought. Thus he made atonement for the dead that they might be freed from this sin."
>
> —2 Maccabees 12:44–45

It was Advent of 2005. While in contemplative prayer before the Blessed Sacrament, Rob heard the rustle of a jacket. He then saw a young boy of twelve years old walking up to the front of the chapel where we were kneeling. Wearing a grey winter jacket with a scarf around his neck, the boy asked if we would pray for him to be in heaven with Jesus for Christmas. How this touched my heart, praying fervently for this child throughout the duration of Lent to receive his Christmas wish.

On another evening in the Chapel of Divine Mercy, he was shown a very large warehouse. Tacked to an inside wall, he saw a sheet of paper with names going down two columns. Unable to read them, he then saw an enormous log hanging lengthwise from the ceiling that was fastened by large chains. Swinging back and forth, it forcefully slammed into the exit doors from one side of the warehouse to the other, unable to break through. Interiorly, it was revealed that the list consisted of the names of holy souls who were being brought to us for prayer. The log that was vigorously banging on the exit doors was indicative of their strong desire for the prayers necessary for them to break out of the chains of sin that still separated them from God's presence. Vigilant in praying for them every day, we also began enrolling them into the SMA.

In ongoing visions, Rob would see groups of holy souls filling up the seats around us in the Chapel of Divine Mercy. Kneeling down, they'd petition for prayer. On Christmas Day, he was shown a vision of the souls in purgatory filling the church and lining themselves up three-deep against the walls in want of Masses offered for the repose of their souls. Grateful for our prayers, he'd often see them stopping by to thank us on the day of their final purification. "It cannot be compared with the anguish of Hell where suffering is a despairing fruit of hatred while the suffering of Purgatory is a hope-filled suffering of love"[12] (St. Catherine of Genoa).

On another occasion, Rob was shown a scene in which he saw the two of us seated in the lobby of a high-rise hotel. From our vantage point, we could see a woman standing at the elevators. Unable to operate the push-button panel to get to the top floor, she walked over to where we were sitting to ask for our assistance. The woman was in purgatory. In the knowledge that she could zoom up the elevator to heaven much faster with the help of our prayers, she explained that without them, she'd have to take the long and winding staircase to the top, one painstaking step at a time. Without the prayers of the Church militant here on earth, it would be for her a much longer and painful way to reach her eternal resting place in paradise.

Other times, he'd be shown various scenes or faces of complete strangers right before their death, carrying with them a sense of urgency to pray for the salvation of their souls. "Be assured that the grace of eternal salvation for certain souls in their final moment depends on your prayer"[13] (*Diary*, 1777). Sometimes given the wisdom of how our prayers had resulted in the salvation of a soul, he'd see looks of relief and gratitude in the knowledge of what God's mercy had spared them. With what greater zeal we persisted in praying for God's people, both for those still on earth and for those detained in purgatory.

While in contemplative prayer in Eucharistic adoration, Rob has been shown panoramic views of us being taken by angels or saints on a guided walkthrough of purgatory. With the lowest level being void of God's light, he described the anguish of the souls suffering there. Shown the various levels in comparison to a room darkening shade, as the soul enters into higher levels of purification, it's through the prayers of the faithful that the light-filtering shade becomes less effective until it is washed pure and clean.

> "Dear children, today I wish to call you to pray daily for the souls in purgatory. For every soul prayer and grace is necessary to reach God and the love of God. By doing this, dear children, you obtain new intercessors who will help you in life to realize that all earthly things are not important for you, that only heaven is that for which it is necessary to strive. Therefore, dear children, pray without ceasing that you may be able to help yourselves and the others, to whom your prayers will bring joy."[14]
>
> —Message of Our Lady of Medjugorje

Going to our usual spot in the front middle row of the Divine Mercy Chapel, we knelt down before the Blessed Sacrament. Looking up at the Eucharistic Jesus, I saw within the Host a still-life portrait of my grandmother. Uncertain as to what it meant, I began to pray for the repose of her soul, suggesting for family members to do the same. Seeing her image again and again on subsequent visits, Jenelle told me of a dream she had. In it, my grandmother was calling me with a phone message saying, "I want to go home." Deciding right away to have a Mass offered for her, my grandmother's image no longer appeared.

It was in early January 2007 when within myself I felt a strong sense to pray before the statue of Our Lady of Grace at St. Pius. Having knelt before the beautiful statue on multiple occasions, I didn't know why I was drawn to go there. Driving across town after the noon Mass at St. Joe's, I knelt down in the chapel within the darkened church. Surrounded by the candles aglow with petitions on either side of Our Lady, I could see perfectly the tall glowing red candle burning alongside Jesus in the Tabernacle. I suddenly had a keen sense of Mary's intercession in bringing all of my prayers to her Son. With a tear rolling down my cheek, I thanked her from the bottom of my heart. Blowing her a kiss before leaving, I professed my love before blowing her a second kiss to bring to Jesus.

I had hoped to be home by three o'clock to pray the Divine Mercy Chaplet before tidying up the house for the prayer meeting. Turning southbound on a road that took me by the same hospital my mother had passed away in nearly nine months prior, I began praying a Hail Mary to benefit the soul in most need of salvation, asking Mary to be at their side at the hour of death. Immediately upon finishing, I noticed a white cloud in the sky that was drifting very slowly across the front of the sun. With the right side of the cloud looking delicate and feathery, it was in the perfect shape an angel wing. Even more astounding was that the angel wing was bright-red in color! "Lord, what is it?" I exclaimed.

Approaching the intersection, I was relieved that the stoplight had turned red. Watching very intently as the cloud continued to pass to the left of the sun in a downwardly direction, the sun became fully visible. With a portion of the cloud still gradually drifting by below it, I then saw two rays extending forth from beneath the sun, one red, and one the translucent white of the cloud. Close to the 3:00 p.m. hour, I prayed out loud, "Oh blood and water which gushed forth from the Heart of Jesus as a font of mercy, I trust in You!"[15] (*Diary*, 187). Returning home, I turned on the Divine Mercy Chaplet and got down on my knees before the Divine Mercy image of Jesus. As I was praying, a specific Scripture verse came to my mind: "But for you who revere My name, the Sun of righteousness will rise with healing in its wings. And you will go out and leap like calves released from the stall" (Malachi 3:20, NIV) In the sky that day, I had seen the rays of mercy coming from the Sun of righteousness.

Three weeks following this incident, in the early morning hours of January 31 while I was in the state of sleep right before waking up, I was shown a vision. It was of a calendar. With no month visible, the only date I saw on it was the fifth, and it was on a Friday. On the date shown to me was a shiny gold medallion shimmering back and forth. Interiorly, I received the knowledge that the date had to do with the healing of my kidneys. Getting out of bed, I walked straight over to my calendar in the kitchen. Flipping through the pages for a month that the fifth landed on a Friday, I stopped on October 5, 2007. Sensing all along that I wouldn't require dialysis, with my kidney function fluctuating around the 9 percent mark, I wondered how they'd possibly last another eight months! As an act of faith, I drew a circular medallion on the date of Friday, October 5, writing on my calendar in all caps: "SUE'S HEALING!"

When telling this to a friend and committed prayer warrior of the Intercessors of Light, Bonnie smiled and said, "October 5 is my birthday, and it's also the feast of Saint Faustina." Her words sent chills down my spine, thinking of seeing rays of divine mercy coming from the sun just a few weeks prior following my visit with Our Lady of Grace. What it all had to do with the cloud that had formed into a wing of an angel, I didn't yet know. And though I had absolutely no idea of how it was all going to play out, I believed our Lord had a wondrous plan already laid out for my healing.

My nephrologist at UW Madison ordered a battery of tests to be repeated from when I'd first been seen over four years prior. Necessary to be completed prior to my May appointment, I scheduled them throughout the course of Lent. With little kidney function remaining, I strategically scheduled the test most threatening to be done during Holy Week. With the potential of dehydration, the relatively low-risk colonoscopy for someone on the brink of renal failure could have devastating results. What better time, I thought, than in the holiest week of the Church-year leading up to the Passion, Death, and the Resurrection of Jesus Christ to rely completely on the mercy of God.

On the evening before the colonoscopy, I went with Rob to the Chapel of Divine Mercy. Placing my trust in Jesus, I implored Mary's intercession. Asking her to accompany me to my test, I asked also for the protection of the holy archangels Michael, Gabriel, and Raphael, as well as all the holy angels of heaven. Completely unaware of my impulsive plea to Mary and the angels, Rob told me of a vision he'd been shown.

"I saw you kneeling in Eucharistic adoration when a burst of brilliant light shone forth, and then there were angels hovering all around you." "Make yourself familiar with the angels, and behold them frequently in spirit; for without being seen, they are present with you"[16] (St. Francis de Sales).

In the habit of praying to my guardian angel each day, I also prayed the Angelus in honor of the Archangel Gabriel's announcement to Mary, combined with an ongoing novena prayer to St. Michael the Archangel, and a beautiful prayer to Maria Rosa Mystica with the holy Archangel Raphael. Viewing the heavenly choirs of angels as my protectors and mentors in discerning good and evil, I credit a near tragic incident from my childhood to the protection of my guardian angel.

Learning to swim at a young age, I'd become a fairly good swimmer. A member of the swim team and diving club, I soon became aware that I could hold my breath longer than most of my peers in the games we played. Standing on the ledge of the fifteen-foot deep section of the pool that required a swim pass to enter, my friends and I decided to "up the ante" in our ongoing contest of who could hold their breath the longest. We were to all dive into the water at the same time and swim as far as we could beneath the water. Whoever swam the farthest without coming up for air would be deemed the winner.

Taking a deep breath, I dove in at the count of "One, two, three, go!" Feeling confident in the quest at hand, I speedily swam underwater as fast as I possibly could, being sure to swim below the water according to the rules set out. Holding my breath for what seemed to be longer than I'd ever held it before, I saved the exhale for my final ascent.

Unable to hold my breath any longer, I was horrified in not being able to break the water's surface! Using my arms to push myself upward combined with the strong leg kick I'd learned in swim class, try as I might, I simply could not reach the top! Without realizing it, I'd been swimming as fast as I could on a diagonal slope toward the bottom of the fifteen-foot-deep pool! Relieved for having saved my exhale to swim back up to the water's surface, I instinctively released only small amounts of air at a time. Becoming almost frantic as my lungs felt as though they were about to burst, a sickening thought came to my mind. Confused as to why I could not reach the top, I wondered if I was swimming up or down. Swimming with all of my might, I broke surface at last! "See, I am sending an angel before you, to guard you on the way and bring you to the place I have prepared. Be attentive to him and heed his voice" (Exodus 23:20–21).

With one breath of air, I swam across the entire length of the pool, beneath the buoys, and halfway through the swim team section. Having already blown his whistle to clear the pool, the lifeguard called out, "Can you make it back on your own?"

Exhausted, I shook my head yes while hanging on to a buoy to catch my breath. Having had the presence of mind to conserve my exhale, I believe it was my faithful companion, my guardian angel, who guided me safely back up to the water's surface. "The angels are here they are at your side, they are with you, present on your behalf. They are here to protect you and to serve you"[17] (St. Bernard, Doctor of the Church).

Traveling to UW Madison Hospital, we met with the head of Nephrology to discuss the results of my tests. With my total kidney function dipping to a mere 7 percent, we prayed for St. Joseph's intercession to impart God's wisdom to the doctor. Sitting back in his chair, he advised that we get into the surgery lineup sometime in June, July, or August.

Escorted to a small room, the surgeon assigned to my case held out his hand and introduced himself. Shaking his hand, I said, "Nice to finally meet you. We've been praying for you for a long time."

Holding up both hands, he professed, "They're instruments of the Lord." I gave Rob a high five as we headed out to meet with my pretransplant coordinator. What better reassurance could I have than for my surgeon to declare his hands as the tools of God's handiwork?

"When would you like to schedule your surgeries?" the nurse coordinator asked as she told us the open dates.

"Could we pray about it before deciding?" I asked.

"Sure," she said while reaching for a yellow Post-it note. Writing down the open dates in June, July, and August, she cautioned; "Be sure to call me back within a week or so, because the dates fill up fast."

"I will," I assured her as we headed out the door for home.

Getting back into town, we stopped off at the Chapel of Divine Mercy to pray for God's wisdom in choosing the date for our surgeries. As we were leaving, Rob shared a vision he had of a pair of white, straight-legged jeans with a zip-up front. "They were suspended in midair, and they were for you," he said. Given the fact that I didn't own a pair of white jeans and that my enlarged kidneys made it extremely uncomfortable for me to wear zip-up jeans, I was excited.

"How about we put our faith into action and go buy a pair right now?" I suggested. Despite the long day and four-hour roundtrip, we stopped off to buy a pair of white jeans. Selecting a size that didn't even come close to zipping up around my waist, I placed them on my closet shelf in the spot that I'd previously removed the two pair of "kidney pants." From my heart, I prayed, "Jesus, I promise not be as the nine lepers who didn't come back to thank You. Wearing these white jeans, I will prostrate myself before You in the Blessed Sacrament of the Altar."

As Rob was reading the second book of the four-volume set of *The Mystical City of God*[18] the very next day, something caught his interest. "Read this," he said. Reading the instruction given by Our Blessed Mother to Venerable Mary of Agreda, Our Lady told of the value of seeking "Divine Wisdom" in all things big or small. For those who do, she promises either to come with an answer herself, or that God will shed on it His divine light. In Eucharistic adoration that evening, we asked Mary to reveal the date most pleasing to God for us to schedule our surgeries. Vowing not to proceed in choosing a date before receiving the answer to our petition, our surrender into God's Will brought us such peace.

Conscious of telling my nurse coordinator I'd be punctual in getting back to her, a week had passed by without receiving an answer to the constant prayer on our lips. Frequenting the Chapel of Divine Mercy, we continued placing our request before the Altar of the Lord. Relieved when Saturday finally arrived, I knew my coordinator wouldn't be calling on the weekend. It was at Mass the next morning on the feast of Mary's Immaculate Heart that I made my second plea, "*Please*, Mary, come quickly with an answer!" Later that evening as we prayed before the Blessed Sacrament, Rob was shown an interior locution of Our Lady opening a white door for me. Interiorly, he was told our answer from Mary was forthcoming. Asking, seeking, and knocking every night in our Novena to the Sacred Heart, I instantly felt the weight of my concern lifted in the unwavering belief that, indeed, the door would be opened!

Arising early the next day, what a glorious Sunday it was! With rosaries and Bibles in hand, walking onto our deck felt like we'd stepped into a little taste of paradise. The birds were singing, the sky was a gorgeous, and the sun poked through the deciduous trees outlining our backyard. Spending the first half hour delving into Scripture, Rob lifted his head and asked, "Hon, was August 2 one of the dates written down for us to choose from?"

"I'm not sure. Why?" I asked.

"It's the date we're to have our surgeries on," he said.

"How do you know?" I asked enthusiastically.

"Because as I was reading the Scripture verses tagged in my Bible, the moment I read Matthew 8:2, I received an interior message that "8/2," August 2, is the date we're to schedule our surgeries."

Of all the healing Scriptures we had faithfully read each day for nearly five years, Matthew 8:2 was the only verse we claimed specifically for me. Having cried out to God in similar words as the leper's plea back at the onset of my diagnosis, I had penciled my name next to the verse to claim it as my very own. "And then a leper approached, did him homage, and said, "Lord, if you wish, you can make me clean" (Matthew 8:2). Picking up our coffee mugs to replenish, I couldn't rush into the house fast enough to retrieve the little yellow Post-it note. On it, the nurse coordinator had written "8/2" as one of the dates for us to choose from. Checking whose feast was celebrated on August 2, I was elated to learn it was the feast of "Our Lady of the Angels!"

"Look!" I said to Rob while holding out the Post-it-note. "Do you remember the interior message Jenelle had at the grotto of Our Lady in asking Mary when I'd be healed?"

"The angels will sing!" we said in unison.

"And remember the red angel wing I saw in the cloud as it passed in front of the sun five months ago, and the red and white rays extending down from the sun?" I asked.

"Oh, that's right!" he said in amazement.

"And what about the spontaneous prayer that formed in my heart while we were in Eucharistic adoration a couple of months ago on the night before my colonoscopy?" I added. "Remember how I found myself pleading with St. Michael and the angels of heaven to be at my side, and the vision you saw of the burst of radiant light followed by angels hovering all around me?"

Smiling, he said, "I do remember, praise God!"

Going back into the house, I quickly dialed the number of my nurse coordinator to leave a message for her to schedule August

2 for our surgeries. In joyous thanksgiving to Mary for answered prayer, I went back outside to pray the Glorious Mysteries of the rosary with Rob.

Though still uncertain as to how St. Faustina's feast day of October 5, the date I'd been shown as the date of my healing, fit in with the kidney transplant date of August 2, I was able to see the correlation to St. Faustina with the August 2 date. It had been on the vigil of the feast of Our Lady of the Angels back in 1925 that she'd been accepted into the Congregation of the Sisters of Our Lady of Mercy.

After Mass that evening, we strolled over to the Chapel of Divine Mercy to thank Jesus in person for the spiritually magnificent day. But there was more. Upon leaving, Rob told me the Lord had asked something very special of us.

"What's that?" I asked, remembering back to a time when He instructed us to pray for the gift of love.

"As I was brought into contemplative prayer," he said very seriously, "within the silence of my heart God presented to us a request."

Sitting on the edge of my seat, I questioned, "What was it?"

"He asked if we'd be willing to ask Him 'for things not to be easy.'"

For reasons I can't explain, I felt an implosion of joy within my heart. "What did you tell Him?" I asked.

"Well, nothing at first. I really didn't want to ask for more trials."

"Yeah, I know. But you know that God loves us more than we could ever imagine, and that He wouldn't ask this of us unless it was for His greater glory, right?" I added.

"I know," Rob conceded.

"Besides, I've already given Him my yes." Telling him of the rush of happiness I felt upon hearing God's invitation, I speculated it was a result of the faith I'd gained in the amazing way Mary had answered our prayer. "Thank You, Jesus, for the graces and the pieces of the Cross which You give me at each moment of my life"[19] (*Diary*, 382).

Our acceptance of the Lord's appeal had been, for me, a turning point. It helped me to realize that, in order for us to grow in the virtues we're striving to attain, means surrendering to Him every trial, every hardship, and every pain. Encouraged to let go of what remained of my will, I better understood that to be united perfectly as one with Him meant to unite my free will perfectly within the divine Will of God, not by mere words, but with a sincere heart, with no strings attached.

God was beckoning us for a deeper surrender, to trust Him with a childlike faith in the knowledge that our daddy, "Abba Father," wishes for us, His beloved children, only that which is good. It had been almost five years of walking alongside Jesus on the path of adversity that He was teaching me firsthand that the same Cross that gained our salvation is often what He uses to help His people accept it! How tremendously grateful I was for the aid of His Holy Mother, and the angels and saints in helping us to get there! "Therefore, since we are surrounded by so great a cloud of witnesses, let us rid ourselves of every burden and sin that clings to us and persevere in running the race that lies before us while keeping our eyes fixed on Jesus, the leader and perfecter of faith" (Hebrews 12:1-2).

Be to me, O Virgin, nigh,
Lest in flames I burn and die,
  In his awful judgment day.

—Stabat Mater

Oh, my Lord! How true it is that whoever works for you is paid in troubles! And what a precious price to those who love You if we understand its value.

—Saint Teresa of Avila[20]

Stations of the Cross

Fourteenth Station
Jesus Is Placed in the Tomb

Do not fear adversity, because by it, your soul is placed at the foot of the Cross which takes you to the doors of Heaven. There you will find Him who triumphed over death, who will introduce you to eternal happiness... the Passion of Christ should always be present in your mind if you want to participate in His triumphs.

—Padre Pio

8:2

It was during the time we spent in Assisi nearly two years prior that Rob and I had knelt before the tomb of St. Francis to pray for his intercession for the healing of my kidneys. Shortly after the date of "8/2" had been finalized for our surgeries to take place on the feast of Our Lady of the Angels, I read of the Portiuncula Indulgence.[1] Established by Saint Francis in the early 1200s, the Portiuncula is an old church dedicated to Mary under the title of Our Lady of the Angels, and was the place where he lived and died. Because of St. Francis's love for Mary and his reverence for the angels, the abandoned church was gifted to him by the Benedictine monks. It was Jesus Himself who had given Francis the date of August 2 for the great pardon to take place on the special feast. Those completing its requirements would be freed from all temporal punishment, becoming as pure from the stain of sin as on the day they were baptized!

It also occurred to me another reason why our Lord had chosen this same date of August 2 for me to receive one of Rob's healthy kidneys. A date set aside to receive God's mercy nearly eight centuries prior, the indulgence was established in commemoration with the chains of St. Peter being removed and his release from prison. The first Plenary Indulgence ever granted to the Church, its purpose was to remove the chains of sin for those faithfully seeking it. Reading Fr. Robert DeGrandis's book entitled *Intergenerational Healing*,[2] how I wanted to be freed from the chains of PKD that had held my family captive throughout four generations. Ever since, I realized the importance of praying for healing within the family tree.

With August 2 just a little over a month away, I found myself longing to visit the Solanus Casey Center[3] in Detroit. Some five hundred miles away, I was elated to have Rob on board with my ambition. My only concern for our three-day excursion was in being able to fulfill the promise I'd made to God over a year prior in praying my monthly "Novena to The Blessed Sacrament." Arriving early at the Divine Mercy Chapel before our departure, we planned to come back to the chapel on our return trip home no matter how late. Coming up short on the calls I made in trying to find out where Eucharistic adoration was offered on our full day in Detroit, I resorted to relying fully on God's divine providence. In true Solanus form, I began "thanking God ahead of time" in believing it would happen. Arriving at the Solanus Casey Center, my heart smiled as I read the words engraved upon the glass entrance doors.

Ask, Seek, Knock

Standing on the same Scripture verse in our nightly novena to the Sacred Heart, they were words by which this humble priest had centered his life around. Prior to my inspiration to travel to the center, it was before the Blessed Sacrament that Rob had received another prophetic vision of a holy place where we'd be going. In his journal, he sketched a picture of what looked to be a metal structure resembling the framing of a small house. Rectangular in shape, a cross was erected on the peak of its gable.

As we viewed the bronze figures portrayed in correlation with the scriptural Beatitudes, Rob said, "Sue, look over there. That looks like the same structure shown to me in the chapel a couple of weeks ago!" On our walkthrough, it was a wooden-framed replica of the first St. Bonaventure Church built in 1883.[4] Painted in a silvery grey, it had the appearance of metal. Standing within its frame, we looked up at the skylight directly above, marveling at the way in which the prophetic vision had come to fruition! What consolation we took in knowing we were at the holy place where God foretold we would be! Kneeling down before Solanus' casket,[5] I hand wrote numerous prayer requests of those entrusting to us their needs to lie atop the wooden monument. Praying together the Divine Mercy Chaplet, we went into the church to spend time with Jesus in the quiet of the Tabernacle.

Returning on the following morning, we received the Sacrament of Confession. What a blessing it was to have one of the brothers unlock the St. Bonaventure Chapel for us to pray before the very altar in which the Venerable Solanus had celebrated Mass. I had read of the many accounts of him praying all night long before that very same altar. I thought of the numerous times I spent with Jesus before the Tabernacle at St. Joe's, in the same church he had offered his first Mass following his ordination. Within my heart, I pondered the image shown to Rob on Christmas Eve of Solanus Casey hovering with St. Charbel above the spot in our home enthroned to the Sacred and Immaculate Hearts of Jesus and Mary.

Visiting the gift shop before leaving, a seven-inch ivory angel with sparkling wings perched on a frame caught my eye. Not an impulsive shopper, I felt within me a strong desire to purchase it though I was quite sure I didn't have an appropriate-sized frame to place it on.

"Why don't you get it?" Rob encouraged. "If you can't find a home for it you can always give it as a gift."

Heading off to attend a noon Mass at St. Anne's Church in Detroit, it was the day I was relying on God to help me fulfill my monthly novena to Jesus. Preceding the Mass at the beautiful Gothic-styled cathedral, I prayed for the intercession of St. Anne and her daughter Mary to intercede in helping us find the exposition of the Blessed Sacrament. Following Mass, we asked the man who had assisted the priest if he knew where we could go for Eucharistic adoration.

"Yes!" he said, telling us of a church that offered it on Friday afternoons. "It's a bit tricky to get there," he told us, "but I'm on my lunch hour and will lead you there." Having thanked God ahead of time, He was certainly true in helping me not to miss a single day of my novena!

Driving back to our motel, Rob suggested we take an underground bus to Ontario to have dinner in Canada. Discovering the drop-off point was not in close proximity to the shops and restaurants, I took extra care to do periodic leg stretches and to stay hydrated. Nonetheless, the night to follow would prove to be the most horrific of all the cramps I ever suffered. Awaking at 1:00 a.m., I broke out in a cold sweat from the multiple spasms relentlessly ravaging my legs. "Mary, bring my suffering to Jesus!" I prayed, as Rob rushed to the cooler for ice. It felt as though giant king cobras were biting down on my inner thighs. Other areas felt like my muscles were being ripped from the bone. With the arches of my feet contorting and my toes curling, I lost control of the pain. My nightgown was wringing wet as I began to shiver nonstop. When the pain subsided in what felt like an eternity, Rob retrieved a dry nightgown for me. Laying his hand on my head, he said a prayer of thanksgiving. Completely exhausted, I instantly fell asleep.

Unpacking the suitcase upon returning home, I was unable to find the right-sized frame to place the angel on. A few days later, I received an unexpected package from Father Charles over in Italy. Serving as our tour guide in Rome two years prior, I'd become accustomed to receiving his occasional phone calls. Unwrapping from him a 5"x7" picture of the Pieta rendering of Our Lady portrayed from the bodice up, the destination of my ivory angel with the glittery wings had been determined!

Five days before our surgeries were to take place, I received a call from my friend Debbie.

"Sue," she said, "I was praying a rosary for you before the Blessed Sacrament last night and was inspired to organize a rosary marathon for you and Rob."

Telling me of her plan to begin and end it at the Divine Mercy hour, I was overjoyed. Set to start at 3:00 p.m. on the day before our surgeries, at the hour in which Jesus promises to refuse no one His mercy, rosaries would be prayed for us every hour around the clock until 3:00 p.m. on the third day. Thinking of the special request the Lord had made of us to "ask for things not to be easy," I found her words very consoling. I was also feeling greatly blessed with the four-inch crucifix containing a true relic of the Sacred Cross of Christ that Joyce had entrusted me to wear in the days surrounding the transplant.

On the evening of July 31, Rob and I went to the Chapel of Divine Mercy after meeting with Father Kieran to receive the Anointing of the Sick. Scheduled to be at the hospital early the next morning for our presurgery workups, it was the ninth day of my monthly Novena to the Blessed Sacrament. Filled with peace as I knelt before Jesus, I had a deep sense that I was going to see His wondrous and mighty deeds. In adoration, Rob was shown a vision of a calendar. To the left of the page he saw the face of Mary and to the right, my face.

"Your cheeks looked rosy and healthy," he told me, "and your faces were tilted toward each other."

Continually praying for Mary's intercession, how it warmed my heart to envision myself next to her. I couldn't help but think back to the calendar vision shown to me several months prior of the gold medal shining brightly on Friday, October 5, the date foretold of my healing. Still uncertain of its meaning, I prayed persistently for God's wisdom concerning it.

As we prepared to leave for the hospital, I quickly gathered some sacramentals from Medjugorje to bring along, and seeing the framed picture of the Pieta with the angel atop, I placed it in my suitcase as well. On the two-hour drive, I read out loud the

Scripture verses we'd been reading faithfully every day for five-years. "[God] will shelter you with pinions,/ spread wings that you may take refuge;/ God's faithfulness is a protecting shield" (Psalm 91:4). As I read my favorite psalm in its entirety, Rob received an interior locution telling him that God had formed a protective shield around us through the prayers of his faithful ones. Through the three-day rosary marathon, we'd be cushioned with feathers and tucked safely beneath the powerful wingspan of Almighty God!

Having completed all of our tests by noon, we were free to leave the hospital until our scheduled return time the following day. Stopping off at the registration desk, we asked for directions to the nearest Catholic Church. As Rob drove up to St. Bernard's, he observed its distinctive architectural design. "Look at the roof," he pointed out. "It looks like the prophetic vision shown to me a few weeks ago."

Remembering the sketch he'd drawn in his journal of a "holy place" we'd be going, I shook my head while saying, "That's incredible!" Once again, I was secure in knowing we were exactly where the Lord had shown we would be.

Entering a small chapel, we knelt down before the Tabernacle of the Lord. On the wall directly to the left, a sculpted rendering of Our Lady as depicted in the Pieta was hanging. Molded from the bodice up, it was precisely the same rendition sent to me by Father Charles. Tears formed in my eyes as I thought of my last-minute impulse to bring the picture along in celebration of the feast of Our Lady of the Angels. I felt such peace in the thought of Mary and the angels surrounding us on the special feast. Upon leaving, Rob told me of a Scripture verse that was brought to his heart during our visit with Jesus. "For I will restore you to health;/ of your wounds I will heal you, says the Lord" (Jeremiah 30:17).

The day was Thursday, August 2, 2007. It had been nearly five years since I first penciled in my name next to the Bible passage of Matthew 8:2. In my wildest dreams, I never would have imagined that my husband of thirty-three years would "match" my antigens as though he was my brother! More so, I could never have fathomed that God would choose the date for us to undergo surgery that would also "match" the very Scripture verse we'd prayed especially for me! By seeking His Will in all things, we fully relied on Mary's intercession even concerning the date. The simple plea of a leper had so much resembled the spontaneous petition of my own heart in saying, *"Lord, if You're willing, You can heal me,"* that it inspired me to take God at His word and claim the verse as my very own. "And then a leper approached, did him homage, and said, "Lord, if you wish, you can make me clean" (Matthew 8:2). Standing firmly on the promise of this one little verse in Scripture, the same as the leper who came before Jesus in homage, we also had approached Jesus in reverence before the Tabernacle and in Eucharistic adoration. And just as the leper had an incurable disease in his time, I, too, suffered from an incurable disease in mine. Our prayer to Jesus was the same, and whether through a miracle or through the hands of the surgeon, all healing comes from God.

Arriving early for Rob's 9:30 a.m. admittance, I was happy to be able to spend some time with him prior to my admit time an hour later. Promptly checked into one of the presurgery rooms, he was hooked up to an IV, but as the 10:30 a.m. time for my admittance came and went, Jenelle and I remained in Rob's room as the clock continued to tick by. Three hours after Rob's check-in, I asked a third time, "Shouldn't I be checked in and put on an IV?" Telling three different nurses of the precaution given to me by the nephrology nurse the previous day that I should be hooked up to an IV right away to keep me hydrated, I heard the same answer, "There's not a room available for us to put you in." Having had no liquids after midnight, my concern was growing.

Closing in on half past twelve, a doctor entered Rob's room while calling out, "Susan." But before I could answer, he asked, "Where's Susan?"

"That's me," I said.

Puzzled, he probed further, "Why are you still in your street clothes and not in a room?"

"From what they're telling me, it's because there's not a room available."

Becoming instantly agitated, he walked out. Exhorting his authority, he ordered that I be placed in a room at once. Before I knew it, I was being whisked away and brought into the room directly across from Rob. With an urgent undertone, the nurse handed me a hospital gown to change into.

"Mom," Jenelle said, "while you're doing that, I'm going to find a bathroom."

"Sounds good, Bell," I answered.

As I was changing, I could hear someone apologizing to Rob in regard to a mistake that had been made. It sounded serious. Crossing the hallway back over to his room, I asked, "What's wrong?"

Turning to me, the doctor said apologetically, "Your husband was mistakenly prepped for surgery first when it should have been you, which means you'll be going into surgery within the next few minutes." The look on Rob's face said it all, and I knew his concern was for me. Walking over to his bed, I reassured him that God was in control.

"I love you," I said. "And thanks for what you're putting yourself through out of love for me."

Embracing me, he professed his love back and added, "Remember, hon, I'll be praying for you."

The new turn of events made much more sense. I was having two major surgeries—first to excise both of my kidneys, and second, the delicate and skilled surgical procedure of transplanting Rob's kidney into my body. His operation would be timed in accordance with mine, so that within fifteen minutes of excising his left kidney, it would be relocated within me. Walking back into my room, a scurry of activity unfolded as a surplus of nurses descended upon me. Rushing about to prep me for surgery, they poked and prodded, trying hastily to hook me up to IV lines. Failing on every attempt, they resorted to inserting an IV port in the base of my neck.

"How soon before I'm taken into surgery?" I inquired.

"Very soon!" a nurse replied.

Pleadingly I said, "Please don't take me off before my daughter returns from the bathroom. She's still under the assumption that my surgery is at least an hour away, and I'm certain she'll feel terrible if she's not able to see me beforehand."

"When will she be back?" the nurse asked apprehensively.

"Soon," I replied.

Things were happening fast. To the nurse closest to me, I asked, "May I keep my scapular on?"

"No, I'm sorry. That won't be possible," she said straightforwardly. "There's nowhere on your entire body that doesn't need to be clear."

Remembering the pledge we'd made to God in asking "for things not to be easy," I surrendered my heart's desire back into His Holy Will.

"Our Lady of the Angels," I prayed, "please be with me throughout."

Just then, one of the other nurses said assertively, "Why can't we tape her scapular to the top of her right foot? It won't be in the way of anything there."

With no arguments heard, I thanked her from the bottom of my heart. Within myself, I prayed, "Thank you, Queen of the Angels!"

Looking rather perplexed with all of the commotion going on, I breathed a sigh of relief as Jenelle walked in.

"Bell," I said tenderly, "they need to take me into surgery first, and they're going to be wheeling me off any moment now."

Seeing her beautiful blue eyes tear up, she bent down. Wrapping her arms around me, she said, "Mom, I'll be praying for you the whole time." Standing back up, her face suddenly lit up as she told of what she discovered. "As I was walking down the hallway, I noticed the five-inch room numbers mounted above each room. And guess what the room numbers are that you and dad are in?"

"What?" I asked curiously.

"You're in room number 8 and dad is right across from you in room number 2!"

"Oh my goodness!" I exclaimed. This time it was my turn to get teary-eyed of the way God's preordained plan was unfolding. After claiming Matthew 8:2 everyday as my very own, combined with the amazing way in which we were led to schedule our surgeries on 8/2, it was also in His divine providence that we now found ourselves awaiting our surgeries in rooms numbered 8 and 2! Elated, I took hold of my darling daughter's hand in reassurance that God was heartening us that He was in complete control. "O Most High, when I am afraid,/ in you I place my trust" (Psalm 56:3).

It was time for me to go, and just as I was removing Joyce's large Crucifix from around my neck to give to Jenelle for safekeeping, in walked my surgeon. Looking up in total surprise to see him standing at the foot of my bed, I automatically held it out to him, saying, "Within this Crucifix is contained a true relic of the Cross of Christ. Would you like to hold it?"

Smiling, he replied, "Yes. I would." Having already proclaimed to us months earlier that his hands were vessels of the Lord, I wondered how it could possibly get any better than this. To witness my physician closing his eyes momentarily while holding a sacred relic of the same Cross the Divine Physician hung from to heal the wounds of the world—in the *same* hands that would soon be performing surgery on me, I felt like I was on top of the world! Handing it back, he left to prep for surgery. Kissing the Crucifix before passing it off to Jenelle, I said to her, "Hold on to this in faith."

"I will, Mom," she promised. "Love you."

"I love you too, sweetie," I said as I reached out to squeeze her hand. "Take good care of dad, and remember that Mary and the angels will be right in there with me." As they rolled the gurney toward the surgery unit, I prayed silently, "Jesus, I trust in You!"

Opening my eyes some ten hours later, the first thing I saw was Jenelle standing near my bed. Feeling calm and relaxed, she, on the other hand, looked completely exhausted. Immediately perking up to see me awake, she rushed to my side.

"Mom," she said in her gentle manner, "you're in the intensive care unit. I'm so relieved that you're okay!"

"I'm fine," I responded. "Why am I in the ICU?"

Filling me in on the harrowing details, she told me that things didn't go the way they had planned. Following the excision of my kidneys, she said of how relieved she'd been to receive a call from my doctor to report that everything had gone very smoothly. They just had to wait to receive Rob's kidney before doing the transplant surgery, ideally, within the calculated fifteen-minute time period. "The doctor promised to call me again when your kidney transplant was completed," she said. "But over two hours later, I got a call from dad's surgeon telling me they had trouble removing his kidney through the scope procedure. He was fine, but it had taken much longer than planned."

Her heart dropped into her stomach as her concern for me grew in knowing that I was likely dehydrated, and that I'd already been without any kidney function for two and a half hours. With the five-plus hour surgery time required to perform the transplant surgery, she wondered how I'd possibly be able to maintain life. Feeling a burden too heavy to carry on her own, she first called her brother before proceeding to to call family, friends, and everyone she could think of to petition for prayer. The word of her plea spread quickly throughout the surrounding towns, with various prayer chains set into motion. Taking comfort in the around-the-clock rosary marathon already orchestrated on our behalf, she held on tightly to the Crucifix in her possession. "In my rosaries, I asked Mary and the angels to come to your aid," she told me.

"I'm sorry you had to go through all that," I said as I squeezed her hand.

"I'm just so happy you're all right, she replied. "The doctor told me that your new kidney is working great, but that your blood pressure nearly bottomed out in surgery. That's the reason you're in the ICU."

Upon first meeting my surgeon, he had presented me with the option of having both my kidneys removed or just one of them. In the event that something went wrong, to leave one in would allow kidney function enough to keep me alive. Explaining very carefully the pros and cons of each, I asked what he thought would be the best choice.

"If you leave the kidney in, it can become infected and require another surgery down the road to remove it," he told me. "I'd recommend you get both of them excised." Considering that we'd been praying for St. Joseph's intercession to impart God's wisdom to our doctors, in faith, I went along with his recommendation. And though something had gone terribly wrong in the lengthy delay of receiving Rob's kidney, never did I second guess my decision. Having accepted our Lord's invitation for things "not to be easy," I thought of how very blessed we'd been to have had the shield of God's protection through the prayers of His righteous ones, and of the hearts of others that had been opened in seeing power of prayer, some who hadn't prayed a rosary in years.

Thinking of Our Lady and the angels keeping a very close watch on me in the operating room, I asked Jenelle to remove the picture of Mary with the angel adorning its frame from my suitcase to display. Thanking her, I asked, "Bell, do you remember the words you heard spoken in your heart at the Marian grotto at St. Joe's when you asked Mary when I'd be healed?"

"The angels will sing," she said, smiling.

"Today, the angels were singing," I affirmed.

Early the next morning, I heard a group of doctors standing just inside my door, separated by only a small partition. Going over my chart and discussing my case, my surgeon's tone of voice sounded particularly uplifting as he told the team of essentially what had transpired in the surgery room the day before. Having teetered on the balance of life and death, with zero kidney function and blood pressure plummeting, I had been in imminent danger of going into shock and probable death. Walking over to the foot of my bed, he held up high the chart containing the excellent readings of my lab results. Exuberantly pleased, my surgeon said, "No matter what anyone ever tells you about their transplant, I want you to know that you'll always be in a class of your own!"

What was so remarkable about what had transpired in the ICU that morning was in remembering a prophetic vision Rob had recorded in his journal several weeks earlier. It was before the Blessed Sacrament that he'd been shown a scene in which a doctor was looking at my chart in absolute amazement.

"It had to do with your healing," he told me, "and the doctor couldn't believe his eyes."

Realizing the prophetic vision had been fulfilled the day after my surgery, on August 3, I saw the connection it had to the Bible verse in Matthew 8:3, in Jesus' response to the leper's plea. "He stretched out his hand, touched him, and said, 'I will do it. Be made clean.' His leprosy was cleansed immediately" (Matthew 8:3). The verse was key in answer to the prayer of the leper, and in answer to the prayer of my heart that had so closely resembled his. I thought of the many times in my five-year journey that I had felt Jesus' outstretched hand always there in helping me carry my cross.

"Thank You, sweet Jesus," I prayed from my heart, "for Your willingness to heal me."

Receiving a visit from my son and his wife that same afternoon, Eric was relieved to see for himself that his mom was going to be all right. Elated in the expectancy of the soon-to-be arrival of our third grandchild, I placed a kiss on my hand to rest on Kelly's tummy.

"God bless you, little one," I said. "How blessed I've been in the chance to watch you grow." Having prayed to be blessed with grandchildren, the favor of the Lord was upon us.

There was a young nurse assigned to my care who came in at the change of shifts. Though she was doing a very good and thorough job, I could see in her eyes that her heart was void of love in the work she was doing. In my heart I felt very sad, asking Jesus to bless her. Seeing my scapular around my neck, she commented, "Oh, I remember those! My grandmother gave one to me when I was little, but I lost it in third grade." Thinking of how she must have treasured the gift to remember exactly when she lost it, I wondered if perhaps the loss of her grandmother had something to do with her lack of love in her chosen profession. It was then that I remembered placing a scapular in my suitcase with the other sacramentals I brought along. Aware that her shift was nearing its end, I asked, "Would you mind coming back before you leave?"

"Sure," she answered.

I asked Jenelle to retrieve the scapular and a miraculous medal from my suitcase.

"Sweetie," I said as she placed it on the bedside table, "would you mind praying a rosary with me for Janie?"

"Who's that?" she asked.

"Oh, she's one of the women back from the bus trip to the Medjugorje Conference who we've been praying for ever since, and she's not doing too well. I suddenly feel the need to pray for her."

Together, we lifted Janie up in prayer. It was getting late, and before going off to the lounge for the night, Jenelle said to me; "Mom, promise me you'll buzz the nurse to come and get me for any reason. I'm just on the other side of the ICU and I'll be there if you need me." Aware that I was having trouble sleeping with the mega-doses of meds and the sounding alarms in blood pressure drops, she added, "I can come and pray with you some more if you want."

"We'll see," I answered. "First and foremost is for you to get some much needed rest."

Unwilling to stay at a hotel until I was out of intensive care, she headed off to the lounge.

A short time later, the nurse returned at the end of her shift. Giving her the blessed scapular from Italy, I told her of how I was prompted to put it in my suitcase the morning before. "I had to bring it for you," I told her. Visibly touched, she held onto it affectionately. "This is also yours," I said, giving her a miraculous medal, explaining of how it held Our Lady's Motherly blessing as well as that of a priest. Talking with her briefly about Mary's messages, she genuinely thanked me. Walking slowly out of my room, she stared down into her hands.

Since waking up from the anesthetic the evening before, I hadn't slept a wink. Suffering the ill effects of the drugs, I also had a nagging backache in my lower spine, presumably from the hours spent on the operating table. Deducing that a bulged disc in the lumbar area of my spine from years back must have become agitated, as the hours and minutes ticked by on my second sleepless night in the ICU, though I couldn't concentrate on prayer as normal, I prayed continuous little prayers to Jesus and Mary. Waiting until early morning to take Jenelle up on her offer to pray with me, I noticed that my call button had been mistakenly set down out of my reach.

That afternoon as the day nurses were busy changing my IV bags and catheter, the nurse who I'd given the scapular to the previous night had come in early for her shift. Though she wasn't assigned to my care, with nurses on either side of me, she reached over from the end of my bed. Extending out her arm, she squeezed my hand, saying, "How can I ever thank you enough for the kindness you've shown me?" Flowing out from her eyes, I saw love.

I wanted desperately to be moved out of the ICU to the transplant floor closer to Rob. I couldn't wait to see him! But as the day wore on, I started to think that perhaps it wasn't going to happen in the way I'd hoped. Placing the outcome into God's Holy Will, I prayed over and over to myself, "Thy Will be done." How delighted I was when, in late afternoon, my nurse relayed that my blood pressure was stable enough for them to remove the IV bag containing the medication to control it!

Arriving in my new room in the transplant unit, the first thing I did was to ask my nurse if I could see Rob. First helping me to sit up in a chair, the moment she left, I became acutely aware of the need to pray for the woman in the room next to me. Hearing her chronic cough, I sensed it was something very serious. Immediately, I began pleading for the Precious Blood of Jesus to be poured out upon the woman, asking Mary to intercede on her behalf. Feeling light-headed from sitting up for the first time since surgery, I closed my eyes. Interiorly, I saw Our Lady of Grace. Wearing a white gown with a soft blue mantle, she was beautiful! Inwardly, I pronounced, "Mary, I'm so happy to see you!" Seconds later as her image disappeared, my heart overflowed with joy and peace.

I thought back to six months earlier, when I'd been drawn to pray before the life-sized statue of Our Lady of Grace at St. Pius. I remembered the amazing grace of seeing the miracle of the sun on my way home from church, and of the red cloud in the shape of an angel wing. Truly a foreshadow of the mercy I'd receive in the red and white rays I saw extending down from the sun, I reminisced of the Scripture that had come to my mind that day while praying the Divine Mercy Chaplet: "But for you who fear my name, there will arise/ the sun of justice with its healing rays;/ And you will gambol like calves out of the stall" (Malachi 3:20).

Into my room I saw walking my beloved Rob! Elated to finally see each other, he bent down to hug me as best he could.

"Thanks, hon," I said softly. "I love you so much for what you've done."

"I love you too," he replied softly. Noticing how weak he looked, I shared with him of my vision of Mary before persuading him to get some rest.

"I will, hon, but I first want to tell you that I received a word of knowledge the morning after surgery that I need to offer my sufferings to Jesus." Smiling, I nodded in agreement. Giving me a kiss before leaving, he added "Sue, we need to pray for that lady in the room next to you who's coughing."

Shortly after he left, I could smell the wonderful aroma of the dinner trays being distributed to the surrounding rooms. From the time of my required fast the night before surgery, it had been three days since I had food or water, with the exception of the tiny sips allowed me to take my medications. Not overly thrilled at the prospect of taking lifelong antirejection drugs, it occurred to me of how even taking the medicine prescribed to me could bring honor to God. From that day on, I decided that every pill I would ever take for the rest of my life I'd offer for His glory. Every time I took them, I prayed, "Jesus, Mary, Joseph, I love you. Save souls."

The following day, I was happy to learn that I'd been upgraded to "clear liquids," and I was looking forward to having some broth and Jell-o. It was Sunday, and even more so, I found myself craving the spiritual nourishment of the Bread of Life. Having gone without receiving Jesus in the Eucharist for three days, I was happy when a Catholic priest walked into my room. Administering to me the Sacrament of Holy Communion, I was filled with joy. Talking with him, I learned that the church that had fulfilled the prophetic vision shown to Rob the day before our surgeries had been the same parish he'd belonged to in his youth. Returning back to my room a half hour later, he said, "I've downloaded Pope John Paul II's apostolic letter, *Salvifici Doloris*,[6] for you to read. It's written on the value of human suffering and it'll help you understand the co-redemptive power of suffering with Jesus." Never having disclosed to him my affection for John Paul II or of my devotion to Mary, the true co-redemptrice of Christ's sufferings, I was astonished at his insight. "Now I rejoice in my sufferings for your sake, and in my flesh I am filling up what is lacking in the afflictions of Christ on behalf of his body, which is the church" (Colossians 1:24).

In his Apostolic Letter on Human Suffering entitled *Salvifici Doloris*, John Paul II said:

> Human suffering evokes compassion; it also evokes respect, and in its own way it intimidates. For in suffering is contained the greatness of a specific mystery. This special respect for every form of human suffering must be set at the beginning of what will be expressed here later by the deepest need of the heart, and also by the deep imperative of faith.[7]
>
> —The Supreme Pontiff Pope John Paul II

On morning two following my transfer to the transplant unit I was allowed to have food. The problem was, in my attempt to eat breakfast, I got a terrible stomachache and dysentery.

"That's okay," my surgeon advised. "We'll give you something for that, but it's imperative that you eat, even if its food brought in from the outside if that's what you prefer. You have to eat."

In combination with my trouble eating, every time I tried to get up to walk or to attend one of the tutorial classes that were being offered, I'd start to black out from the low blood pressure that still resulted from the complications of surgery.

Asking if I'd like to take a shower, the nurse cautioned me to press the button if I was in need of help. Feeling the lightheadedness come on soon after getting in, I quickly rinsed the shampoo from my hair. Realizing I was about to faint, I pressed the help button before managing to get out of the shower and sit down. Seconds later, I saw the curtain of black coming down before my eyes, as my nurse swiftly held on to me, assisting me back into bed. Bound and determined to make it to at least one of the educational classes recommended for optimum home care, I voiced to Rob of my goal to attend the afternoon class the following day.

Feeling very weak and shaky, I walked with the assistance of my nurse and portable IV cart on one side and Rob and Jenelle on the other down the hallway to where the class was being held. Halfway there I said in alarm, "I'm feeling really lightheaded!"

Calmly, my nurse persuaded, "It's not too much farther."

With determination, I continued pressing on as she encouraged. Arriving at my destination at last, I was pleased with my achievement. Sitting down on the chair, I felt shaky and incredibly weak, when suddenly the black curtain began coming down before my eyes.

"I'm going to faint!" I said with urgency. Lifting me back into a wheelchair, my nurse hurriedly started pushing me back to my room. The instant the burst of fresh air hit my face, the blackness dissipated. Taking my blood pressure once back at my room, medication was put into my IV to bring it back up. Other occasions when my blood pressure didn't dip quite as low, I'd be given high-sodium broth to elevate it enough to keep me from fainting.

Aside from the woman with the cough in the room next to me, who Rob and I had been praying for from the beginning, there was another woman in my wing of the transplant unit who I was also praying for. A kidney transplant recipient from a few years prior, not only was her kidney rejecting, but her liver was also failing. Family members had gathered in the lounge located near my room, speaking of their mother's life-threatening condition with Jenelle and her friend. Relaying this to me, my heart went out to the poor woman as I began lifting up her needs to the Lord.

Later that evening, the night shift nurse assigned to my care shared with me of the heartache she suffered in the health concerns involving her nine-year-old son, and of the torments of his precious little heart in getting picked on at school.

"I'll pray for him," I promised, assuring her that his needs would be continually lifted up in the prayers of the Intercessors of Light as well. Retrieving a medal from the blessed sacramentals I'd brought from home, I asked, "Would you like this blessed medal to give to your son?"

Tearing up, she bent down to give me a hug. "I'd love it," she answered. "Thank you so much."

The following morning, as my surgeon made his rounds, marked the first day I could walk without feeling the lightheadedness.

"When do you think I'll be able to go home?" I questioned.

"That's what I like to hear!" he commented. "Maybe tomorrow, but we have to wait for one more test to come back before we can release you."

Voicing to him my concern of being behind the other transplant patients who'd been walking about since day one, he responded, "Not to worry, that will take care of itself now that you're able to eat. The bottom line is that your lab results are excellent. You're doing great, but because of the complications of your surgery, the date of your healing will be extended out an extra week from the usual eight weeks."

Not having attended any of the educational classes, I was unaware of an eight-week time period of recovery set in place for transplant patients. At the very instant my doctor voiced to me that he was extending out my healing date one week, I knew exactly the date it would be! Remembering the "calendar vision" that was shown to me over six months prior in seeing

Friday, October 5 as the date of my predestined healing, I knew instantaneously that the nine-week projected healing time would coincide perfectly with the same date. Thinking of the "shiny gold medallion" foretelling the date of my healing, I also connected the dots to what one of the nurses in the ICU told me the day after my surgery.

"Today is day one of your healing," she had said. "We begin counting the first day of healing on the first day following surgery."

Given that my operation was on a Thursday, August 2, that would mean I'd begin counting out the weeks of my recovery beginning on Friday, August 3. Confirming what I already knew in my heart to be true, my surgeon's nine-week date-of-healing brought me to Friday, October 5, on the feast of St. Faustina! I thought of my devotion to praying the Chaplet of Divine Mercy each day at 3:00 p.m. in correlation with the three days that I could not eat or drink, and of the three days I'd gone without receiving the Bread of Life in the Eucharist.

Springing up from my heart, I felt a strong desire to ask Rob if we could make plans to celebrate October 5 at Holy Hill. Located a scant two hours from our home, we'd gone to the Basilica of the National Shrine of Mary, Help of Christians on numerous occasions. Aside from attending Mass and confession, we loved hiking outdoors to the top of Holy Hill to pray the Stations of the Cross.

All at once, my thoughts were interrupted as I became aware of the woman in the room next to me whose cough was getting progressively worse. Politely asking the nursing staff if they'd mind closing my door behind them each time they left my room, they'd always assure me that it was protocol for no one "contagious" to be admitted into the transplant ward. Though completely sincere, I sensed from the very beginning the woman was critically ill. With my door left open more than it was closed, I resigned myself to relying on the care and protection of Mary and the angels.

With Rob's release from the hospital two days prior, Jenelle was driving him to a nearby hotel to sleep, while insisting that she stay in the lounge close to my room. Earlier that same evening as the two of them came back to be with me after dinner, Jenny, my favorite nurse, came in and offered to assist me in going for a nice long walk with them. Standing just outside of the door to my room with Rob and Jenelle upon returning, we overheard a doctor gently breaking the news to the woman with the cough that the bacteria causing her problems had been identified. Going into my room, we closed the door and lifted her up in prayer.

"Jenelle," I said, pointing to the large vase of flowers sitting on the counter. "Ever since receiving this gorgeous bouquet earlier today, I've felt inspired to give it to the woman whose transplanted kidney and liver are failing. Would you mind bringing them to her family when you see them in the lounge?"

"Sure," she responded.

Sitting down, I quickly wrote the woman a note, telling her that I'd been praying for her since she'd first been brought in, and that despite the fact that I hoped to be released the next day, her needs would be continually lifted up by the Intercessors of Light. "When good things begin to happen in regard to your healing," I wrote, "give thanks to God for answered prayer."

As I finished the last line, Jenelle said, "I'm pretty sure her family is in the lounge right now."

"Perfect timing," I replied, sealing the envelope.

Excited at the prospect of being able to go home, the three of us decided to make it an early night to catch up on some much-needed sleep. Still quite weak, Rob's arm was hurting at the IV site where phlebitis had developed, with a three-inch red streak traveling up his arm. Once back at the motel, he'd ice it before going to sleep. It had been a good day for me, and for the first time since my admittance six days prior, Jenelle agreed to stay at the hotel where she could get a better night's sleep.

"Mom, be sure to call me for any reason," she said before leaving.

"I will, sweetie," I promised. As I walked to my bed after seeing them out, I heard interiorly within my heart, "If you awake during the night, pray for the dying."

Though I could still feel tenderness on both sides of my back where my kidneys had been removed, as well as in the area where the surgeon placed Rob's kidney, it was my lumbar spine that was causing me the most aggravation. Having felt the pain throughout the entire duration of the time I was on the strong narcotics, it was growing worse. Situating myself in a way that I hoped to be able to read my Bible, I just couldn't get comfortable. At midnight, when my nurse came in with my dose of Tylenol, I managed to fall asleep shortly after taking it.

Awakening during the night with severe back pain, I buzzed my nurse to ask for more pain reliever. Entering my darkened room, she bent down close to my face and said, "I'm sorry, but it's only 1:30 a.m. and too soon for you to have it again." Surprised that I'd only been sleeping for an hour before waking up with pain, I instantly remembered the interior message of the night before, instructing me to pray for the dying. Closing my eyes, as I began praying first for Janie, I was shown a vision of Rob standing next to me in the back center of St. Francis Xavier Cathedral. Located in the city where she lived, we were overlooking her funeral Mass. Seeing her casket placed in the middle front aisle before the altar, I felt an overwhelming sense of peace as I watched those in attendance filing out of their seats to receive Communion.

Lying awake in my hospital bed, I heard the organ-donation helicopter descending down upon the landing pad located on the rooftop outside of my room. Right away, I began praying for the repose of the soul from whom the organ(s) had come, as well as for those whose life hung in the balance in wait of a life-saving organ transplant.

Next, as I lay praying, I heard a code-blue alert sound throughout the hospital corridors. From the depth of my heart I prayed three Hail Marys, "Pray for us sinners, now and at the hour of our death,"[8] asking our dear Blessed Mother to intercede on behalf of the dying soul. Offering my pain to Jesus through Mary, I prayed throughout the night, never again thinking of buzzing the nurse for more pain medication. "Every pain we endure with love, every cross borne with resignation, benefits every man, woman and child in the Mystical Body of Christ"[9] (Mother M. Angelica).

At 4:30 a.m., the hospital attendants came to get the woman in the room next to me who was coughing incessantly. With my door wide open, I heard them tell her she was being taken to have a test done of some sort. I thought it rather odd to be doing it in the middle of the night. Feeling deep compassion for her, I prayed with all my heart. With the picture from Father Charles sitting on the shelf next to me, I thought of our sorrowful Mother's tears as she held the lifeless body of her Son in her arms. Though His human Heart would beat no more, I thought of how Jesus' divine Heart would never stop beating for souls. I thought of how Mary longs to hold her children who've drifted away from the faith and how her tears will wash away their hardened hearts, enabling the Light of Christ to shine in. For the "woman with the cough," I prayed for the Blood of Jesus to be poured out upon her.

As morning neared, a specific Scripture verse kept going over and over in my mind. Within my heart, I knew it was intended for Jenny, the young nurse who I favored the most. Working at the hospital part-time while she was still finishing up her nursing degree, I saw the love and genuine affection that flowed out from her to her patients. In conversations regarding faith, she told me she was still searching. "I just don't see the love," she voiced. Exploring various movements with a friend on campus, I cautioned her of the lures and traps that certain religions lend themselves to in changing one's whole belief system.

"Be sure to have your spiritual ladder firmly planted up against the right wall," I advised. "When you do, your love will bring many souls up the rungs of faith with you to God's kingdom."

Because nurses were not assigned to the same patient two days in a row, I knew that Jenny wouldn't be my nurse, and furthermore, I had no idea if she was even scheduled to work. What I did know was that I needed to write down the Scripture verse the Spirit was placing on my heart to give to her. At 5:45 a.m., I got out of bed to retrieve my note cards from the shelf. Opening my Bible, I wrote her a little note followed by God's inspired word. "For I know well the plans I have in mind for you, says the Lord, plans for your welfare, not for woe! plans to give you a future full of hope. When you call me, when you go to pray to me, I will listen to you" (Jeremiah 29:11–12). As I wrote the last verse, tears formed in my eyes in the knowledge that our Lord had His designs on Jenny, and that she would find what she was searching for. "When you look for me, you will find me. Yes, when you seek me with all your heart, you will find me with you, says the Lord" (Jeremiah 29:13–14).

Stopping by my room before the start of her morning shift, I was delighted to see Jenny!

"Assuming you'll be going home today," she said cheerfully, "I decided to stop in to say good-bye."

"I'm so glad you did," I replied. "I have a card for you."

Looking surprised, she said, "Thank you! I'll open it on my break."

Around midmorning, she returned to thank me for the words of encouragement. I said, "Jenny, early this morning I was prompted to write down that passage for you because God wanted to speak to you directly through Scripture."

Visibly moved, she hugged me before returning to her duties.

It was day seven of my hospital stay, and I was elated to hear of my approved release. Picking up the phone, I immediately called Rob and Jenelle to tell them the news.

"That's great, hon," Rob said. "We'll check out right now and will be on our way over."

Jenelle's face beamed as they walked into my room. She wore a bright pink T-shirt which read, "I LOVE MOM." My eyes watered in remembering the Scripture verse I had shared with her the night before our surgeries: "For I will restore you to health;/ of your wounds I will heal you, says the Lord" (Jeremiah 30:17).

"Thanks for being there for us, Bell," I said, knowing she wouldn't have had it any other way. Turning to embrace my husband of thirty-three years, my heart spilled over with love and gratitude of the precious gift he'd given me. Though organ donation is referred to as the "gift of life," I didn't know exactly why, but I could only refer to my husband's selfless gift as the "gift of love." It was God's love flowing out from him that he gave to me his kidney, and it was God, the giver of all life, who had given me the "gift of life," both of which I'd be eternally grateful for.

Christian Wedding quilt, *Quilting Cause*

With one hospital personnel filing into my room after another, they attempted to give me a crash course on all I missed out on in not being able to attend any of the home healthcare classes. Somehow, I had an intrinsic understanding of everything I needed to do. Lunchtime came and went, until the moment I'd been waiting for had finally arrived. Sitting down in the wheelchair to exit my room, I noticed the door of the room previously occupied by the "woman with the cough" was tightly closed.

"Look," I said to Rob. Posted on the door was a biohazard sign that read "Do Not Enter."

We made our way down the hallway to the elevator. There was a group of people in street clothes standing by the nurse's station. Smiling, it appeared as though they were as happy with my release as I was. Lining up, they extended their hands out to me as we passed by, wishing me well and giving me high fives along the way. With a send-off such as that, I was certain that Mary and the triumphant choirs of angels were singing along in jubilation!

"Mom," Jenelle whispered as we approached the elevator, "do you know who those people were?"

"No, I have no idea," I answered.

"They're the family of the woman you gave your vase of flowers to," she revealed. Happy tears welled up in my eyes in the joyfulness I felt for listening to the inspiration that offered such hope to God's people.

Stopping off at the hospital pharmacy to get my meds before leaving, there were lines of people waiting to be served. Upon finishing up with that, Rob suddenly remembered that we forgot all of the wonderful fruit baskets we'd been given. Much more than we could possibly consume, I planned to give them to Father Carr's Place-2-B.

"How about I go up to retrieve them from the fridge while you two wait at the revolving doors?" Rob suggested.

"Do you think you're up to it?" I asked.

"I'll walk slow and put them on a cart," he assured.

Wheeling me toward the exit doors, Jenelle found a nice little nook for us to wait for Rob's return. As people hustled in and out of the revolving doors, I experienced something unlike anything I've ever experienced before. Emanating out from the eyes of the people who walked by from both directions, the Lord allowed me to see the hollowed emptiness of those who were living in the ways of the world in His absence. There were many. And though I could see their person and the clothes they had on, their outside appearance was secondary to the barrenness I saw radiating out from the darkness of their souls. To myself, I began praying for their conversion. "Therefore I tell you, do not worry about your life, what you will eat [or drink], or about your body, what you will wear. Is not life more than food and the body more than clothing?" (Matthew 6:25). "But seek first the kingdom [of God] and his righteousness, and all these things will be given you besides" (Matthew 6:33).

At long last, how excited I was to see Rob walking toward us with the cart full of fruit! As valet parking drove up with our vehicle, Jenelle assisted in helping us get in before proceeding to drive us home. Looking at the clock on the dashboard, it was exactly 3:00 p.m.! Astounded at the God-incidence of the numerous time delays that added up for us to leave the hospital right at the Divine Mercy hour, I was so incredibly happy that tears of joy rolled down my face. Recipients of God's mercy, we began praying together the Divine Mercy Chaplet.

Getting out of the traffic and onto the interstate, Jenelle asked, "Mom, were you awake at 1:30 this morning?"

Thinking it peculiar for her to ask me specifically if I was awake at the precise time I awoke to pray for the dying, I said yes.

"Oh," she went on. "I remember you asking me to pray with you for someone named Janie when you first came out of the anesthetic from surgery, and so I thought that if you were awake at 1:30 a.m. this morning that you'd probably be praying for her again."

"As a matter of fact, I *was* praying for Janie at 1:30 this morning, but why do you ask?"

"It's because your friend Mary left a message on my cell phone this morning, asking me to let you know that Janie passed away at 1:30 a.m."

Tears immediately began flowing down my cheeks.

"Oh, I'm sorry," Jenelle apologized. "I didn't know if I should tell you right away or not."

Reassuring her, I said, "There's no need for you to feel bad for telling me. Though I'm deeply saddened at her passing, I'm overjoyed at the same time." Telling them of the interior locution I received right after they left for the hotel the night before, I articulated to them how I awoke with pain and of my nurse reporting to me that it was 1:30 a.m. before leaving my room. Shown a vision of Janie's funeral, how blessed I was for the privilege of praying for her at the very moment of her death.

As we traveled home that warm and humid August day, I couldn't help but notice the white and wispy cumulous clouds that gently floated across the blue sky. In the form of angel wings, it seemed as though they were moving right along with us. With joyful hearts, we talked, rested, and prayed together the Joyful Mysteries of the rosary.

"Look at the angel in the sky!" I exclaimed as we turned onto our street. It appeared that Mary and the angels not only oversaw our surgeries, but they also escorted us safely back home! Already after five o'clock, the first task at hand for me was to sort through the prescriptions we'd just picked up from the pharmacy in order to take my scheduled 6:00 p.m. medications on time. As Jenelle went to the stove to fix dinner, her dear friend sat down at the table with me to help. Looking at the conglomeration of medication, I took consolation in knowing that I'd eventually be taken off some, and significantly reduced on the others.

As I was going about doing all of this, our dear friend, Nestor, called to see how we were doing. Though we were unable to talk with him much during our hospitalization, he'd been in constant communication with Jenelle. Along with my sisters and my friend, Debbie, what a tremendous support they were to her in the ordeal she suffered. It was Wednesday, the same day that the Intercessors of Light met each week in our home. With a change of venue during our time of recovery, I gave Nestor the list of the names I compiled during our hospital stay of those in need of prayer.

"Oh, Nestor," I added, "I don't know her name, but could you please write down 'woman with a cough' under the categories of 'Blessings of the Lord' and 'Salvation.' I don't think she's going to make it."

That first evening home, I awoke at 2:40 a.m. with a strong sense that I needed to pray for someone who was dying. There'd been numerous times before that I awakened at 3:00 a.m. to pray the Chaplet of Divine Mercy for the salvation of souls, but this time I sensed that it was someone specific I needed to pray for. Unaware of who it was or why I was to pray it twenty minutes early, I began reciting the chaplet for whoever it was in need of God's mercy. Upon finishing, I received interiorly the knowledge that the "woman with the cough" had just passed from this life and into the next. As I turned to look at the alarm clock, it was 3:00 a.m. Thinking of our Lord's promise to St. Faustina, what a privilege and blessing it was for me to be called upon to pray her home. "At the hour of their death, I defend as My own glory every soul that will say this chaplet; or when others say it for a dying person, the indulgence is the same"[10] (*Diary*, 811).

In the problems and difficulties of life, we're offered opportunity after opportunity to grow in the sanctification of our souls by uniting our pain with the pain that Jesus bore for us. It was with a sincere heart that Rob and I had accepted God's invitation of asking Him for things "not to be easy." We agreed to His offer not because we were looking for more trials and tribulation, but because we were seeking to infuse our free will as one with the

Divine Will of God, in full trust of His mercy. "If we knew the power of suffering, we would pray for it," said Mother Theresa of Calcutta.[11] We were learning that it's in deciding completely for Jesus in the daily unrestrained surrender of our will that we would receive the grace of seeing His wondrous works unfolding in our lives. "But if you are patient when you suffer for doing what is good, this is a grace before God. For to this you have been called, because Christ also suffered for you, leaving you an example that you should follow in his footsteps" (1 Peter 2:20–21).

> Christ, when you shall call me hence,
> Be your Mother my defense,
>   Be your cross my victory.
>
> —Stabat Mater

If God gives you an abundant harvest of trials, it is a sign of great holiness which He desires you to attain. Do you want to become a great saint? Ask God to send you many sufferings. The flame of Divine Love never rises higher than when fed with the wood of the Cross, which the infinite charity of the Savior used to finish His sacrifice. All the pleasures of the world are nothing compared with the sweetness found in the gall and vinegar offered to Jesus Christ. That is, hard and painful things endured for Jesus Christ and with Jesus Christ.

—Saint Ignatius of Loyola[12]

Stations of the Cross

Fifteenth Station
Jesus Is Risen

Let us ascend Calvary, burdened with the Cross but without tiring. And let us be convinced that our ascent will lead us to the Heavenly vision of our sweetest Savior.

—Padre Pio

Jesus, I Trust in You!

Though our struggles didn't come to an end when we returned home from the hospital, it was during this period of our affliction that I saw God's grace abound in ways I never before imagined. By relying completely on grace to get me over each hurdle as it presented itself, I saw firsthand that God's grace truly was sufficient to get me through. But in order for grace to take effect, it required cooperation on my part. Understanding that it's so often in the crossroads of our lives that the cross of adversity is found, it's in deciding to walk with Jesus in those very hardships that one will begin to see their struggles as opportunities of spiritual growth. In viewing suffering as circumstances that God uses to further transform the hearts of His people and change their lives for the better, we'll begin to see our trials as ways that can keep us from veering off of the path that leads to heaven. In the quest of sorting through the things in life that really matter, what matters the most is getting to heaven. "But the path of the just is like shining light,/ that grows in brilliance till perfect day" (Proverbs 4:18).

The day after returning home from the hospital, Jenelle came down with a terrible respiratory infection. Concerned in taking the precautions necessary so as to not to spread it to me, though she planned to be at our beck and call day and night, with my compromised immune system she decided it best to back off until her prescribed antibiotic could take effect. During the time she strategically kept her distance, we saw God's love operating through those around us in the daily witness of corporal and spiritual acts of mercy.

With Rob unable to drive, my friend Debbie offered to bring me to have my blood work drawn locally to be faxed to my nurse coordinator at UW Madison. But trying to get out of bed, the all-too familiar black curtain began coming down before my eyes. Quickly lying back down to prevent from fainting, I waited a bit before trying to get up again. Sitting up very slowly, I carefully placed my feet on the floor. But as soon as I tried standing up, the blackness started coming down once again. In my third attempt, I was able to stand up.

"Are you okay to walk?" Rob asked.

"I think so," I responded. "I still feel a little lightheaded, but I need to go in for my labs."

The next thing I knew, I was opening my eyes to see myself lying on a wood floor. Since most of the floors in our home are wooden, I calmly asked, "Where am I?"

With phone in hand about to call 911, Rob responded, "You're on the floor of our bedroom! Are you hurt?"

Sounding panicked, I assured him I was all right. Soon realizing how dangerously close I came to hitting my head on the sharp corner protruding out from of the armoire where I had fallen, there was only a small scrape above my ear. With nearly fifty staples in my stomach, not one was bleeding or out of place. In the quiet of my heart, I thanked my faithful guardian angel for protecting me in the fall. Unable to leave the house, a lab technician came to our home.

Sipping on some broth to elevate my blood pressure, Rob expressed to me his craving for pancakes. Now able to eat whole-wheat products, I suggested we make them from scratch with pecans and fresh blueberries once we could get out to buy the ingredients. That same morning, we received a call from one of the women in our Intercessors of Light prayer group.

"Is there anything I can do?" Johanna asked. "I have a healthy whole-wheat pancake recipe that I'd love to make for you." I could hardly believe my ears! Continuing, she said, "I'll put them in a

Ziploc bag for you to freeze, and whenever you want pancakes, you can pop them in the toaster."

"We'd love them!" I told her.

With Jenelle sick, Rob came to me at 5:00 p.m. and asked, "What are we going to do about dinner?"

"Don't worry," I said reassuringly, "God will provide."

A short time later, the phone rang with an offer to bring us a meal. At the peak of harvest season, I articulated to Rob after dinner how much I was craving fresh melon. No sooner were the words out of my mouth when the doorbell rang. But before Rob could get to the door, he saw from the window a car backing out of our driveway. How pleasantly surprised we were to find a large bag filled with a variety of fresh grown melons—watermelon, musk melon, and honey dew! During the time of our recovery, the Lord's provisions abounded in every way to the point in which even my thoughts were being answered in the most remarkable ways!

Learning that Janie's funeral Mass was going to be held at St. Francis Xavier Cathedral, I reflected back on the vision shown to me of her funeral in the very same church. I thought of how I'd been prompted to pray for her so soon after awaking from surgery as I laid in the ICU following my own brush with death. Having prayed for her faithfully in the three and a half years since we first met, in the reality of my own set of circumstances, I took consolation in the vision of Rob and me in the back of the cathedral overseeing her funeral Mass. It occurred to me that the Lord was showing me in advance that we were not going to be among those in attendance. How overjoyed I was to learn that the time of her funeral Mass coincided with the same time I could watch Mass on EWTN. I also took solace in knowing that Grace, a dear woman from our Cross and Crown prayer group, was coming over to administer Holy Communion to us. How incredibly blessed we were to have such wonderful friends who never missed a single day of bringing Jesus to us during our recovery! Planning to offer my Mass in union with Janie's funeral Mass, I tuned in early to pray the rosary with Mother Angelica and her sisters at "Our Lady of the Angels" Monastery.[1]

As the feast of Mary's Assumption drew near, I felt my heart squeeze in the realization that we wouldn't be able to partake in the outdoor Mass on the holy grounds of Our Lady of Good Help. Due to chronic dizzy spells caused by the frequent drops in blood pressure, my lightheadedness and fainting spells continued. With my muscles beginning to atrophy, such simple tasks as sitting up at the table at mealtime were difficult, feeling the muscles around the surgical wound in my stomach literally shaking. Extremely weak, it was becoming a challenge just to get up from the chair. At the advice of my nurse coordinator, I began sipping on high-sodium broth throughout the day to prevent my blood pressure from plummeting and eating healthy snacks in between meals to help me regain strength.

The doorbell rang constantly with delivered meals and homemade goodies, while numerous get-well cards and Mass enrollments poured in. Thankful for God's mercy of sparing my life, Jenelle handed out nearly fifty rosaries she made from beautiful crystal gems and supplies purchased in Medjugorje. When Rob was able to drive, I began setting goals for myself to attend Mass with him, but somehow, they'd always have to be pushed back. As an effect of the high doses of antirejection medication, all five of my senses were adversely affected in one way or another. As soon as one issue would subside, another would be quick to take its place. Referring to these difficulties as "boulders" in connection to the huge boulders we scaled on Cross Mountain, through surrender and grace, I was able to hurdle over them with ease.

Despite the obstacles placed in my path, Rob's kidney was functioning perfectly inside of me. Because of my blurred vision from the high doses of prednisone, he'd read out loud the Bible passages that now held for me a deeper understanding. "Indeed, the word of God is living and effective, sharper than any two-edged sword, penetrating even between soul and spirit, joints and marrow, and able to discern reflections and thoughts of the heart" (Hebrews 4:12). Astounded at the many ways in which the biblical promises we'd been reading for so long had come full circle, I felt within myself an ever growing "fear of the Lord." The utmost desire of my heart was to never again offend God.

Aside from the physical trials I was suffering and the immense emotional anguish Jenelle had endured, Rob was called to undergo a spiritually painful ordeal. Having agreed for things "not to be easy," it was soon after our surgeries that he entered into a spiritual "dark night of the senses." In the trials we suffered, I saw a connection to the countless people we prayed for as Intercessors of Light in relation to the areas of suffering we were now called to bear in mind, body, and spirit. By accepting God's Will beforehand, I was keenly aware that our struggles were bringing Him glory in the co-redemptive power they held. "So I ask you not to lose heart over my afflictions for you; this is your glory" (Ephesians 3:13).

How Rob had relished the grace of being brought into such close union with God following his conversion, treasuring the gift of contemplative prayer. Now, his soul deeply lamented over the absence of being able to feel God's love within his soul. As his bitter agony became heavier to bear, I remember very clearly the first time he fell under the weight of his cross. Though the Lord continued showing him prophetic visions and of people to pray for, he felt an intense spiritual dryness, as though he'd been placed in the scorch of the desert sun.

Being witness to the intense inner torment he was suffering, it was especially hard for me to watch him retreat within himself. Becoming almost robot-like in the numerous acts of love he did for me each day, I could see within his eyes his spiritual void and interior pain. I recalled the prophetic vision he'd seen of himself walking amongst tortured and martyred saints, and of God's foretelling that I'd be for him his "rock." With all my heart, I prayed for him in his great trial. Though observing his inner pain on a day-to-day basis was far more difficult for me to endure than any physical pain I ever suffered, it was during this same time period that I could feel the Lord's presence magnified within my soul more than ever before.

One morning shortly after Rob returned to work, I became very weak and shaky after taking my morning shower. Home alone and feeling as though I was about to faint, I quickly grabbed my robe and made my way into the bedroom. As I gingerly lay on the bed, I impulsively raised my arms in thanksgiving of the many ways in which our Lord revealed to us His wonders. But without the stamina or strength to hold up my arms, I plopped them back down on the bed. Lying flat on my back, I closed my eyes in pure exhaustion. Interiorly, I saw an image of Jesus hanging from the Cross. Within my heart, I heard, "You are crucified with Christ. You are crucified with Christ. You are crucified with Christ." As I opened my eyes, I felt a tremendous source of peace flowing throughout my body. In awe of what I'd been shown, I noticed that my arms had fallen onto the bed extended out as though I was literally hanging on the Cross with Jesus! In His words to St. Faustina, Jesus said, "My daughter, know that if I allow you to feel and have a more profound knowledge of My sufferings, that is a grace from Me. But when your mind is dimmed and your sufferings are great, it is then that you take an active part in My Passion, and I am conforming you more fully to Myself. It is your task to submit yourself to My will at such times, more than at others"[2] (*Diary*, 1697).

During my recovery, Andrew's mother sent me some of his recorded inspirational CDs. In hearing his beautiful voice singing the words to the song "Testify to Love," it suddenly dawned on me the reason why I could only refer to Rob's selfless gift to me as the "gift of love" rather than as the gift of life. I was immediately reminded of a promise I had made to God, telling him I would not be like the nine lepers who didn't come back in thanksgiving. Instead, I promised Him that for all the days of my life, I would tell of His wondrous deeds. Fully aware that I would not even have breath in my lungs if God had not willed it to be so, I knew at that moment that as long as I would live, I would testify to God's Love.

It was mid-afternoon on Friday, September 14, the feast of the Exaltation of the Holy Cross, that Rob fell with his cross a second time. In the anguish that tore away at his heart, nothing I could say or do could ease the emptiness he felt inside. Feeling alone and abandoned, the only thing that alleviated his interior suffering was to spend one-on-one time with Jesus before the Blessed Sacrament.

> I have understood that at certain and most difficult moments I shall be alone, deserted by everyone, and that I must face all the storms and fight with all the strength of my soul, even with those from whom I expected to get help. But I am not alone, because Jesus is with me, and with Him I fear nothing. I am well aware of everything, and I know what God is demanding of me. Suffering, contempt, ridicule, persecution, and humiliation will be my constant lot. I know no other way. For sincere love—ingratitude; this is my path, marked out by the footprints of Jesus.[3]
>
> —*Diary*, 746

It pained me in the times he seemingly loathed the blessing God desired for him in the personal apostolic cross he received. Unable to feel God's love, it was in the times he fell with his cross that it felt as though he was rescinding his love from me. As he went off by himself to the Chapel of Divine Mercy that evening, I went before the pictures of the Two Hearts of Jesus and Mary placed upon our mantle. From my heart, I prayed, "Lord, what am I supposed to do?" Interiorly, I heard His reply: "Don't go on what you feel, but on what you know."

Pondering His words in my heart, I knew with all certainty that Rob loved God above all else. And with the same blessed assurance, I knew that he held a love for me more deeply than for any other person on the face of the earth, having given to me his self-sacrificing "gift of love." With certainty, I knew of the committed love he held for his family, and at that moment, I also knew that my beloved husband was in need of my prayers.

"Thank You, Jesus," I said, as I began praying for Rob the Sorrowful Mysteries of the rosary, uniting my prayers with his as though I was right alongside of him in the chapel. Later apologizing for his need to go off to pray alone, he told me how awful he felt that I had to suffer with him.

"You were there to help me carry my cross for five years, and you gave me your kidney, remember?" I comforted.

"I'd give you my other one too if you ever needed it," he said softly. Tearing at the implication of his words, he suddenly said, "Oh, I forgot to tell you. While I was in adoration, I received the same message I heard within my heart the morning after our surgeries, that I'm to offer my suffering to Jesus."

> "If we are afflicted, it is for your encouragement and salvation; if we are encouraged, it is for your encouragement, which enables you to endure the same sufferings that we suffer." (2 Corinthians 1:6)

It was on the following morning that I heard interiorly the words, "Invite Clare Marie over for a visit." In the happenstances of seeing her at St. Joe's, where we first met, I'd never before thought to invite her over. In response to the interior prompting, I thought, *I should do that sometime.* In not having spoken with her since well before our surgeries, how surprised I was to receive an e-mail from her two days later, asking if she could come over for a visit! Telling her of the Spirit's prompting for me to invite her over just a couple of day prior, she revealed to me that when she returned to her pew after receiving Holy Communion that day, she heard within her heart the words, "Go visit Sue."

A few days after her visit, I was praying the Divine Mercy Chaplet when I started thinking of a specific Scripture verse: "[I] will shelter you with pinions,/ spread wings that you may take refuge" (Psalm 91:4). An image formed in my mind of beautiful white velvety feathers shaped into the form of a heart.

"Jesus," I prayed. "Place me within your merciful Heart, me and my whole family."

Two hours later, Clare Marie called. To that point, few were the occasions that she and I had ever spoken on the phone.

"Sue," she began. "I hope I'm not disturbing your dinner hour."

"No, it's quite all right," I assured.

"Well," she went on, "I was at a book study this afternoon, and we're reading St. Faustina's *Diary*. I have to tell you that there was one thing that stood out to me today that I sensed was Jesus' message to you."

"What was it?" I inquired.

"I can e-mail it to you so you have it, but right now, I'll just read it to you over the phone if that's okay?"

"Yes," I responded. "I can't wait to hear!"

"'My daughter, let your heart be filled with joy. I, the Lord, am with you. Fear nothing. You are in my heart.'"[4] (*Diary*, 1133)

I was humbled to think that in close proximity to the same time I had asked Jesus to place me within His merciful Heart while listening to the Chaplet of Divine Mercy, that He would answer my special request through my friend in the same words He spoke to St. Faustina!

October 5 was fast approaching. The date preordained as the date of my healing nearly eight months prior in the calendar vision shown to me, I was especially enthusiastic about going to Holy Hill to celebrate. I thought back on the numerous times I had voiced to our friends in saying, "I don't know exactly what God has planned for me. I only know that I will see His wondrous deeds!" The reason I was able to believe and profess this bold statement from my heart as truth was because I read and proclaimed it to be true in the Scripture promises I read each day. "We do not keep them from our children;/ we recite them to the next generation,/ The praiseworthy and mighty deeds of the LORD,/ the wonders that he performed" (Psalm 78:4).

Though greatly looking forward to our day of celebration, I had within me a growing concern as to how my legs were ever going to make the climb up Holy Hill to pray the Stations of the Cross. Despite walking every day and gaining strength with each passing week, my legs were still very weak. Getting down on the floor to wipe off the base of a stool one day, I found that I didn't have the strength enough to get myself back up. On other occasions when I'd venture down the basement stairs to retrieve something, halfway back up my legs would begin to shake unstoppably. Every day, I began praying with all my heart that my legs would be strong enough to make the climb up Holy Hill.

As I awakened from sleep five days before our planned outing, I was shown a scene in which I saw myself inside a church. Sensing that Mass had just ended, I noticed a room off to the right. Through its glass doors, I could see two people kneeling down inside. As I left the church, I inadvertently exited the small back door instead of going out of the front doors as usual. I found that in order for me to get to my car in the parking lot, I had to climb up a very steep hill. Though I knew if I went back into the church to exit from the other side I would be able to get to my car much easier, for some reason, I chose to climb the hill instead. But in attempting to do so, after climbing only a third of the way up, I found myself to be in complete dismay. The incline of the hill had become so steep that I felt as though I were going to tumble over backward! Realizing it was impossible for me to go on, the vision ended. Unsure as to what it all meant, I was certain that the Lord had shown to me something quite profound. Was the steep hill indicative of another great trial I'd have to undergo? I found myself wondering. I didn't know. Saying a little prayer before getting out of bed, I yielded it into God's Will, placing any trepidation I felt about it back into His mighty hands.

A beautiful warm and sunny autumn day, Friday, October 5 had arrived! Anticipating this day for so long, I couldn't help but think of the very first Scripture verse the Lord had spoken to me in the desolation of my heart five years prior: "This is the day the LORD has made;/ let us rejoice in it and be glad" (Psalm 118:24). God had made it known that by trusting in His Merciful Heart, I could maintain inner joy and peace. Not only in the hills of my life when everything was going good, but in the valleys of suffering as well. He taught me that it is in the climb up Mt. Tabor that we are truly transformed, and on this day, I felt myself to be high up on the top of the mountain! Truly a day for rejoicing, I had ordered a special gift to give Rob while at Holy Hill in gratitude of the extraordinary "gift of love" he'd given me. Having purchased for him a shiny gold medallion like the one I had seen in the "calendar vision" marking this very date, I chose for him a beautiful gold medal of St. Michael the Archangel, his favorite. Noticing a priest stationed just outside of the gift shop when we walked in, as soon as Rob parted for the restroom, I seized the moment to get the momentous medallion blessed. Swiftly tucking it back into my purse for just the right time to present it to him, we headed to the St. Therese Chapel where the Sacrament of Reconciliation was being offered. Afterward, we proceeded up to the gorgeous cathedral where Mass was being celebrated on the feast of St. Faustina. Receiving Jesus in Holy Communion, my heart was consumed in the overwhelming joy of being a recipient of His mercy!

In the exuberance of the day, we were eager to do the hike along the wooded path leading up Holy Hill. As we began our walk along the Way of the Cross, our surroundings were seemingly transformed into our own little paradise. Encircled in the scenic beauty of nature, bursts of sunlight streamed out through the amber-colored leaves. Parallel to the path that Jesus walked in His sorrowful Passion, I understood the similarity of being called to walk with Him along the way to holiness in the five years leading up to the significance of this day. I thought back to the start of my journey, of the extreme brokenness I felt and of feeling the security of God's arms wrapping me in the beams of sunlight that broke through the black clouds. I pondered the ways in which Jesus taught me to trust in Him with the faith of a child by embracing the small portion of His Cross measured out especially for me.

> "Then Jesus said to his disciples, 'Whoever wishes to come after me must deny himself, take up his cross, and follow me.'" (Matthew 16:24)

As we prayed together the Stations of the Cross, my legs grew weaker and I was becoming increasingly aware of my laborious steps. Because I didn't want to turn back, I said nothing to Rob of how difficult the climb was becoming for me. Step after strenuous step, I tried instead to focus my thoughts on placing my feet in the footprints left behind by Jesus for us to follow on His grueling walk up Mount Calvary. Approaching the Fifth Station, where Simon of Cyrene helps Jesus carry His Cross, my legs began shaking uncontrollably.

Noticing that I could barely hold myself up, Rob said very caringly, "Hon, this just isn't working out for you to make this climb."

Knowing how much I'd been looking forward to praying the Stations, he proposed that we walk back down the hill where I could sit down on a picnic table while he went back up to get the car.

"I'll come and pick you up and we'll do the Stations from the top going down," he heartened. "It'll be much easier on your legs."

In all practicality, I knew he was right, and that I truly could not go on. But at that point, my legs had become so weak and shaky that I wasn't even sure I had strength enough in them to pray the Stations of the Cross going downhill. Having carried the cross of my failing kidneys with Jesus for five years to the very month, my heart literally ached in wanting to finish our commemorative walk in honor of the way in which our Lord revealed to me the value of the Cross. Feeling defeated in the limitations of my human condition, my ambition had become for me an impossible feat to accomplish. Perceiving my reluctance to turn back, Rob extended his arm upward to the top of the hill while saying, "Sue, we're only a third of the way up the hill and the climb is only going to get steeper." To drive his point home, he added, "There's no way possible that you're going to be able to walk up the sharp incline of those steps up ahead. They go practically straight up!"

Hearing Rob's spoken words, I instantly remembered my vision of five days prior, as the dots began to connect in my head. The same as in the scene shown to me, I'd just gotten out of Mass and was walking up a hill toward the parking lot where our car was parked. And just like in the vision, I could only make it a third of the way up the hill because it was much too steep for me to climb. I remembered that while the Lord was showing to me the prophetic scene, I considered taking the easier and more practical way of getting to the parking lot by going back into the church and exiting out of the door on the other side. But despite that knowledge, I had decided to attempt to climb the hill. Just like in the vision, I now found myself realizing at the very same point in my ascent up Holy Hill, a third of the way up, that it was simply impossible for me to climb! And strikingly similar to the revelation shown me in relation to the situation I now found myself in, how true that it would be so much easier for me to turn back in favor of the easier way of praying the Stations from the top of the hill going down.

"Rob!" I exclaimed in the elation of realizing the correlation of what the Lord had revealed to me in advance. "Remember the vision I told you about a few days back? I know this climb seems impossible for me to do on my own, but I really think that God is asking me to believe that, through Him, all things are possible! For us to turn back now doesn't really require us to use our faith," I said eagerly, "and I'm not even so sure that I'd be able to walk down those stairs at this point either. You know of all the amazing ways that we've been seeing an abundance of God's grace, right?"

"Well, yes," he responded, still lacking in the same enthusiasm as me.

"Hon," I said pleadingly. "I really think that I was shown myself in a similar predicament so that, with the faith of a child, I'd be able to surrender my physical limitations back to God. If we trust that His grace will provide me the strength to walk up the steep incline of Holy Hill, then He'll make possible for me the impossible! If you think about it, it was what allowed me to walk with Jesus along the cross of my failing kidneys, and I really want to walk along the Way of the Cross today in thanksgiving. What Jesus is asking of us today is for our trust!"

"All right," Rob conceded. "Let's give it a try."

Tears of happiness filled my eyes as we began praying together the fifth Station of the Cross. It was surreal for me to think that we were at Holy Hill in celebration of the date predestined by God Himself as the date of my healing. In His magnificent design, it would turn out to be on the feast day of St. Faustina, and in His splendid foresight, we would be called to complete "trust" on the feast of the saint who Jesus chose to give His message of trust to the world. If the graces of God's mercy are dependent on our trust, then the greater our trust, the greater mercy we will receive.

And if the "container" in which I was to receive God's mercy was my trust, then I needed to step out in faith in a literal sense, by picking up my feet to walk! "I keep my steps from every evil path,/ that I may obey your word" (Psalm 119:101).

Suddenly remembering the gift I had for Rob, I said, "Honey, I brought this along to give to you in thanksgiving for the gift that you've given me." I took out the little black velvet pouch from my purse.

He asked, "What's that?"

Handing it to him, I said excitedly, "Here, open it to find out!"

As he removed the gold medallion, he smiled, saying, "I really like this."

"Remember the shiny gold medallion I saw placed on this date in the 'calendar vision?'" I asked.

"Oh yeah," he answered. "How did you know to choose Saint Michael?"

"Oh, I know," I bantered in giving him a big hug. Before moving on to the sixth station, I petitioned for God to change the impossible into the possible, believing that it would happen. Taking my hand in his to proceed onward, I glanced back at Simon of Cyrene helping Jesus to carry His Cross. There was something spiritually profound about the particular spot in which my legs would move no more. "Jesus, I Trust in You!"[5] (*Diary*, 47) I said out loud as we began our walk of faith to the top of Holy Hill.

"Jesus, I Trust in You!"[6] Rob affirmed.

At each of the remaining stations, we said a prayer for God's grace to allow me the strength to continue our uphill walk along the Stations of the Cross. How astonished we were to discover that, instead of growing weaker, my legs were essentially gaining strength as we went along! Climbing with ease up the steep staircase, it was in going up the final flight of stairs that we counted out thirty-three steps. Pondering Jesus' age when He gave the ultimate gift of His love to humanity in climbing the bitter path to Calvary, I considered our five-year climb of faith in the face of adversity with Jesus along the Way of the Cross. As though the entire ordeal was compiled into this one day, I thought also of the thirty-three years of marriage that Rob and I had celebrated prior to my receiving his "gift of love" and "God's gift of new life."

Reaching the parking lot on top of the hill near to where our car was parked, we were unaware that the most incredible ending to our spiritual day of celebration had yet to take place. Going back up to the beautiful basilica, we planned to attend the First Friday Exposition of the Blessed Sacrament before leaving for home. Upon entering the empty church where we attended Mass earlier, I immediately took note of something I had not observed when the church was full. Focusing my eyes on the glass doors of the adoration room located off to the right of the church, I suddenly remembered the room with the glass doors that I'd seen off to the right of the church in the prophetic vision shown to me days prior. Having seen two people inside of the room, a sudden realization came over me in the knowledge that the two people I saw were me and Rob kneeling before Jesus in Eucharistic adoration! Approaching the front of the altar, we dropped to our knees before the "Fountain of all Mercy" in humble thanksgiving. Bowing to the floor, tears of joy flooded my eyes in awe of His tender loving mercy. "I will bless the LORD at all times;/ praise shall be always in my mouth./ My soul will glory in the LORD/ that the poor may hear and be glad" (Psalm 34:2–3).

In attempt to get up from the floor, I found that I did not have a single ounce of strength left in my legs to lift myself up. As I looked up to Rob for help, it occurred to me the significance of my legs giving out at the fifth station where Simon of Cyrene helps Jesus to carry His Cross. It was in God's perfect timing and in His holy arrangements that Rob and I were allowed the opportunity to grow in holiness in the trial allowed me, both in my acceptance to embrace my cross and in Rob's willingness to accept his role as "Simon of Cyrene" in helping me carry it. The same as with the Cyrenean, Rob had been thrust into a role he neither asked for nor desired. But yet he chose to embrace the portion of Jesus' Cross that had been singled out just for him. Reaching down to help me up from the floor, what solace I took in the immensity of blessings we found in the cross that brought us straight into the Heart of Christ.

A few days later, Rob asked me, "What do you want for your birthday?"

Quick to respond, I said, "To go to the Shrine of Our Lady of Good Help."[7]

Since October 16 marked the five-year date of first learning of my failing kidneys, it was a perfect opportunity for me to thank our dear Blessed Mother for all the wonderful ways she had interceded on my behalf.

"We can do that," Rob replied cheerfully. "And then we'll go out for that birthday dinner you didn't get to enjoy five years ago."

The day couldn't have been lovelier for us to walk the holy grounds while praying a rosary of thanksgiving. How perfectly fitting was the shiny gold medallion of St. Raphael, God's "healing" Archangel, that I received from Rob as a birthday gift to commemorate my healing. Before going down to the crypt below the church, we decided first to walk the paved cobblestone around the Stations of the Cross. It was at the ninth station where "Jesus Falls the Third Time" that I sensed Rob would fall again and again under the weight of his cross. But we had grown to learn that in the hardships of life, it's not the falling that matters, but rather it is the "getting up again" to walk with Jesus in our trial that's most important. In the drought of his suffering, we'd come to discover that beautiful flowery blossoms really do grow in the scorched desert sand when they're soaked in the rays of God's love. How I'll always remember the love I saw pour forth from Father Kieran's eyes as he prayed over Rob in the deprivation of his soul.

All of us are called to carry the Cross of Christ's love at various times in life's journey. Other times, we're asked to be Simon of Cyrene and help someone else carry theirs. Just as Veronica affectionately wiped the wounds of Jesus on His way to Calvary, Jesus beckons each of us to reach out in love to ease the sufferings of those around us. "Those who trust in him shall understand truth,/ and the faithful shall abide with him in love:/ Because grace and mercy are with his holy ones,/ and his care is with his elect" (Wisdom 3:9).

It was the first day I was strong enough to get back to attending daily Mass on my own. Staying on afterward to spend a holy hour before Jesus in the Tabernacle, I suddenly found myself wishing that I had brought money along to light a candle of thanksgiving. Kneeling down to pray before the beautiful statue of Mary, a young woman approached who I'd never seen before.

"Excuse me," she said, "I feel as though I'm supposed to give you money to light a candle."

Telling her of the desire that had sprung up in my heart just moments before, she said, "Oh my goodness, providing you this candle has made my day!"

"What is your name?" I asked. "I'll pray for you."

With tears forming in her eyes, she told of her great need for prayer. Embracing her in a hug, I found it amazing how God blesses those who seek first to be a blessing to others.

The following Saturday upon returning home from morning Mass with Rob, I went to my top closet shelf with a special purpose in mind. Having waited for just the right time, I removed the pair of white jeans that we purchased in faith several months prior. Putting them on for the very first time, my intent was to wear them to the Chapel of Divine Mercy that same evening.

Just as I promised Jesus I would do, I laid down prostrate on the floor before Him in Eucharistic adoration.

"Jesus," I said, as I paid homage to the King of all kings, "I promised that I would return to You in thanksgiving and I am here to fulfill that promise. All the days of my life, I will tell of Your glorious and wondrous deeds." "Magnify the Lord with me;/ let us exalt his name together./ I sought the Lord, who answered me,/ delivered me from all my fears" (Psalm 34:4–5).

Another day as I was praying before the Grotto of Mary after Mass, there was a woman of about forty who was also there praying a rosary. Though I didn't know her, I felt as though Mary was prompting me to go over and ask if I could pray for her. Because I didn't feel at all comfortable in doing that, I continued in praying my rosary. Receiving the same inspiration a second time, I began to pray for the woman from right where I was, making a mental note to place her in the Intercessors of Light prayer binder when I got home. With the third prompting, however, I knew that I needed to step out of my comfort zone and do what Our Lady was asking of me. Turning to look at me as I approached, I could see the Light of God in her eyes. Completely receptive to my offer to pray for her needs, she confided in me the concerns she had of her family.

"I'll pray for them," I promised. Telling her of a Holy Communion novena she could pray as a source of protection for her loved ones, she was enthusiastic to find out more. "Are you going to be here tomorrow?" I asked.

"Yes, I can be," she replied.

"I'll get a copy of the novena to give to you then."

"Oh, thank you so much," she said before leaving.

That night as I lay sleeping, I had a dream. It was one of spiritual warfare, and it was very clear to me that the opponent of salvation was not at all happy with me. Interiorly, I knew the dream was somehow connected to the prayer commitment I had made to the woman at the Marian Grotto the day before.

In retrieving the novena prayer I promised her, I asked Mary to guide me in bringing whatever else she needed. Instantly, the miraculous medal came to my mind, as well as one of the beautiful holy cards of Our Lady of Medjugorje with the "Five Stones of Conversion"[8] listed on back. Meeting up with Rob at noon Mass, I told him of the menacing dream.

"I'll be praying for you," he promised as he headed back to work.

Meeting up with the woman after Mass, I gave her the novena and the blessed sacramentals. Examining the holy card, she asked, "Is this Our Lady of Medjugorje?"

"Yes," I answered.

Suddenly becoming very excited, she told me of what had happened two weeks prior while praying her rosary at the same grotto. "When I asked Mary what I could do to help my family, I heard within my heart, 'Remember the five stones of conversion.' I read of them a couple of years ago, but had forgotten what they were. But here they are written on the back of this holy card!" Standing up, she asked if she could tell me of a dream she had when she was nine years old.

Since the reading at Mass that day had been of the Prophet Daniel's interpretation of King Nebuchadnezzar's dream, I immediately prayed within myself, "Daniel, please help me to interpret her dream!"

Telling me the vivid memory of her childhood dream, I clearly understood the hope it offered in the power of good over evil. Involving sorcery going back through previous generations, I told her of the tremendous power of the Precious Blood of Jesus, suggesting for her to have intergenerational healing Masses offered to break the chains of spiritual oppression within her family. Now understanding the reason why Our Lady's request was for me to go to the woman instead of simply praying for her from my pew, I also understood explicitly the reason why I had come under attack. The evil one does not want God's people interceding in prayer for those whose souls he already considers as his own.

Though my new kidney was functioning exceptionally well, it was detected on one of my regular lab draws that a potentially harmful virus, otherwise dormant in 98 percent of the population, had become active within my body. For those on antirejection medication following a transplant, there's a fine line between balancing the right amount of immune-suppressant drugs to prevent an organ from rejecting, while at the same time trying not to oversuppress one's system in allowing the BK virus to become active. At the onset of detecting the virus, my nurse coordinator cut the dosage of a particular antirejection drug in half. Despite it, however, the BK virus continued to be active in the follow-up urinalysis.

"What does BK stand for?" I asked my nurse.

"I believe it's the initials of the person who discovered the virus," she told me.

Deciding to lay my BK virus **B**efore the **K**ing, I surrendered the "boulder" back over to God. After several weeks of monitoring the virus in my regular labs, a special blood test was ordered to ensure that the potentially life-threatening viral infection had not spread into my bloodstream. On December 26, the results came back, indicating that it had, indeed, become systemic. This was not good news.

How thankful I was for my faith, and of my choice to put my faith into action by constantly surrendering my need before the King of all kings. "Rejoice in hope, endure in affliction, persevere in prayer" (Romans 12:12). The peace that comes from submission to God's Will is in not having to worry about "what could happen." I knew that absolutely nothing could happen to me unless He first allowed it. The constant prayer on my heart was, "Jesus, I trust in You," asking for faith even greater than the size of a mustard seed. "I say to you, if you have faith the size of a mustard seed, you will say to this mountain, 'Move from here to there,' and it will move. Nothing will be impossible for you" (Matthew 17:20).

In early January I received an e-mail from a friend, telling me of a yearly tradition of letting a patron saint "choose you." In going to the blog to discern as to whether or not I would partake, my interest peaked in learning that the "Patron Saint of the Year" devotion was one that St. Faustina recorded in her diary dated on New Year 1935. "There is a custom among us of drawing by lot, on New Year's Day, special Patrons for ourselves for the whole year"[9] (*Diary*, 360). Instantly, I recollected the times in the Chapel of Divine Mercy when, in venerating the first-class relic of St. Faustina, I beseeched her to stay by my side, subsequently asking for her help in choosing for me other patrons as well. Wasting no time in seeking out the saint who would choose to be my companion for the year 2008, I was astounded in learning it was "Saint Stephen" who chose to be my patron. A man of great faith, he taught the faith and was the first to be martyred for the faith. Considering that he'd chosen to be patron over me during a time when I was praying to receive a greater faith, I was already amazed. But even more remarkable was in learning that his traditional feast date is August 2, the date I received Rob's kidney, with his nontraditional feast day being celebrated on December 26, the date I received the news that the BK viral infection had ominously invaded my bloodstream.

Convinced that St. Stephen was the saint for me, my spirit was elevated. From then on, I prayed every day for his intercession to receive the gift of faith, so that I could believe without a shadow of a doubt that the BK virus would become dormant once again. "Let it be done for you according to your faith" (Matthew 9:29). I was praying for the faith to believe not only that God could, but that He would! With my early January labs indicating that the infection in my blood had doubled, I was shocked to learn later in the month that it had quadrupled since first having been discovered the day after Christmas. Receiving the news just moments before Rob arrived home from work, my heart was heavy as I relayed it to him.

"Come here," he said while pulling me down on his lap. "We need to trust that God is overseeing everything."

"I know," I replied. "It's the reason why I'm praying for a stronger faith! But the infection in my blood is getting worse instead of better."

With no time to spare, we quickly headed out the door to get to the 4:30 p.m. Mass in Green Bay, a half-hour drive from our home. Standing for the Gospel, the priest read St. Luke's account of the same Scripture passage that I had claimed for five years from Matthew 8:2. "And when he saw Jesus, he fell prostrate, pleaded with him and said, 'Lord, if you wish, you can make me clean'" (Luke 5:12). What I noticed different in the two versions of the same gospel story was that in Luke's account, the leper "fell prostrate" before Jesus. Thinking of how I had honored my promise to lay prostrate before Jesus in the Blessed Sacrament offered me great encouragement! No longer was I troubled of the BK virus that lurked within my bloodstream. My heart was as light as a feather. Instead, I thanked Jesus for the Gospel message that so perfectly coincided with the discouraging news I had received. In faith, I prayed, "Jesus, I trust in You!"

In the numerous trials we faced postsurgery, Father Kieran had come to our home for a visit, advising us to take out our journals to read as a reminder of the ways in which our Lord had revealed Himself to us. How enlightening it was for us to go back and read of the goodness of God in showing to us His glorious wonders. Walking back into the house after returning home from Mass, I saw that I had left one of my journals lying out on the table. Randomly opening it, I found myself looking at an entry that was made on May 2, 2006, one year and three months prior to the date of receiving Rob's kidney. My mouth dropped wide open as I read of a vision shown to Rob on that date while in Eucharistic adoration: "I was shown a scene in which Sue was lying on an operating table before going into surgery. Placed on the lower right side of her abdomen, I saw the hand of God."

Never having received God's wisdom as to what the prophetic vision meant, I had remained puzzled concerning the area in which God's hand was resting on my abdomen. Nowhere near the location of my diseased kidneys, how often I had prayed for enlightenment concerning it. In awe of His infinite goodness, I was humbled to think that our merciful Lord had reserved His reply for the moment it would benefit me the most! What I hadn't been aware of at the time of the vision was that Rob's kidney would be transplanted into my lower right abdomen in the exact spot where he was shown the hand of God resting on me! I was reminded once again of Jesus' response to the leper's plea: "Jesus stretched out his hand, touched him, and said, 'I do will it'" (Luke 5:13). The same as He had stretched out His hand to touch the leper, Jesus had His hand stretched out in protection of my kidney! With spirits soaring, we decided to take a drive over to the Chapel of Divine Mercy that evening to thank Jesus for lifting the weight of my burden. Just before leaving, I asked if He had anything else to say to me. Picking up my Bible, I opened it randomly to read: "Jesus said to them in reply, 'Have faith in God'" (Mark 11:22). With St. Stephen at my side, I was praying for the faith to move mountains!

It was during the time I was infected with the BK virus that I received a phone call from Kristin. No one I ever encountered had endured greater misery in their affliction than she.

"Sue," she said on speakerphone, "I heard you were suffering from a blood infection."

"Yes," I confirmed.

"I'm sorry to hear that," she replied. "I'm back in ICU with another blood infection myself, and Ginny is up here visiting. We'd like to pray for you over the phone."

My heart melted in hearing the love of her words. There was nothing I had ever suffered that even remotely compared to what she had endured for so many years, but yet she was on the other end of the line with the sole purpose of praying for me!

"I'd love for you and Ginny to pray with me," I responded, "but only if we can include your needs in on our prayers as well."

Still vivid in my mind is the beautiful speakerphone prayer spoken through the airwaves that day with my dear sisters in Christ. Over the span of two decades, the heavier Kristin's cross had become for her in the progression of lupus, the greater strength and grace she was provided to persevere.

With the start of Lent right around the corner, Rob felt called in his prayer time once again to offer the same difficult forty-day fast he'd been inspired to do in the previous three years. Telling me he also felt called to get up at 5:00 a.m. every day to spend time in Eucharistic adoration before going to work, I immediately became enthusiastic about doing it with him. Gently reminding me of the predicted "late flu season" and of the times we'd encountered people in the chapel with colds, I was disheartened not to be able to join in. There was no question that I didn't like being immune-suppressed. But I came to look at it as another little thorn that I could offer back to Jesus. I knew that Rob was right in that I shouldn't spend an hour in closed quarters with other people in the midst of flu season, but I felt my heart being squeezed nonetheless.

But as divine providence would have it, God would give to me once again the desires of my heart. In reading *Thy Kingdom Come*[10] concerning the life and mission of Luisa Picaretta, a victim soul whose cause is up for sainthood, the words that Jesus spoke to her in regard to her home confinement during her illness jumped off the page to me as I read. "Thus, in gratitude for My infinite love, I want you to visit Me thirty-three times a day in honor of the years I spent on earth for you and for all…You will make these thirty-three visits at all times, each day, wherever you may be; and I will accept them as if they were made in My sacramental presence."[11] My heart leaped with joy! Kneeling down before a crucifix in my home, I beseeched Jesus, asking if I too could come before Him thirty-three times a day in the confinement of my home. I asked Him to accept each of my visits as though I was with Rob in His presence before the Blessed Sacrament of the Altar. In preparation for my daily visits with Jesus, I arranged an altar in a spare room, positioning it directly below a large Divine Mercy image that hung on the wall. Draping over a beautiful lace cloth, I placed on it my open Bible, a Crucifix, blessed candles, and a few relics I had acquired. Ordering for me another one of Luisa's books, *The Hours of the Passion of Our Lord Jesus Christ*,[12] I was delighted to have my friend Mary show up at my door the day before Lent to drop it off!

Calling home on his morning break on Ash Wednesday after getting up an hour early for his Eucharistic holy hour, I asked Rob, "Do you remember back five and a half years ago when I first found out my kidneys were failing when the Bible story of the vine and the branches stood out to me?"

"Yeah, you mean when we were on Mackinaw Island with your mom?" he asked.

"Yes," I replied. "Well, in my prayers this morning, I had a strong sense that God is again pruning us to bear more fruit in all of the difficulties we've been encountering since our surgeries."

A short time after conversing with Rob, I stopped what I was doing to pay another visit with Jesus. Kneeling before the makeshift altar in my home, I felt prompted to open up my Bible. I read the following:

> "My lover speaks; he says to me,/ 'Arise, my beloved, my beautiful one,/ and come!/ 'For see, the winter is past/, the rains are over and gone./ The flowers appear on the earth,/ the time of pruning vines has come,/ and the song of the dove is heard in our land./ The fig tree puts forth its figs/ and the vines, in bloom, give forth fragrance./ Arise, my beloved, my beautiful one,/ and come!
>
> 'O my dove in the clefts of the rock,/ in the secret recesses of the cliff,/ Let me see you,/ let me hear your voice,/ For your voice is sweet/, and you are lovely.'/ Catch us the foxes, the little foxes / that damage the vineyards; for our vineyards are in bloom!"
>
> —Song of Songs 2:10–15

Reading the beautiful passage, I truly felt as though my heart was going to burst with joy! The Lord is the lover who speaks to us in the book of Songs, and it's to His followers that He addresses as His "beloved." He desires to guide His beloved into elevated degrees of holiness, and into an advanced spiritual union with Himself, as His bride. Reflecting on how we could catch for Jesus the foxes that threaten to damage the vineyards, I thought of the value of prayer, and of the great merit of walking with Him in our trials. Seeking to live hidden away within "the secret recesses of the cliff," I thought of Jesus' Sacred Heart and of the magnificent treasure that's hidden away in every Tabernacle around the world.

Our three-year-old grandson had come to stay with us for a few days that Lent, and from the other room I suddenly heard him shouting, "Grandma! Grandma! Come here!" Coming quickly to see what was wrong, I saw little Jacob kneeling upright on the chair where he was coloring. Leaning over toward the hardcover book that was set off to the side of the countertop where he was, he was pointing to the glossy front cover of *The Hours of the Passion*.[13]

Reaching over to get the book, I asked, "What is it, honey?"

Looking at the image depicting the crucified Christ, he placed his finger directly on the spot where the sword had pierced the Heart of Jesus. "Who did this to Him?" he demanded to know.

Pausing for a moment in not quite knowing exactly how to explain to a small child that it was the sins of mankind that had nailed Jesus to the Cross, before I could answer, he moved his pointer finger to the Roman soldier with the spear in his hand.

"Look!" he exclaimed. "Did he do it?"

"Yes, sweetheart" I replied softly. "He was a bad soldier. He didn't believe that Jesus was God, and he didn't have any love in his heart." "But one soldier thrust his lance into his side, and immediately blood and water flowed out" (John 19:34).

Pointing to the Blood and Water that came forth from the Heart of Jesus in the form of red and white transparent rays, I continued. "But later, the soldier did believe that Jesus was the Son of God, and he was very sorry for what he had done to hurt Him. Jesus had mercy on him and forgave him. Then the soldier was able to show love for others, the same as Jesus had shown love to him."

"The centurion and the men with him who were keeping watch over Jesus feared greatly when they saw the earthquake and all that was happening, and they said, 'Truly, this was the Son of God!'" (Matthew 27:54).

Absorbing my words like a sponge, I looked into the sadness of his big brown eyes and further explained, "When we do bad things and don't love one another as we should, we hurt Jesus too."

Shaking his head, Jacob stared intently at the picture. With firm resolve, he added, "When I get big, I'm going to help Him!"

Hugging my precious little grandson, I said, "I know you will, sweetheart. Jesus loves you so much!"

It was also during Lent that year that I received an e-mail from a woman we met on our Medjugorje pilgrimage, telling of a bus trip she was organizing to bring women from the Fox Cities to a "Magnificat Retreat" in Milwaukee. Taking place in March, I knew it had to be concerning a prophetic vision shown to Rob months earlier.

"You were on a bus of all women that was traveling to someplace of a religious nature," he had told me. "And you looked very happy."

Since I'd never before been on a bus of all women, I remember being perplexed. "You and I are pretty much 'joined at the hip' in going on spiritual excursions together, right?" I'd asked.

"Right," he had responded.

"So then where would I be going without you on a bus full of women?"

"I don't know," he answered. "I just know that you were very happy to be going."

Admittedly, hearing of a retreat entitled after Mary's Magnificat did spark a desire within my heart to attend. Saying a prayer to Mary, I said, "Holy Mother, it's been in faith that I've laid my BK virus 'Before the King.' If this is the 'bus of all women' that I'm called to be on, please ask Jesus for my next blood draw to be completely free of the virus." Afterward, I opened my Bible to read the Canticle of Mary: And Mary said: "My soul proclaims the greatness of the Lord;/ my spirit rejoices in God my savior./ For he has looked upon his handmaid's lowliness;/ behold, from now on will all ages call me blessed" (Luke 1:46–48).

It was through the intercession of St. Stephen that I'd been praying for a deeper faith to "believe without seeing" that my BK virus would be gone. Waiting for my lab results before committing myself to the bus pilgrimage, the tests showed that, although the infection was still detected in my bloodstream, it had dropped to a level "too low to be calculated." This was terrific news! But then I suddenly thought, "What am I to do about the bus trip?" My prayer in regard to whether or not I would attend the retreat was for the virus to be completely gone, but my labs revealed it was not yet entirely out of my system. Taking the matter back to prayer, the answer became crystal clear. The Lord had done His part in bringing the BK virus down to a level so low as not to be measured, and now, the ball was in my court. Faith is an "action word," and I knew that I needed to put my faith in action by trusting that God would finish what He started. Stepping out in faith, I picked up the phone to reserve a seat on the bus, sending in my payment. It was on the day before the retreat that my blood work revealed that not a trace of the BK virus remained in my system. Going before the altar in my home, I knelt down in homage 'Before the King.' How happy I was to attend the Magnificat retreat in fulfillment of what God had foretold!

As I was awaking from sleep on the day preceding Divine Mercy Sunday, the Lord showed to me a vision of a structure. Colossal in size, it resembled that of an oval football stadium. Instead of a playing turf, however, I saw what looked to be a bottomless bog of stagnant sludge. Nowhere around it was there any indication of life whatsoever. My eyes then focused on a man on a rope ladder, having already traveled three-quarters of the way down to the hideous looking miry pit. Hovering right next to him, I saw a strange-looking creature suspended in midair, noticing that its head was extremely large. I sensed that throughout the course of the man's lifetime, he had stifled the voice of conscience in choosing evil over good, darkness over light. Though deep down he had known all along that he was treading down the wrong path, he still thought himself to be in control. In the flawed thinking that "he could always turn back," he had convinced himself that there was plenty of time to change the error of his ways. Watching the scene unfold, I then saw the man stop to look downward in the direction he was heading. Terrified, he suddenly became aware of what he had failed to notice, in that the repulsive sludge had been very slowly creeping up to consume him! With the sewage nearly reaching his feet, the man quickly turned back in great fear. Scurrying back up the ladder as fast as he could, I saw that the huge dome was rapidly closing in on him. With his escape appearing to be hopeless, I opened my eyes. Thinking of how bleak his predicament seemed to be, before getting out of bed to get ready for Mass that Saturday morning, I prayed for God's wisdom in discerning exactly what it all meant.

At 3:00 p.m. that afternoon, I picked up the handbook on Divine Mercy to say the prayer of the ninth and final day of the novena leading up to Mercy Sunday. As I began reading, I clearly understood the meaning of what the Lord had shown me earlier that morning. Jesus said to St. Faustina;

> Today, bring to Me SOULS WHO HAVE BECOME LUKEWARM and immerse them in the abyss of My mercy. These souls wound My Heart most painfully. My soul suffered the most dreadful loathing in the Garden of Olives because of lukewarm souls. They were the reason I cried out: 'Father, take this cup away from Me, if it be Your will.' For them, the last hope of salvation is to flee to My mercy.[14]
>
> —*Diary*, 1228

Speaking to St. Faustina of lukewarm souls who had become to Him like corpses, Jesus defined to her:

> These are souls who thwart My efforts…[15] Souls without love and without devotion, souls full of egoism and self-love, souls full of pride and arrogance, souls full of deceit and hypocrisy, lukewarm souls who have just enough warmth to keep them alive: My heart cannot bear this. All the graces that I pour out upon them flow off them because they are neither good or bad.[16]
>
> —*Diary*, 1682, 1702

Divine Mercy image

I knew in my heart that the sludge represented the devil's playing turf. The creature with the oversized head identified the sin of pride, a sin that is present in all sin. When souls slip outside of the state of sanctifying grace and begin to think of themselves as their own god, they at the same time relinquish the boundaries that keep their consciences in check. Away from the saving grace of God pertinent to their salvation, they eventually succumb into the evil temptations that abound in the world around them. The enormous stadium was indicative of the vast amounts of souls that the devil and his agents are working feverishly to lead astray in every moment of every day. The fast closing dome was symbolic of God's Divine Justice that is quickly closing in on those who still refuse to accept His mercy in a time of abundant grace. As a corpse dead in his faith, the last hope of salvation for the man shown to me in the vision was to run to the mercy of God. For some, it will be too late.

Pondering the desperation of the dismal scene the Lord had shown to me, it appeared on the surface as though the devil was succeeding in bringing numerous souls with him into the fiery pit of hell for all of eternity. But I knew that God had a much greater plan for the salvation of humanity. I thought back to a time of grace in my own life when upon praying the Act of Contrition, I had first realized that I could not tell Jesus with my whole heart that I was sorry for my sins. Though I had regretted my sins enough to pray for God's forgiveness, it was in telling Him that I was "heartily sorry for my sins" that had opened up to me the acute awareness that I had been fooled into thinking that I was not much of a sinner. It was through God's redeeming grace in receiving the Sacraments of the Church that I was convinced otherwise. I thought of how Rob, too, had become a recipient of God's mercy and grace after drifting away from the faith to the point of simply "going through the motions" in attending Mass each Sunday. My eyes were teary as I thought of the great honor and privilege we now had to pray for others to receive the grace of conversion. Within my heart, I understood what God was asking of us was for continued and fervent prayer, to bring back to Him the lukewarm souls who've become stagnant in their faith. In the magnitude of sin gone rampant in our families, our country, and in the whole world, I better understood the myriad of love in which God calls His people back to Himself. With full trust in the unfathomable mercy of God, I began praying in song the Chaplet of Divine Mercy. "For the sake of His sorrowful Passion, Have Mercy on us and on the whole world"[17] (*Diary*, 475).

At my pastor's request, I was honored to go up to the podium that Divine Mercy Sunday to tell of how I had been a recipient of God's mercy. Deciding to pay a visit to the Shrine of Our Lady of Good Help that afternoon, we attended the Eucharistic holy hour before going down to the crypt to pray the Divine Mercy Chaplet at 3:00 p.m. In his meditation, Rob was shown a vision of St. John Vianney. He saw the saint walking up the side aisles of the "Prayer Cenecle for Priests" that met on the second Sunday of every month, and in his hands he was carrying a basket. In it, he was collecting the prayers that were being said for priests. Interiorly, Rob received the message that we were to return to the monthly prayer cenacle. With our lengthy recovery time followed by the ominous BK infection and the late flu season that year, now was the time for us to begin attending it once again.

It was before the Blessed Sacrament that Rob received an interior locution telling him the Lord was going to be bringing to us three people to pray over. Though we had resumed hosting the weekly Intercessors of Light prayer meeting in our home after temporarily changing the venue to Elizabeth Ministries[18] during our recovery time, we'd not yet been called on to lay hands over anyone since our surgeries. In the message received, Rob was told that "we need not worry, nor be afraid."

Telling me this, I responded, "The only thing that may cause us fear would be if there was evil involved. And now, with my suppressed immune system, the thing that might be cause for us to worry would be if the person in need of prayer had something contagious that could be potentially life threatening."

It was on the following morning that we received a request of someone who wanted to meet up with us for prayer. A holy and devout person, she was experiencing diabolical attack. Knowing ahead of time that it was God's Will for us to pray with the woman, we made arrangements to pray with her. The second request came from a young woman asking if she could talk to us about discerning religious vocation, and of personal complications surrounding her decision. After meeting with her, she asked, "Could you please pray over me?" The third request came in being sought to pray over a woman who had become very sick just prior to learning she had terminal cancer. In the knowledge that she also was suffering from a serious skin infection that was contagious and potentially life threatening, we didn't hesitate in going to her bedside to pray, fully trusting in the Lord's protection through the message received.

On a subsequent visit to the adoration chapel, Rob was shown a scene in which the two of us were walking through a dimly lit hallway that led into a large auditorium. There were people sitting in chairs who were captivated in listening to someone speak. "I had a sense that it was a special group of people and that it's someplace that you and I are going to be." He was also shown a side view of a woman he believed to be a saint. "She was wearing a red velvet dress and was kneeling inside of the chapel, praying with us." Following our night prayers that evening, Rob relayed to me that the Lord had put on his heart that "something really good" was going to be happening before the end of May.

While driving home from the Chapel of Divine Mercy on the following evening, Rob shared with me a vision shown him in which he saw himself standing inside of a bus full of people.

"Another bus?" I interjected.

"Yes, believe it or not," he confirmed. "I was standing up in the middle aisle in the front of the bus, facing the people who were on it, and you were sitting in the front seat right next to me. What stood out to me was the bright and colorful clothing that many of them were wearing."

"Where were we going?" I asked.

"I don't know," he responded. "But I had a sense that it was to a religious event of some sort."

Calling me from work the next morning, Rob asked, "Can you call the local bus companies to get some pricing to find out what it would take for someone to bring a bus to the Medjugorje Conference?"

"Why?" I asked.

"While I was in adoration this morning before work, I received an interior message that you and I are to bring a bus of pilgrims to the National Medjugorje Conference for Mary."

"Oh my goodness," I said. "The vision you were shown of the two of us in the front of a bus filled with people!"

"Yes," he replied.

"I'll call the bus companies right away this morning," I promised.

While organizing a three-day bus pilgrimage was definitely not on either of our "wish lists," I thought of the amazing way the Holy Spirit had made Himself manifest to us at the same conference five years prior. How could we pass up the opportunity to be Mary's true apostles by helping others to experience the same? With limited time to fill the bus, the very first thing we did was to ask Our Lady to be in charge of hand selecting every pilgrim who was to be on the bus. I thought of how often I had looked with love upon the hand-painted image of Mary under the title of "Maria Rosa Mystica" in the entrance of the Divine Mercy Chapel over the years, in the assurance of receiving her aide. To honor her as the Mystical Rose, I reserved both the bus and the sleeping room block under the same title. Before entering the chapel each time thereafter, I placed a kiss upon my fingertips before touching the three roses of white, gold, and red aligned across the top of Mary's bodice.

> But if you call her a rose, white is the color of her purity; gold, the tint of her royalty; red, the hue of her suffering. The rose grows out from a stem of thorns and in the heart of this flower, the red of the Cross of her son was forming. Indeed, without thorns a rose is not a rose, and without the thorn of great suffering, Mary could not have become the Mystical Rose of God's Paradise.[19]
> —Rosa Mystica

It was on the Thursday after Easter that Rob told me of the interior promptings he'd been receiving all week that he should do a second forty-day fast. Being less than thrilled with the notion, he admitted to pushing the inspiration to the back of his mind.

"What do you think I should do?" he asked.

Keeping in mind that his inspired Lenten fast was an extremely difficult one in which he was able to accomplish only by grace,

I replied. "Well, we sure don't want you to lose your health. I think it would be wise for us to go before Jesus in the Blessed Sacrament tomorrow night to pray for confirmation on whatever it is that God is asking of you."

With his mind set at ease in the plan to further discern before going forward with the second fast, he suddenly said out of nowhere, "Oh, and what's up with St. Rita?"

Chuckling, I asked, "Where did that come from?"

"It's just that, in the last couple of days, I've also been sensing that we need to ask for St. Rita's intercession for the bus pilgrimage."

"Hmmm," I pondered out loud. "She's the saint of impossible causes, and with our lack of experience in organizing a bus pilgrimage and the little amount of time we have to do it, that sounds impossible enough to me! You could read the book on her life that we gave to Jenelle for Christmas," I suggested. "I know she really enjoyed it."

"Oh, that's right," he commented. "I'll ask her."

The next evening, we went before Jesus in Eucharistic adoration in the joint purpose of praying to discern God's Will concerning Rob's back-to-back forty-day fast. While in the state of contemplative prayer, he was shown a vision of himself with his arms held straight out in front of him. It depicted his resistance of willingly opening his arms to be nailed to the cross of the second fast the Lord was asking of him. Instantly upon receiving this self-knowledge, he felt within himself a deep peace and sudden readiness to do the fast. Sharing this with me after our holy hour, I vowed to do my Lenten fast for a second time as well. "When do we begin?" I asked.

"We'll start it on Monday," he said. Telling Father Kieran of what we were being led to do, he gave us his blessing.

Picking up the book on St. Rita,[20] Rob learned that her feast day was on May 22, the day before our bus trip to the Medjugorje Conference. Counting out on the calendar when our forty-day fast would end, he found it incredible that the last day of our fast also landed on May 22! We were amazed as the dots began to connect. First in realizing that the vision of the "mystery saint" in the red velvet dress who was praying with us in the chapel was St. Rita, and secondly, in the dual inspirations of needing to do another forty-day fast leading up to the bus trip and to call on St. Rita for her help!

After sending out a copy of a novena prayer to St. Rita to those who signed up for the bus, a couple of days prior to leaving, I found myself wishing that I would've thought to order St. Rita holy cards to pass out to the pilgrims. As God's amazing providence would have it, when my friend Debbie came over to pick up food for Father Carr's Place-2-B, she held out something in her hand, saying, "Here. I found these down in my basement after forgetting I even had them."

Handing me a large stack of bifold holy cards of St. Rita she had brought back from Medjugorje, I was amazed to think that they also held Our Lady's Mother blessing!

"Thank you so much!" I said excitedly.

"Oh, you're welcome," she responded modestly, handing me a small Ziploc bag. "Here are some medals from Medjugorje for you to pass out as well." Opening the bag, a plume of rose scent filled the air.

Having successfully completed our fasts within the same forty days leading up to the feast of St. Rita as well as to the conference, how fitting it was that Our Lady chose exactly forty pilgrims to be on the bus! Marking the fifth anniversary of our "call to ministry," what a privilege it was to be bringing a bus of pilgrims back for Mary! Walking with Rob through the narrowed off darkened area alongside of the stage that led into the auditorium for the opening ceremony of the conference, I suddenly remembered the prophetic vision shown to him a couple of months back, seeing us walking through a dimly lit hallway into an auditorium. I instantly became aware that the

Lord was fulfilling the "something wonderful" that Rob had sensed would be happening before the end of May. Taking our seats, I knew that we were sitting amongst a very special group of God's people. How humbling it was to think of the beautiful way in which Our Dear Blessed Mother had called us back to the same place in which we had been summoned to come five years prior. To think of the amazing and wondrous things that had transpired in between, what a great honor and tribute it was for me to begin carrying out the vow that I had made to God in promising I would always be as the one leper who came back to Him in thanksgiving.

As the bus departed for home, I began to think of the special plan our Blessed Mother had for each of her beloved sons and daughters, a plan that would ultimately lead them further up the Mount of Transformation and closer to her Son. In the example set by Joyce, we asked those who'd been spiritually and profoundly touched to come to the front and give witness. One by one for nearly an hour, Mary's pilgrims came forth to share their testimony. A couple of minutes before three o'clock, Rob stood up in the front of the bus to insert the Divine Mercy CD.

"Look, hon!" I said while sitting in the seat next to where he was standing.

"What's that?" he questioned.

Pointing down the center aisle of the bus, I exclaimed, "Look at the colorful spring clothing they're all wearing!" Filled with awe, the prophetic vision he'd been shown prior to our call to bring a bus back to the conference for Mary had come to fruition.

"Can you hold on a minute before putting in the CD?" I quickly asked.

"Sure," he said without questioning the reason why.

Knowing that Kristin was nearing the end of her life, my heart ached in thinking of her ardent desire to live long enough for her daughter's wedding, which had taken place the day before. Having kept her close in prayer throughout the weekend, since the first time we met, I prayed for her in my chaplet every day. Standing up to take hold of the mic, I beckoned for those on Mary's bus to remember our dear friend in singing the Chaplet of Divine Mercy, briefly telling of her courageous longtime suffering. Little did I know that it would be in the "Hour of Mercy" on that very day that she would meet up with her Savior. To St. Faustina, our Lord stated: "At the hour of their death, I defend as My own glory every soul that will say this chaplet; or when others say it for a dying person, the indulgence is the same"[21] (*Diary*, 811).

In the days following her death, the Lord showed me a vision of Kristin. I saw her standing behind a desk and facing outward toward a classroom of students, looking healthy, happy, and content. Within my soul, I understood what was shown me. As a conduit of Jesus' love, it was under His tutelage that she served as an example for others to follow in the classroom of life. In the constant flare-ups of her disease, she taught others to strive to see the good that can come from every hardship. In striving always to walk with Jesus in her long-suffering, Kristin was able to learn the valuable lessons our Divine Teacher often uses to draw His people closer to Him. A predestined soul whose name was forever written in the Heart of Christ, what a privilege it had been to be an observer of one who had surrendered herself to share in His sufferings. "As gold in the furnace, he proved them,/ and as sacrificial offerings he took them to himself" (Wisdom 3:6).

There will be times in our lives when each of us will be called to travel with Jesus along *The Forgotten Way*, on a path that leads to holiness. How one responds will determine the spiritual merit they will either gain or lose. As a recipient of God's mercy, how slight was my conception of the magnanimous way in which He would respond to my plea. Love replaces fear while despair turns into hope when one chooses to follow Jesus along the Way of the Cross in times of trial. Utilizing the Sacraments and praying Holy Scripture with an expectant faith is what enabled me to believe in what I could not see.

Spending countless hours before the Blessed Sacrament in The Chapel of Divine Mercy, our souls craved the outpouring of love and peace that being in Jesus' true presence never failed to bring. Praying The Divine Mercy Chaplet each day, we pled for the Father's mercy based solely on the meritorious act of His Son. Reflecting on St. Faustina, a Sister of Mercy, I think of the amazing ways in which her intercession was made known. In considering the tremendous blessing we had in kneeling before the tomb of Pope John Paul II at St. Peter's Basilica in petition of his intercession, and of the revelation that the Pope of Mercy was interceding on our behalf, I once again marveled at the divine providence of his entrance into eternal glory on the vigil of Divine Mercy Sunday. "The message of divine mercy has always been very close and precious to me. I thank divine providence because I was able to contribute personally to carrying out Christ's will, by instituting the feast of Divine Mercy"[22] (Words of Pope John Paul II following the beatification of St. Faustina). With a great love for Mary, John Paul II's life's mission was *Totus Tous*, meaning "All for you, Maria." What tremendous value there is to be found in consecrating oneself to Jesus through Mary, the Mother of Mercy. She wants to be for us the guiding light to help us stay the path that directly leads to the Heart of her Son.

Jesus is the "Fountain of Mercy" through which all mercy flows. He is the source and summit of our faith at the table of every Eucharistic banquet celebrated in all of the Holy Masses offered around the entire world each day. Jesus is the Living Word in Holy Scripture, the Word made flesh, who came to die so that we might live. He is the one who invites us to walk with Him in our trials, and who constantly reaches out to us in our pain. It is He who serves as our strength in times when we are weak, our healing and wholeness. He is the great "I am" who we need only to turn to in the hardships of life, crying out, "Jesus, I trust in You!"

> Eternal God, in whom mercy is endless and the treasure of compassion inexhaustible, look kindly upon us and increase Your mercy in us, that in difficult moments we might not despair nor become despondent, but with great confidence submit ourselves to Your holy will, which is Love and Mercy itself.[23]
>
> —*Diary*, 950

While my body here decays,
May my soul your goodness praise,
   Safe in heaven eternally.
Amen. (Alleluia)

—Stabat Mater

O human souls, where are you going to hide on the day of God's anger: Take refuge now in the fount of God's mercy.[24]

—St. Faustina (*Diary*, 848)

They Will See God

> "Come and hear, all you who fear God,/ while I recount what has been done for me./ I called to the Lord with my mouth;/ praise was upon my tongue./ Had I cherished evil in my heart,/ the Lord would not have heard./ But God did hear/ and listened to my voice in prayer./ Blessed be God, who did not refuse me/ the kindness I sought in prayer."
>
> —Psalm 66:16–20

Transformation takes place in the trials and sorrows of life. When God's people cry out to Him in their adversity, these are the times He uses to draw His children deeper into the Heart of Christ. Our trials are often the means most effective in catapulting us onto the path of holiness. In the midst of my anguish, I was able to see God more clearly than ever before. It was only in recognizing the cross I received on my 49th birthday as a true gift from God that I was able to embrace my walk with Jesus along the Way of the Cross. A present that most would not consider to be a gift at all; I would grow to understand its significance in relation to the *greatest* gift ever given to mankind. But in order for me to find calm amidst the storms of my life, I needed to hold on tightly to the Rock of my salvation.

> "To you, Lord, I call;/ my Rock, do not be deaf to me./ If you fail to answer me,/ I will join those who do down to the pit./ Hear the sound of my pleading when I cry to you,/ lifting my hands toward your holy place" (Psalm 28:1-2).

At the onset of my trial, I prayed according to what my own wishes were, without regard as to what God's Will might be for me. Wanting to be healed "yesterday," I failed to consider that the length of my trial was accurately measured out ahead of time in order that I would see the mercy of God. Miracles can and do happen every day. But in God's Divine knowledge, the walk of conversion is most often a process that takes time in order to for life-long transformation to take hold. How much more grateful is the person who is set free of their infirmity after suffering for a longer period of time in comparison to one who has endured very little hardship?

While no one will escape the challenges of life, it's vital for one to remember that whether in times of physical pain resulting from sickness, accident or injury, our safe haven is always in God. In war, in famine, in the agony of poverty and the uncertainty of addictions, Jesus is the answer. In our failures and criticisms, or in the emptiness of depression, we need only to look up to God for help. In the aches and pains of growing old, or in the grief caused by the loss of a loved one, it's in reaching out to our Creator that we will feel His loving embrace. "At the time, all discipline seems a cause not for joy but for pain, yet later it brings the peaceful fruit of righteousness to those who are trained by it" (Hebrews 12:11).

It is important for us to remember that God is not a sadist, nor does He take pleasure in our suffering. To accept all circumstances as providential means to believe that nothing can happen to us unless God permits it. In some instances, He allows or sends various trials for corrective purposes. Sometimes He prunes His people to bear more fruit, and other times He disciplines those who are not bearing any fruit at all. The Lord permits various trials to further purify His people by the perfecting of their faith. When His people as a nation turn from Him and take God out of their life, disciplinary measures are sometime the only way through which His people will be saved. "So shall your rule be known upon the earth,/ your saving power among all the nations./ May the peoples praise you, God; /may all the peoples praise you!" (Psalm 67:3–4).

In Jesus' transformation on Mount Tabor, His Heavenly Father commanded the apostles to "Listen to Him." Similar to our Pentecost experience following the Medjugorje Conference, after receiving the word-of-knowledge for Rob and me to *"listen,"* Jesus was preparing His Apostles to live their lives transformed by the Holy Spirit in preparing them for Calvary, teaching them the fruit of the Cross. I could see the parallel of the way Jesus prepared us to see the value of my cross, resulting in the fruit of transformation. Our Lord still beckons the people of today to walk with Him along the only path that leads to holiness and eternal life. Promising His disciples that His Father would send the *Spirit of Truth* to those who observed His commandments; the same holds true today. "Jesus took Peter, James, and John his brother, and led them up a high mountain by themselves. And he was transfigured before them; his face shone like the sun and his clothes became white as light" (Matt 17:1–2). Jesus is the Truth. His Word is Truth, and He is always true to His Word.

For Rob and I to journey up Mount Tabor on the path chosen for us, it demanded self-sacrifice and detachment from things considered of value to those living in the world. The treasures we were seeking, however, were no longer of this world. Transformed through a deeper infilling of the Holy Spirit following the Life in the Spirit Seminar we attended, God bid us to *"listen"* for His voice. Calling us out of our comfort zone while commissioning us to pray for His people, He drew us out of ourselves and away from focusing too much on our own problems to better serve Him. He taught us to surrender our worries and concerns in the hope of one day seeing His ever-merciful face. As we traveled willingly with Jesus along the path of adversity, He walked with us, talked with us and showed us that a servant is never greater than his Master. Washing our feet before leading us into ministry and service for the good of our neighbor, we responded in agreement with His summons to live a life of prayer. "Strive for peace with everyone, and for that holiness without which no one will see the Lord" (Hebrews 12:14).

Having prayed relentlessly for Rob's conversion, never did I think the news of my failing kidneys would serve as the very means by which Our Lord would place us onto the fast-track to sanctity. Little did I know that the cross gifted to me on my birthday would forever change our lives to the point of being able to profess our greatest adversity as our greatest blessing! It was in my extreme misery that I cried out to God, and over the course of our five-year climb-of-faith up the Mount of Transfiguration, we would see the Lord's goodness and love in the various mountain-top experiences we shared. "Come, let us climb the mount of the Lord,/ to the house of the God of Jacob,/ That he may instruct us in his ways,/ that we may walk in his paths" (Micah 4 2).

At the very onset of my diagnosis, it was in my decision to honor the promise I had made to my mother in spite of the great turmoil I was feeling inside, that I encountered my Heavenly Father upon reaching the top of Mackinac Island. Symbolic of the great turbulence going on in my own life, the extreme weather conditions of wind, rain, sleet and snow just seemed to add to the intensity of the anguish of what I was feeling inside. But it was in pushing forward in doing what I knew in my heart I should do rather than what I wanted to do, which was to wallow alone in self-pity, that allowed me the splendor of feeling the comfort of God's love. It was there on the summit of the historic Fort Mackinac that marked my first "mountain-top-experience" on my journey up Mount Tabor. The unveiling of what would forever change my perspective on suffering, I saw the Sun break forth from the menacing sky to wrap me in the warmth and security of my Father's arms.

> "But we also boast in our sufferings, knowing that suffering produces endurance, and endurance produces character, and character produces hope, and hope does not

disappoint us, because God's love has been poured into our hearts through the Holy Spirit that has been given to us." (Romans 5:3–5)

Though it's in the most trying times of our lives that we're called to walk with Jesus along the Way of the Cross, it's important to remember that in doing so, we share in His Resurrection! It is in looking for Divine help in our trials rather than succumbing to the emptiness and bleakness of despair that we'll begin to see God in our suffering. What the opponent of salvation does not want God's people to know, is that when they're in danger of losing their way, it's the Lord's utmost desire to guide them back to safety. "Make known to me your ways, Lord;/ teach me your paths./ Guide me in your truth and teach me,/ for you are God my savior" (Psalm 25:4–5). For us to think that joy and suffering can be experienced by the same person at the same time seems an oxymoron of sorts. But yet, in the spirit of hope, that's exactly what God intends for us in the trials we encounter.

The more that we submitted ourselves to changing our lives in pursuit of holiness, the more we could see the Face of Christ in our adversities. In the grace offered to us in the Sacrament of Confession, our hearts were opened to see the Sun even on days when it wasn't shining; to see the light of God's love shining through in even the darkest of circumstances. In frequenting the Holy Sacrifice of the Mass each day, we were brought deeper into the fullness of our faith and into the fullness of the love of Christ. My cross was made lighter in the day-to-day surrender of my burden back to Jesus. What I couldn't do alone, I could do with God. Whether before the Tabernacle after Mass, or before the Blessed Sacrament at night, I simply laid down all my troubles at the foot of the Cross. "Thank you for adoring my Son in the sacred host. That touches me very much. I ask you to pray, for I desire to see you happy"[1] (Our Lady of Medjugorje, 1-26-84).

In traveling along the uphill journey of sanctification in the hardships of life, I would meet up with God once again halfway around the world in the small little mountain village of Medjugorje. It was in reaching the top of Apparition Hill that I would see the radiant smile of His Heavenly Mother after being allowed the grace to smell the lovely scent of roses at each of the Mysteries of the Rosary we prayed along the way up. In the brightness of the mid-day Sun, I saw Mary's resplendent face smiling at me in the statue marking the spot where she first appeared to the visionaries.

This extraordinary mountain top experience was what gave way to an unwavering faith in deciding to attempt the much steeper climb of the treacherous rocks leading up Cross Mountain. My new found confidence had nothing to do with what I could do for myself to succeed in making the ascent, but rather in the assurance of what the grace of God would do for me. Praying quietly with Rob at each of the Station of the Cross, we held hands all the way to the top! Feeling exhilarated, we remained there for as long as possible before having to head back down to the village for Mass. Getting down on my knees before the Cross erected on the summit of Mt. Krizevac, I felt a close and intimate bond with God and Mother Mary, the *Queen of Peace*.

Achieving victory in my climb up Mr. Krizevac, I better understood that it's in the most difficult climbs of our faith that we will see Jesus in our suffering. To the visionaries Marija and Ivan on June 24th of 1986, the following message was given during the time they were up on Mt. Krizevac with their prayer group:

> You are on (Mt.) Tabor. Here you receive blessings, strength and love. Carry them into your families and into your homes. To each one of you, I grant a special blessing. Continue in joy, prayer, and reconciliation. (Our Lady of Medjugorje)[2]

Until the day when we meet God face to face, the more one accepts everything that comes along their way as providential, the greater they will see His Kingdom come on earth. "Such are the people that love the Lord,/ that seek the face of the God of Jacob" (Psalm 24:6).

In thinking back to the very first scripture verse our Lord spoke to my heart when I found myself weighed down under the burden of my failing kidneys; *"This is the day the Lord hast made, let us rejoice and be glad in it,"* what didn't make sense to me then made perfect sense to me now. Not only was it an invitation to ask for the grace necessary for me to sustain inner peace and joy in my struggles, but it was also a call to *rejoice* in the very means by which God had willed to make me holy. And though it may take a lifetime to perfect, it's in deciding to walk within the Holy Will of God in our trials that we will be provided the grace to become holy. "In difficulties, when you carry the cross, sing, be full of joy!"[3] (Our Lady of Medjugorje, 1986).

We would learn that God doesn't intend for us to wait to become holy until we reach Heaven, but that holiness is a gift He wishes to clothe us in while we are still yet pilgrims here on this earth! Our entire life is a pilgrimage. Mary tells us that we must long for Heaven and strive for holiness. In sickness and in health, in good times and in bad, God calls each of us to see all of life's circumstances as occasions of His divine providence in order that we would grow in holiness. In all conditions of life, the Hand of our Redeemer is constantly reaching out to help. Though the ransom for our salvation has already been paid on the Cross, it's down in the valley of our trials that one becomes broken enough to reach up and accept what Jesus has offered. "So as to strengthen your hearts, to be blameless in holiness before our God and Father at the coming of our Lord Jesus with all his holy ones" (1 Thessalonians 3:13).

In the grim diagnosis of my failing kidneys, inconceivable to me was the way in which we were shown the magnificence of the Cross. It would be on the very day pre-destined as the day of my healing that I would meet up with God in yet another mountain top experience. He would teach us first-hand that, through Him, absolutely nothing is impossible! We would learn that it is doing what we would otherwise not be able to do that puts our faith into action. In my attempt to hike up Holy Hill to pray the Stations of the Cross, it was grace alone that brought me to reach its pinnacle. Once there, we would see once again the magnanimous wonders of our Lord! With strength enough left over to get down on my knees to thank Jesus in Eucharistic adoration, how beautifully fitting that it was the same way we'd gone before Him for five years in petition!

> "Who may go up the mountain of the Lord?/ Who can stand in his holy place?/ The clean of hand and pure of heart,/ who are not devoted to idols,/ who have not sworn falsely./ They will receive blessings from the Lord,/ and justice from their saving God." (Psalms 24:3–5)

The journey of transformation is as long as a lifetime. In the sometimes rigorous and painstaking trials of life, it was in choosing to walk with Jesus that we learned to tread in the footprints He left behind for us to follow. He waits for each of us, individually, to walk with Him in the hardships we face. In doing so, we will receive special lenses that will allow us to see our troubles in a different light and to see God in the sufferings of others. Our mind will better understand that everything we think, say, or do can be for His greater glory when we offer back to Jesus our every trial, sorrow and pain. As gold tested in fire, every facet of our lives will become meritorious when we live, speak and breathe within the Will of God. When we strive to see Jesus in our suffering, we will discover the true meaning of our lives. "The first end I propose in our daily work is to do the will of God; secondly, to do it in the manner He wills it; and thirdly, to do it because it is His will"[4] (St. Elizabeth Ann Seton).

Only when one wanders off from living their lives within God's holy designs will they lose their inner joy and peace. But in human weakness and frailty in the times we fall and find ourselves veering off the straight path and zigzagging aimlessly along the mountain, we must be quick to turn again and again to the grace of God for the strength to get up, pick up our cross, and follow Jesus. The sooner one does, the lesser the grip of sin will take hold. "Lost sheep were my people,/ their shepherds misled them,/ straggling on the mountains;/ From mountain to hill they wandered,/ losing the way to their fold" (Jeremiah 50:6). When one embraces life's crosses as the very means of gaining them entry into the Kingdom, God's Light will illuminate them in a way that will become radiant for others to see. They will see Jesus shining through God's people as a beacon of light to help them find their way out of the darkness. "Just so, your light must shine before others, that they may see your good deeds and glorify your heavenly Father" (Matthew 5:16).

To grow in holiness doesn't necessitate the need to travel to faraway lands, but it does require us to travel inwardly to the very center of our souls. That's where we will meet up with Jesus, who awaits us there. "Do you not know that you are the temple of God?" (1 Cor 3:16). In the arduous task of striving to become the bride of Christ within the centermost sanctity of our souls, it necessitates dying to oneself daily. Though few are those who achieve perfect union with Jesus during their lifetime on earth, it's something very worthwhile of making every effort to achieve. Many good intentioned Christians become comfortable in wanting to stay put "right where they are" in their walk with the Lord. It's a daily struggle, but in not striving to push forward in faith, one risks the tendency to go backwards into sin.

The secret of sanctity is in striving to surrender our will over to the Divine Will of God. Though we've been given a free-will in which the Lord will not interfere, one must stop and consider what they could possibly decide better for themselves than what the love of God wills for the greater good of their soul. To relinquish and fuse our free-will as one with the Will of the Father, means gaining the freedom to become empowered to do that which we could never do on our own. It was in the witness of our dear friend Katy's total submission to God that I was able to see the true liberty she found in having discovered the secret of "Heaven on earth." To practice living in the Divine Will means to have Jesus' prayer to His Father constantly on our lips in saying; *Thy Will Be Done!* How tempting it can be, at times, to pray the contrary.

It was in taking God up on His promises in Holy Scripture that I began to fully trust that all of my trials would work for my good, receiving the graces proportionate for each trial I was called to undergo. In response to our Lord's holy arrangements for her to become the Mother of God, Mary said, "Behold, the handmaid of the Lord, be it done onto me according to Thy word" (Luke 1:38). Though many sorrows would pierce her Immaculate Heart, Mary accepted God's Will, resulting in the salvation of mankind. In following the example set for us by the Holy Family; in their uncertain times of journeying to the far country to visit Elizabeth, and in their exile into Egypt, Mary and Joseph always stayed the course by holding on tightly to the Word Incarnate. The same holds true in modern day as we travel along the highway of life. In looking up to the great Compass in the sky, which is our Triune God; the Father, Son, and Holy Spirit, we will receive His direction and never become lost. Through prayer and submission to His Holy Will, we will be able walk with Jesus unscathed along the path that leads towards sainthood!

Conversion is ongoing throughout the span of a lifetime. Though it doesn't always exclude pain and suffering, the fruit of the cross is the holiness that leads to eternal life. Through it, one will discover a new path that leads to joy. True joy results not from seeking the happiness the world has to offer, but an inner-most joy that can only be found only in God. It's an elation of spirit that can be felt even when one is experiencing great trial, because it's a fruit attained from bearing ones sufferings with Christ. The call to conversion is to turn from the things that cause one to sin in order to be transformed in Christ.

Through prayer, fasting, reading scripture, receiving Jesus in the Eucharist, and in utilizing the Sacrament of Confession, one will begin the conversion process of Mary's core message in Medjugorje. It was in discovering the true joy of serving God in our obedience to pray for His people that Rob and I were blessed along the way with "spiritual children" to blanket in prayer. Having always desired to have more children, what a blessing it was to be enlightened also of the tremendous graces we'd receive in the prayers that they, in turn, would reciprocate back to us! It was in accepting the spiritual prompting that we were to organize bus trips to bring back to National Medjugorje Conference each year that we saw numerous blessings abound. Passing out literally hundreds of consecration books, rosaries, miraculous medals and other blessed sacramentals, our prayer was to set aflame the hearts of Mother Mary's hand-selected pilgrims. Inspired in prayer, the "Just One Decade" Rosary Campaign[5] took off, as most all of the bus pilgrims and numerous others said "yes" in committing to add just one extra decade onto their daily rosary in dedication to Our Lady's intentions. Becoming just one small link in a large chain of people praying in supplication to Jesus through Mary, our conjoined petitions then take on colossal power.

Essential in the climb up Mt. Tabor, is to possess an unwavering faith and ongoing perseverance. To share in the sufferings of Christ, means also to share in a personal and intimate union with Him. In discovering there is no victory without the Cross, one will comprehend that true love never wants to be apart. In the times of our life when we unite our crosses with Jesus, we're bonded with Him the closest. When fallen away Catholics and Christians alike humble themselves before God, a new outpouring of the Holy Spirit will result and Christians worldwide will be set on fire to lead others along the holy way of transformation. "A highway will be there, called the holy way.... It is for those with a journey to make, and on it the redeemed will walk" (Isaiah 35:8–9). By persevering along this one-lane highway of sanctification, one will discover their earthly sufferings as the means through which Our Lord has called them as His own.

If only all of God's children could grasp onto the tremendous outpouring of grace that is to be found along the way that so few choose. If they knew of its great value, they'd eagerly give up everything in exchange to walk with Jesus along the path of redemption. Instead of looking outwardly to materialistic things to fill the black hole within their soul, which in essence is the void of God, they'd be zealous in seeking the "Bread of Life" for the spiritual nourishment their spirit is craving. "My food is to do the will of the one who sent me and to finish his work" (John 4:33). In choosing to travel along the life long journey up the Mount of Transformation, they'd quickly discover the trials they encounter in this life are what will elevate their status of holiness in preparation for the next. Their minds will be opened to understanding the vital importance of the way they choose to live their lives in the short time spent here on earth, in contrast to where they'll spend time without end in all of eternity; either in Heaven, or in the unquenchable fires of Hell.

In an interior locution shown to Rob on Christmas day in the fifth year of his tremendously painful ordeal of suffering the dark night of the senses, he was shown a scene pertaining to his trial. Standing two thirds of the way up a mountain, he saw Jesus. He was speaking to His followers, who were sporadically positioned at various points on the mountain below Him. Rob then saw a second scene of himself, depicting the times he had rejected the cross of interior suffering. Amidst the jagged rocks and the dreadfully steep cliffs on the mountain, he saw that he had stumbled nearly all the way back down to its base. In his sometimes ominous plunges of faith, however, he saw that Jesus had been standing at his side and protecting him throughout. "Those whose steps are guided by the Lord,/ whose way God approves,/ May stumble, but they will never fall,/ for the Lord holds their hand" (Psalm 37:23-24). In a third vision, he was shown a brightly illuminated path that led three-quarters of the way back up the mountain, past the area in which he'd initially seen Jesus standing. The remaining distance leading to the top, however, was dark and particularly steep. Interiorly, he was told that he would make the ascent back up the lighted way very quickly to the area marking where he was in his spiritual journey before his trial. As for traveling the remainder of the way up to the mountain's summit, it would require of him to accept and embrace his cross, relying solely on God's grace to bring him to its pinnacle. In the final scene shown to him, he saw himself standing on top of the mountain, noticing right away that the ground was nearly flat. The only thing on its summit was a gift; a gift chosen particularly for him. It was a *cross*. Set-out diagonally for him to pick up and follow Jesus, he received the interior knowledge that it's in reaching the mountain's top that one will find the terrain more level and easier to travel. Even in times when the weight of their cross is heavier, it's in persevering to the summit of life's journey that one will ascend to perfect union with Christ. "For it is written, Be holy because I [am] holy.'" (1 Peter 1:16).

How beautiful was the locution given to Rob that Christmas, revealing the exceptional gift he'd been given in the "dryness of his dessert cross." On the very day that the Son of God was born as a "gift" to mankind for the sole purpose of taking up His Cross to die for the salvation of the world, it was made known to Rob that all God's people are all called to emulate Jesus' love by taking up their cross for love of Him. In the virtues attained and merits gained, one will be able it to carry his cross with ease upon reaching the smoother plane of the mountain's top.

> I see that God never tries us beyond what we are able to suffer. Oh, I fear nothing; if God sends such great suffering to a soul. He upholds it with an even greater grace, although we are not aware of it. One act of trust at such moments gives greater glory to God than whole hours passed in prayer filled with consolations.[6] (*Diary*, 78)

Jesus is the Font of all holiness who ardently calls each of us to live a life of holiness. Every opportunity for us to become like Jesus is an opportunity for us to become holy; to love as He loved, to serve as He served, to become holy, as He is holy. To suffer with Jesus in our suffering is the quintessence of what it is to become holy. But holiness doesn't just happen. It takes a long-time commitment on our part to live out God's commandments in our everyday lives. With firm resolve, one must live for righteousness in full reliance of the strength and redeeming grace of God to conquer the habits that are keeping them from becoming holy. When one courageously strives to carry their crosses in patience, as did Jesus for them, they will begin to experience true inner joy in spite of adverse circumstances surrounding them. It is up on the mountain's summit that one day all will fully understand and believe in the Eucharistic Jesus; the source and summit of our Catholic Christian faith. "On this mountain he will destroy/ the veil that veils all peoples,/ The web that is woven over all nations" (Isaiah 25:7).

Over the course of a lifetime, crosses will come in many shapes and sizes. To ask for them to be lightened, would be to ask for God to lessen the merit He wishes for us to gain. Relying fully on God's grace, His consolation will never neglect to soothe our pain. In uncertain times, He will teach us to trust in ways we cannot see. We will be guided safely through the darkness of our sorrows by the steady and gentle Hand of Christ. As we walk with Jesus in a child-like faith along the Way of the Cross, we will be transformed. "Weeping as they come, to seek the Lord, their God;/ to their goal in Zion they shall ask the way./ 'Come, let us join ourselves to the Lord/ with covenant everlasting, never to be forgotten'" (Jeremiah 50:4–5).

Grand are the numbers who will begin their climb up Mount Tabor by following in the example of those who follow Him. In love of the One who first taught us how to love, in service to the One who first taught us how to serve, and in suffering with the One who first taught us how to suffer, others will follow God's people along *"The Forgotten Way"* on the path to holiness. Through faith and perseverance, their hearts will be cleansed, and they will one day see God in all of His Glory. "Blessed are the clean of heart,/ for they will see God" (Matthew 5:8).

Make me feel as you have felt;
Make my soul to glow and melt
   With the love of Christ, my Lord.

—Stabat Mater

Listen, all you people! At Christ's bidding and in His very words, I warn you: We cannot win grace if we do not suffer affliction; toil upon toil must be ours if we are to attain an intimate share in the divine nature, the glory of God's children, and perfect happiness. If only men knew how beautiful, noble, and priceless a thing God's grace is![7]

— Saint Rose of Lima

Notes

The Call
1. Father Patrick Peyton developed the slogan "The family that prays together stays together."
2. The Story of Fatima, www.ourladyoffatima.org/fatima/fatima.htm.
3. Act of Contrition, www.ewtn.com/Devotionals/prayers/contrit.htm.

Walk With Me
1. The Eternal Word Television Network (EWTN) was founded by Mother Mary Angelica in 1980, presenting around-the-clock Catholic-themed programming (*www.ewtn.com*).
2. St. Maria Faustina Kowalska, the Apostle of Divine Mercy, was of the Congregation of the Sisters of Our Lady of Mercy.
3. *Diary of St. Maria Faustina Kowalska: Divine Mercy in My Soul.*
4. Ibid.
5. Ibid.
6. Ibid.
7. Saint John of the Cross, www.catholictradition.org.

Ask, Seek, and Knock
1. Efficacious Novena to the Sacred Heart of Jesus, *www.catholicculture.org*.
2. Memorare, www.CatholiCity.com.

3. Possessing a great love and devotion to St. Joseph, "Brother Andre," as he was commonly known, was canonized on Oct. 17, 2010 (www.americancatholic.org).
4. Totus Tuus Maria, www.catholicsoul.tumblr.com.

Show Me the Righteous!
1. Medjugorje (Croatia) has been the site of reported apparitions of Our Lady of Medjugorje since June 24, 1981 (www.medugorje.org).
2. It is believed that whoever recites the St. Andrew Advent Prayer on Jesus' birth from the feast of St. Andrew, beginning on Nov. 30 through Christmas day, will obtain the favors asked for (www.thepracticingcatholic.com).
3. C. Alan Ames Ministry, *Through the Eyes of JESUS* (USA: Touch of Heaven USA, Oct. 1997).
4. Forgiveness Prayer by Fr. Rbt. DeGrandis SSJ and B. Tapscot (http://mp3pray.com/forgivenessprayer/) is to be prayed to help let go of past hurts.
5. Saint Katharine Drexel, www.centeroftheimmaculateheart.org/foundation/singlenews.

Come
1. Catholic Charismatic Renewal brings those attending into a deep experience of the work of the Holy Spirit, www.charismaticrenewal.org.
2. Eucharistic Adoration is to adore the Eucharistic presence of Jesus.
3. Divine Mercy Sunday is celebrated on the Octave of Easter (the Sunday after Easter Sunday).
4. A first-class relic is the body of portion of the body (bone, flesh, hair) of a saint.
5. Father Carr's Place 2B feeds the hungry and offers a place to stay for the homeless, a shelter for the abused (www.fathercarrsplace2b.com).

6. Sponsored by Queen of Peace Ministries, their mission is to spread the messages of the Blessed Virgin Mary from Medjugorje and of her urgent call to humanity for prayer, fasting, and conversion to her Son, Jesus (www.queenofpeaceministries.com).
7. The DCRC helps people to live the power of Pentecost in their everyday lives (www.charismaticrenewal.org).
8. Founder and president of Vera Cruz Communications, Jim Murphy, transformed lives of those he encountered along the way of his 4,200-mile journey on foot across America (www.christianlifemissions.com).
9. *Diary of St. Maria Faustina Kowalska: Divine Mercy in My Soul.*
10. Title of the Blessed Mother of God as Rosa Mystica (*www.mysticalrose.net*).
11. A monstrance is a vessel in which the consecrated Host is exposed for the adoration of the faithful.
12. Fr. Donald Calloway, MIC, is a convert to Catholicism and a member of the Congregation of Marians of the Immaculate Conception (www.fathercalloway.com).
13. The May Crowning is a celebration of "Mary's month" with a coronation of the Queen of Heaven and earth.
14. VIII Letter of St. Therese to her sister Celine (www.littleflower.org).

Go Out

1. St. Leo the Great, www.holyromancatholicchurch.org.
2. Located within the Roman Catholic Diocese of Green Bay, Wisconsin, it stands on the site of the reported Marian apparition in 1859 to a Belgian-born nun, Sister Adele Brise (www.shrineofourladyofgoodhelp.com).
3. The Peshtigo Fire took place on October 8, 1871, in and around Peshtigo, Wisconsin. It was a forest fire turned firestorm that caused the most deaths by fire in United

States history, with estimated deaths of around 1,500–2,500 people (En.wikipedia.org/wiki/Pestigo Fire).
4. Fr. Machaco, missionary of the Society of Our Lady of the Most Holy Trinity (SOLT). An exorcist trained by Rome, he's an accomplished preacher and evangelist in five continents (www.lovingsaintjoseph.blogspot.com).

Behold, Your Mother

1. *The Catechism of the Catholic Church* (CCC), Second Edition (United States Catholic Conference, Inc. – Libreria Editrice Vaticana, 1997).
2. Preparation for Total Consecration according to St. Louis Marie de Montfort (Montfort Publications, 2005), 52.
3. Saint Maximilian Kolbe, http://whitelilyoftrinity.com/saints_quotes_suffering.
4. Mentioned in three of the four Gospels, Simon of Cyrene is the man impelled by the Roman soldiers to help carry Jesus' cross out of Jerusalem.
5. The Virgin Mary appeared to Juan Diego in Mexico on December 9, 1531, requesting a shrine to be built on the spot where she appeared.
6. http://www.wikihow.com/Say-a-Novena-to-St.-Therese-the-Little-Flower.
7. Encompasses the belief that the Blessed Virgin Mary, as the mother of Jesus Christ, is the source through which all graces (from her Son) flow.
8. Words spoken by Our Lady to the three shepherd children at Fatima, Portugal, on June 13, 1917 (*www.ewtn.com/library/MARY/FIRSTSAT.HTM*).
9. A Catholic title of the Blessed Virgin Mary given by Pope Pius IX, it is associated with a Byzantine icon of the same name dating back from the 15th century (http://en.wikipedia.org/wiki/Our_Lady_of_Perpetual_Help).
10. Saint Vincent de Paul, http://whitelilyoftrinity.com/saints_quotes_suffering.

Intercessors of Light
1. *The Collected Works of St. John of the Cross*, revised edition, trans. Kieran Kavanaugh OCD, Otilio Rodriguez OCD (ICS Publications, 1991).
2. *The Collected Works of St. Teresa of Avila*, volume 2, trans. Kieran Kavanaugh OCD, Otilio Rodriguez OCD (ICS Publications, 1980).
3. Pope Paul VI, www.catholicgarden.com/mass.html.
4. St. Therese, www.goodreads.com.
5. Saint Augustine, www.wf-f.org/StAugustine.html.
6. Intercessors of Light is an inspired prayer group formed to intercede on behalf of the needs of others; it is spiritually led by the Blessed Mother.
7. Fr. Robert J. Fox, *Francis*, Fatima Family Apostolate, second edition (1999), 64.
8. Divine Mercy Sunday is a Catholic devotion to the Divine Mercy that Jesus revealed to St. Faustina Kowalska in a vision, it is associated with the promises of special graces to be attained.
9. *Diary of St. Maria Faustina Kowalska: Divine Mercy in My Soul.*
10. Ibid.
11. Saint Sebastian Valfre, http://whitelilyoftrinity.com/saints_quotes_suffering.

The Apostles Blue
1. www.medjugorje.ws (2005–2014).
2. Pope John Paul II, www.medjugorje.net.
3. Ibid.
4. The Schoenstatt Wayside Shrine Refuge of Sinners is located in the Green Bay Diocese of northeastern Wisconsin (www.refugeofsinners.org).
5. October 2004–October 2005 was proclaimed by Pope John Paul II as the Year of the Eucharist, having devoted

an entire encyclical letter on the Eucharist to remind the faithful that Jesus is really present in the consecrated Host, the Bread of Life.
6. The right to wear the mitre, a type of folding cap, belongs by law only to the pope, the cardinals, and the bishops.
7. St. John Bosco, 1815–1888, founder of the Salesian Order, the Apostle of Youth.
8. The Life of the Blessed Virgin Mary from the Visions of Ven. Anne Catherine Emmerich (TAN Books and Publishers Inc., 1970), 57.
9. Karen Sigler SFO, *Her Name Means Rose*, (EWTN Catholic Publisher, 2000).
10. Raymond Arroyo, *Mother Angelica* (Double Day, 2005).
11. Quote from a booklet written by Rhoda Wise, "My Story," used with the permission of the Rhoda Wise Home. Her Name Means Rose by Karen Sigler S.F.O., Copyright © 2000 by EWTN Catholic Publisher, P. 96
12. World Mission Sunday is celebrated on the third Sunday of October each year, it's a day the Catholic Church sets aside throughout the world to renew its commitment to the missionary movement.
13. OLM, 8-22-1985
14. Rhoda Wise –Wife, Mother, Mystic, Stigmatic, Catholic convert (1888-1948)
15. Therese saw herself as "the Little Flower of Jesus" because she was just like the simple wild flowers in forests and fields, unnoticed by the greater population, yet growing and giving glory to God. Society of the Little Flower @ *www.littleflower.org*;
16. www.ecatholic2000.com/therese
17. OLM, 7-25-90 www.medjugorje.org
18. Millions of the pilgrims that travel on pilgrimage to Medjugorje have witnessed the spinning of the sun since the beginning days of when the apparitions first started.

19. Saint Therese *www.pathsoflove.com/pdf/ThereseLetters.pdf*
20. Our Lady of Medjugorje, *www.maryourmother.org/medjugorje/*
21. Fatima message *www.catholictradition.org/Mary/fatima3.htm*
22. OLM, 4-5-1984. *www.medugorje.org*.
23. OLM, 5-25-1987. *www.medugorje.org*
24. Fr. Jozo Zovko, the parish priest of Medjugorje at the time the visions first began in June of 1981, did not believe at first but later became a crusader for the events that were taking place.
25. The Angelus is a prayer reminding us of the Annunciation (Luke 1:26-38)
26. Zagreb Daily Newspaper, Saturday Evening, August 24, 2002, "The Vercernji List"
27. Krizevac means "Mount of the Cross" and it is the highest mountain in the area.
28. The "Risen Christ" statue in Medjugorje is made by the original sculpture, Andrej Ajdic, from Slovania. The statue in Medjugorje was created in 1998. *www.medugorje.org*.
29. From the year 2000 has been miraculously dripping from the right knee. Physisists have visited the site to investigate and no scientific explanation can be found.
30. OLM, 11-25-2000. *www.medugorje.org*
31. OLM 6-25-1988. *www.medjugorje.com*.
32. Blessed Maria Lopez of Jesus. whitelilyoftrinity.com.

Angels Will Sing
1. OLM 9-26-1982. *www.medjugorje.com*
2. Lectio-divina, *www.lectio-divina.org*
3. Taken from the Hail Mary, it is a traditional Catholic prayer asking for the intercession of the Virgin Mary, the mother of Jesus. *www.catholicplanet.com/catholic/hail*

4. The place of the first apparitions of Our Lady in Medjugorje, today Mt. Podbrdo is called "Apparition Hill."
5. The Story of a Soul; The Autobiography of St. Therese of Lisieux, Michael Day, Cong. Orat. Edited by Mother Agnes of Jesus Tan Books and Publishers, Inc. 1997 P. 44
6. Poems of Sr. Teresa, Carmelite of Lisieux, Copyright, 1907 by Carmelite Convent Pg. 54, "Why I love you Mary" *www.catholicspiritualdirection.org/poemstherese*
7. *Gospa Majka Moja* is written by Dr. Johannes Mikl; English translation; *Lady, My Mother, Queen of Peace*. *www.medjugorje.WS*;
8. Ibid.
9. St. Gertrude the Great. *www.saintpatrickdc.org*.
10. St. Margaret Mary of Alacoque was a Catholic nun and mystic who promoted devotion to the Sacred Heart of Jesus.
11. Twelve Promises of Jesus given to St. Margaret Mary for those devoted to His Sacred Heart. *www.sacredheartdevotion.com*.
12. A worldwide Marian apostolate established to spread the message of Fatima. *www.wafusa.org*.
13. The Blessed Mother specifically stated this to Lucia, one of the three children at Fatima, Portugal, revealing the First Saturday Devotion in reparation for the offenses committed against her Immaculate Heart. *www.fatima.org*.
14. Divine Intimacy by Fr. Gabriel of St. Mary Magdalen, O.C.D.; TAN Books and Publishers, Inc., Copyright 1996
15. A distinction is made between acquired or natural contemplation and infused or supernatural contemplation. *www.wikipedia.org*.
16. A popular Advent prayer, it begins on the feast of St. Andrew (November 30th) and is prayed through to Christmas day.

17. St. Andrew Advent Novena; Imprimatur: +MICHAEL AUGUSTINE, Archbishop of New York, N.Y., February 6, 1897.
18. Ibid.
19. See How Much I Love You. Clarissa Du Montier © 2005 All Rights Reserved. Used by Permission.
20. Ibid.
21. Ibid.
22. Saint Augustine of Hippo *www.saintquotes.blogspot.com*

Four Calling Birds
1. Copyright 1957, Missionaries of the Sacred Heart, page 2
2. Devotional scapulars typically consist of two rectangular pieces of cloth that are connected by bands that drape over the shoulders, with one cloth hanging over the chest and the other resting on the back.
3. Dating back from the late 14th century, the brown scapular has summed up Carmelite devotion to Mary.
4. I Can Only Imagine Bart Millard © 2001 Simpleville Music (ASCAP) (admin. By Simpleville Publishing LLC (c/o Music Services.)) All rights reserved. Used by permission.
5. OLM, 11-29-1983 *www.medugorje.org*
6. *Diary of St. Maria Faustina Kowalska: Divine Mercy in My Soul*
7. In wishing to know something of the Passion of Jesus Christ, St. Elizabeth, Queen of Hungary, together with St. Matilda and St. Bridget, offered fervent and special prayers, upon which Our Lord revealed to them the Devotion to the Drops of Blood He Lost. It was blessed by his Holiness Pope Leo XIII in Rome on April 5, 1890.
8. It involved a legal struggle and the challenges of her parents involving her prolonged life-support.

9. When Our Lady first started to appear in Medjugorje, she asked the visionaries to pray the Peace Chaplet every day.
10. *Diary of St. Maria Faustina Kowalska: Divine Mercy in My Soul*
11. Ibid
12. The Twelve Days of Christmas are the twelve days from the birth of Christ (Christmas, December 25) to the coming of the Magi (Epiphany, January 6, or the Twelfth day of Christmas.)
13. Ibid.
14. St. Therese, the "Little Flower" *www.carmelitesisters.ie/st-therese-of-lisieux/*
15. I Can Only Imagine Bart Millard © 2001 Simpleville Music (ASCAP) (admin. By Simpleville Publishing LLC (c/o Music Services.)) All rights reserved. Used by permission.
16. Saint Margaret Mary of Alacoque *www.catholic.org/prayers*

Hunger for Holiness
1. The Mysteries of Light, or the Luminous Mysteries as they are also called, focus on the public life of Jesus, the Light of the world. They span during the years He was preaching, from His Baptism to His death.
2. Pope John Paul II dedicated an entire year to the Blessed Sacrament, from October 2004 to October 2005, for Catholics worldwide to reflect upon the Eucharist.
3. OLM, 7-24-1986 *www.medugorje.org*
4. Saint Therese of Lisieux *http://whitelilyoftrinity.com/saints_quotes_suffering*

Celestial Choirs
1. *Cenacle* is a word for the upper room where Jesus' apostles gathered together in prayer with his Mother Mary, and the Holy Spirit powerfully descended upon them.
2. To the Priest, Our Lady's Beloved Sons, The Marian Movement of Priests; 18th Edition (2000)
3. Thank God Ahead of Time by Michael H. Crosby, O.F.M.Cap., Franciscan Herald Press, Copyright © 1985, 1989
4. Solanus Casey, a Capuchin friar and priest, is the first United States-born man to be declared "venerable" by the Roman Catholic Church, making him a candidate for beatification. *www.solanuscasey.org*
5. Ibid.
6. The Mystical City of God, Sister Mary of Jesus (Mary of Agreda) Tan Books and Publishers, Inc. Copyright 1914 by Rev. George J. Blatter
7. Founded in 1899, the SMA was formed for the support of Capuchin Franciscan Foreign Missions. Those enrolled in the Association are remembered in prayers and Masses offered by Franciscan Friars.
8. OLM, 10-9-1986 *www.medugorje.org*
9. Venerable Solanus Casey *www.capuchinfranciscans.org*
10. *Diary of St. Maria Faustina Kowalska: Divine Mercy in My Soul*
11. Ibid.
12. Saint Catherine of Genoa *www.americaneedsfatima.org*
13. *St. Maria Faustina Kowalska: Divine Mercy in My Soul*
14. OLM, 11-6-1986 *www.medugorje.org*
15. *Diary of St. Maria Faustina Kowalska: Divine Mercy in My Soul*
16. Saint Francis de Sales *www.quotes.net/quote/17248*
17. Saint Bernard *www.holyspiritinteractive.net/dailysaint/october/1002.asp*

18. Tan Books and Publishers, Inc. Copyright 1914, by Rev. George J. Blatter
19. *Diary of St. Maria Faustina Kowalska: Divine Mercy in My Soul*
20. Saint Teresa of Avila *www.ameriancatholic.org/features/saints*

8:2

1. St Francis obtained the indulgence from Jesus in a vision, in 1216, that was approved by Pope Honorius III.
2. Intergenerational Healing by Fr. Robert DeGrandis, S.S.J. www.marianland.com/queenhealing/7008.html
3. Center leads visitors on a spiritual journey to nurture the spirit and visit the tomb of Venerable Solanus Casey.
4. The monastery was originally intended to serve the area's Catholic clergy and churches, but also provided emergency aid to the poor.
5. On July 8, 1987, Father Solanus Casey's body was exhumed and found to be incorrupt. His body was clothed in a new religious habit, placed in a steel casket, and re-interred beneath the north transept at St. Bonaventure's, where prayers are offered for his intercession.
6. *Salvifici Doloris;* Letter of Pope John Paul II on the Christian Meaning of Human Suffering, 11 February 1984 © LIBRERIA EDITRICE VATICANA. Used by permission.
7. Ibid
8. The Hail Mary; *www.justforcatholics.org*
9. Mother Angelica by Raymond Arroyo; Published by Doubleday, Copyright © 2005
10. *Diary of St. Maria Faustina Kowalska: Divine Mercy in My Soul*
11. Mother Theresa of Calcutta *www.goodreads.com/quotes*
12. Saint Ignatious of Loyola *http://whitelilyoftrinity.com/saints_quotes_suffering*

Jesus, I Trust in You!
1. Mother Angelica founded Our Lady of the Angels Monastery in Irondale, AL in 1962.
2. *Diary of St. Maria Faustina Kowalska: Divine Mercy in My Soul*
3. Ibid.
4. Ibid.
5. Ibid.
6. Ibid.
7. After appointing a team of three Marian experts to study the history of Sister Adele Brise's reported apparition of the Blessed Virgin Mary, on December 8, 2010, the Honorable Bishop David L. Ricken of the Green Bay Diocese in Wisconsin declared the apparition to be authentic.
8. Our Lady of Medjugorje's message is a call to conversion back to God. Mary gives us "Five Stones" as weapons against our goliath, (prayer, fasting, confession, the bible, and the Eucharist) to overcome the temptation of sin and forces of evil.
9. *Diary of St. Maria Faustina Kowalska: Divine Mercy in My Soul*
10. Thy Kingdom Come, by Hugh Owen The Luisa Piccarreta Center for the Divine Will, Copyright © 2007
11. Ibid., 19.
12. The Hours of the Passion of Our Lord Jesus Christ translated from the 4th Italian Edition published by St. Hannibal Di Francia in the 1920's. The Luisa Piccarreta Center for the Divine Will, Copyright © 2006
13. Ibid.
14. *Diary of St. Maria Faustina Kowalska: Divine Mercy in My Soul*
15. Ibid.
16. Ibid.

17. Ibid.
18. Elizabeth Ministry *www.elizabethministry.com*
19. Maria Rosa Mystica, *www.Catholictradition.org/Mary/rosa-mystica.htm*
20. St. Rita of Cascia was a widow, an Italian nun, and saint. She is venerated in the Roman Catholic Church due to various miracles attributed to her intercession.
21. *Diary of St. Maria Faustina Kowalska: Divine Mercy in My Soul*
22. Pope John Paul II Catholic-thoughts.info/saints/Octsaints.htm
23. *Diary of St. Maria Faustina Kowalska: Divine Mercy in My Soul*
24. Ibid.

Epilogue – They Will See God
1. OLM, 1-26-1984 www.reocities.com/olmessages.
2. OLM, 6-24-1986 www.medjugorje.com.
3. OLM, 1-4-1986 jeanneshouseafire.blogspot.com.
4. Saint Elizabeth Ann Seton www.americancatholic.org/features/saints.
5. A campaign to add just one more decade into one's daily Rosary to pray for Our Lady of Medjugorje's intentions.
6. Diary of St. Maria Faustina Kowalska: Divine Mercy in My Soul, Saint Rose of Lima www.marytv/saints-list.
7. Saint Rose of Lima www.marytv.tv/saints-list

Made in the USA
Middletown, DE
21 August 2015